From Smart Cities to the Metaverse

This book offers a comprehensive exploration of the convergence between smart city infrastructure and the emerging metaverse. This book highlights the importance of integrating advanced technologies such as artificial intelligence, virtual reality/augmented reality, and blockchain to enhance urban living experiences while addressing such innovations' security and ethical challenges. Its applications span urban planning, transportation, education, historic preservation, and inclusive city development, making it an essential resource for modern urban development.

The book covers many key areas critical to understanding and implementing smart cities and the metaverse. It starts with both domains' foundational concepts and technological underpinnings, followed by a deep dive into the security infrastructure and challenges smart cities face. Cybersecurity is given special attention, exploring motives and methods of cyberattacks and proposing mitigation techniques and best practices. The book also examines AI chatbots, intelligent transportation, and the integration of digital twins, providing practical case studies and insights. Furthermore, it addresses the socioeconomic implications, governance, and ethical considerations, ensuring a holistic approach to the subject.

The motivation for writing this book stems from the contributors' recognition of the transformative potential of smart cities and the metaverse in creating sustainable, efficient, and inclusive urban environments. By bridging the gap between theoretical research and practical application, the contributors aim to equip researchers, policymakers, and technologists with the knowledge and tools needed to navigate and shape the future of urban living in a digitally interconnected world.

From Smart Cities to the Metaverse

A Journey through Cybersecurity, AI, and Urban Sustainability

Edited by
Norliza Katuk, Noradila Nordin,
and Adib Habbal

CRC Press
Taylor & Francis Group
Boca Raton London New York

CRC Press is an imprint of the
Taylor & Francis Group, an **informa** business

Designed cover image: Shutterstock

First edition published 2026
by CRC Press
2385 NW Executive Center Drive, Suite 320, Boca Raton FL 33431

and by CRC Press
4 Park Square, Milton Park, Abingdon, Oxon, OX14 4RN

CRC Press is an imprint of Taylor & Francis Group, LLC

© 2026 selection and editorial matter, Norliza Katuk, Noradila Nordin, and Adib Habbal; individual chapters, the contributors

ISBN: 978-1-041-02545-0 (hbk)
ISBN: 978-1-041-02543-6 (pbk)
ISBN: 978-1-003-61981-9 (ebk)

DOI: 10.1201/9781003619819

Typeset in Palatino
by KnowledgeWorks Global Ltd.

Contents

Section IV   Sustainability and Inclusivity

Preface

As urban landscapes evolve in the digital era, the intersection of smart cities and the metaverse redefines how we live, work, and interact. *From Smart Cities to the Metaverse: A Journey through Cybersecurity, AI, and Urban Sustainability* explores this transformation, offering a multidisciplinary perspective on integrating AI, cybersecurity, blockchain, IoT, VR/AR, and digital twins in shaping the future of urban environments.

This book is structured into four sections, each addressing critical aspects of smart city development and its convergence with the metaverse:

- **Section I: Foundations and Emerging Trends** lays the groundwork by defining smart cities and the metaverse (Chapter 1), examining their technological underpinnings and societal impact. It delves into the metaverse's core components and economic implications (Chapter 2) and explores how AI powers smart city solutions (Chapter 3). Chapter 4 highlights the role of IoT-enabled smart materials, such as smart concrete, in urban infrastructure.

- **Section II: Security and Resilience** focuses on the vulnerabilities of smart cities. It begins with an overview of security challenges in urban digital ecosystems (Chapter 5) and a detailed analysis of cyberattack motives and methods (Chapter 6). The section also addresses the metaverse's need for governance and ethical frameworks (Chapter 7).

- **Section III: Innovations and Applications** presents practical use cases, including metaverse-driven urban planning and digital twin integration (Chapter 8) and the role of the metaverse in preserving historic sites (Chapter 9). It also examines AI chatbots in intelligent transportation (Chapter 10) and their potential applications in Web 3.0 and metaverse interactions (Chapter 11).

- **Section IV: Sustainability and Inclusivity** emphasises the social dimension of smart cities. It explores how AR and VR technologies support inclusive education for individuals with special needs (Chapter 12) and examines food-sharing initiatives to foster sustainable and inclusive urban communities (Chapter 13).

This book is a valuable resource for researchers, policymakers, urban planners, and technology professionals seeking to navigate the complexities of future urban environments.

We, the editors, extend our gratitude to the contributors, the reviewers, and the institutions that supported this work. Your expertise has been instrumental in shaping this exploration of the digital cities of tomorrow.

Acknowledgements

We extend our deepest gratitude to all the contributors, researchers, and experts who have shared invaluable insights in this book. Your dedication has been essential in shaping this exploration of smart cities, cybersecurity, AI, and the metaverse.

We also thank the peer reviewers and editorial team for their thoughtful feedback, which has strengthened the clarity and impact of this work. Our appreciation goes to the institutions and organisations that have supported this endeavour, fostering research and innovation in this evolving field.

Lastly, to our colleagues, mentors, and loved ones, your encouragement and unwavering support have been instrumental throughout this journey.

Editors

Norliza Katuk is an Associate Professor of cybersecurity at the School of Computing, Universiti Utara Malaysia (UUM). She earned a bachelor's degree in information technology at Universiti Utara Malaysia in 2000, a master's degree in computer science at Universiti Teknologi Malaysia in 2002, and a doctoral degree in information technology at Massey University, New Zealand, in 2012. In her current role as the Deputy Director for Global Engagement at the Centre for International Affairs and Cooperation (CIAC), she leads international partnerships and academic mobility initiatives that enhance the university's global presence. Her research interests include information security and privacy, cybersecurity awareness, internet technology, IoT, disaster management, e-learning, and human-computer interaction. As a prolific scholar, Dr Katuk has published widely in international journals and serves as a reviewer for several esteemed publications. She also has experience editing and writing books, further contributing to the academic discourse in her fields. Additionally, she serves as the Chief Editor of the *Journal of Information and Communication Technology* (JICT).

Noradila Nordin earned a BEng (First Class Hons.) in computer engineering in 2010 and an MSc (with Distinction) in telecommunications engineering in 2011 at Queen Mary University of London. She was awarded the prestigious King's Scholarship by the Government of Malaysia to pursue a PhD, which she earned in 2017 at University College London. Her PhD, awarded by the Department of Electronic and Electrical Engineering, focused on multichannel cross-layer routing for sensor networks. In 2012, she began her academic career as a Lecturer at the School of Engineering and Technology, Insaniah University College, Malaysia. By 2018, she had advanced to Senior Lecturer at the School of Computing, Universiti Utara Malaysia (UUM). Since September 2023, she has been serving as a Lecturer at the School of Games and Creative Technology at the University for the Creative Arts in the United Kingdom.

Adib Habbal (Senior Member, IEEE) earned a PhD in computer science, specialising in networked computing, at Universiti Utara Malaysia (UUM). He is an Associate Professor of computer engineering and the Founding Head of the Innovative Networked Systems (INETs) Research Group at Karabuk University, Türkiye. Dr Habbal's research has garnered significant funding from various prestigious organisations. His prolific output includes over 100 refereed publications in top-tier journals and conference proceedings, particularly in the areas of future internet technologies and cybersecurity. His current research interests include IoT, applied AI/ML, cybersecurity, blockchain technology, and digital trust.

Contributors

Nor Farzana Abd Ghani
School of Computing
Universiti Utara Malaysia
Kedah, Malaysia

Alawiyah Abd Wahab
School of Computing
Universiti Utara Malaysia
Kedah, Malaysia

Nurul Izzah Abdul Aziz
School of Computing
Universiti Utara Malaysia
Sintok, Malaysia

Feras Zen Alden
School of Computing Sciences
College of Computing, Informatics
  and Mathematics
Universiti Teknologi Mara
Shah Alam, Selangor, Malaysia

Fady Alkhateeb
Computer Engineering
  Department
Faculty of Engineering
Karabuk University
Karabuk, Türkiye

Abdulaziz Al-Nahari
Information Technology
  Department
College of Computing and
  Information Sciences
University of Technology and
  Applied Sciences
Nizwa, Oman

Modhawi Alotaibi
College of the Computer Science
  and Engineering
Taibah University
Medina, Saudi Arabia

Mohammed F. Alrifaie
Department of Information in
  Communication Engineering
Alfarqadein University College
Basra, Iraq

Michael Bidollahkhani
Faculty of Mathematics and
  Computer Science
University of Göttingen
Göttingen, Germany

Elif Calik
School of Computer Science
College of Science and Engineering
ADAPT Research Centre
University of Galway
Galway, Ireland

Amna Eleyan
Department of Computing and
  Mathematics
Manchester Metropolitan University
Manchester, United Kingdom

Derar Eleyan
Faculty of Telecommunication and
  Information Technology
Nablus University for Technical and
  Vocational Education
Nablus, Palestine

Osman Ghazali
School of Computing
Universiti Utara Malaysia
Sintok, Kedah, Malaysia

Adib Habbal
Computer Engineering
  Department
Faculty of Engineering
Karabük University
Karabük, Türkiye

Husniza Husni
School of Computing
Universiti Utara Malaysia
Sintok, Kedah, Malaysia

Norliza Katuk
School of Computing
Universiti Utara Malaysia
Sintok, Kedah, Malaysia

Dilshod Kodirov
Department of Power Supply
  and Renewable Energy
  Sources
National Research University
Tashkent, Uzbekistan

Dian Kurnia
Department of Architectural
  Engineering
and
Laboratory for Construction,
  Innovative Structures, and
  Building Physics
Politeknik Negeri Pontianak
Kota Pontianak, Indonesia

Nurul Qalbi Kurniashally
Department of Architectural
  Engineering
Politeknik Negeri Pontianak
Kota Pontianak, Indonesia

Lee Kai Lun
School of Economics, Finance and
  Banking
Universiti Utara Malaysia
Sintok, Kedah, Malaysia

Emy Hazlinda Mohammad Ridzwan
Politeknik Balik Pulau
Pulau Pinang, Malaysia

Mohd Zhafri Mohd Zukhi
College of Computing, Information
  and Mathematics
Universiti Teknologi Mara
Mara, Malaysia

Noradila Nordin
School of Games and Creative
  Technology
University for the Creative Arts
Farnham, United Kingdom

Herry Prabowo
Department of Architectural
  Engineering
and
Laboratory for Construction,
  Innovative Structures, and
  Building Physics
Politeknik Negeri Pontianak
Kota Pontianak, Indonesia

Mhd. Zulfansyuri Siambaton
Fakultas Teknik
Universitas Islam Sumatera
Utara, Indonesia

Bryan Wing Khong Tiew
School of Business Management
Universiti Utara Malaysia
Sintok, Kedah, Malaysia

Ziyodulla Yusupov
Mühendislik Fakültesi
Elektrik-Elektronik Mühendisliği
Elektrik Tesisleri, Türkiye

Section I

Foundations and Emerging Trends

1

Introduction to Smart City and Metaverse

Norliza Katuk, Noradila Nordin, and Adib Habbal

1.1 Defining Smart City and Metaverse

As cities worldwide undergo rapid transformation driven by digital advancements, smart cities and the metaverse have emerged as central themes in urban innovation. These developments are not merely technological but encompass economic, social, and infrastructural dimensions that shape modern urban landscapes. The smart city integrates artificial intelligence (AI), information and communication technologies (ICT), and urban management strategies to enhance quality of life, sustainability, and governance. For example, Singapore has leveraged smart city technologies to enhance mobility and public safety through AI-powered traffic systems and surveillance analytics. Meanwhile, the metaverse introduces a virtual layer extending beyond physical urban planning, providing a new digital interaction paradigm and urban simulation paradigm. Integrating the metaverse in cities like Seoul, which has introduced metaverse-based government services, demonstrates its potential to reshape urban experiences.

A smart city is defined as an urban environment that leverages digital technologies, data analytics, and interconnected infrastructure to optimise resource management and improve the quality of urban life. It is characterised by real-time data processing, automation, and AI-driven decision-making, which enhance public services, governance, mobility, and environmental sustainability. Abu-Rayash and Dincer (2025) believe smart cities are multidisciplinary ecosystems integrating AI, ICT, economic frameworks, societal structures, pandemic resiliency, and infrastructure development. The definition of a smart city varies across nations due to differing urban policies and governance structures (Shao & Min, 2025).

Smart city initiatives generally address six core aspects. The economic aspect fosters innovation-driven urban economies, encourages fintech solutions, and promotes digital entrepreneurship. For instance, Estonia has successfully implemented e-governance and digital banking to enhance economic transparency. The environmental aspect aims to introduce sustainable urban strategies such as green technologies, smart grids, and climate adaptation solutions, as seen in Amsterdam's smart city programme, which utilises the Internet of Things (IoT)-enabled energy-efficient buildings. Governance

DOI: 10.1201/9781003619819-2

in smart cities strengthens participatory decision-making and e-governance, ensuring greater transparency in urban management. The living dimension of smart cities focuses on improving healthcare, education, and public services through digital platforms, as demonstrated by Barcelona's extensive use of IoT-based smart health services. Mobility is enhanced through intelligent transportation systems, including AI-driven traffic management and autonomous vehicles, as successfully implemented in Tokyo's smart transit systems. Lastly, the people aspect promotes inclusivity, digital literacy, and citizen participation, ensuring that urban advancements benefit all social groups (Shao & Min, 2025).

The metaverse is a collective virtual shared space created by converging virtually enhanced physical reality and interactive digital environments. It is facilitated through virtual reality (VR), augmented reality (AR), blockchain, digital twins (DTs), and AI-powered simulations. The metaverse is designed to provide immersive digital experiences where individuals, businesses, and governments can interact, collaborate, and conduct economic or governance-related activities (Kim & Kim, 2025). As urban management technologies evolve, concepts such as u-city, smart city, metaverse, and DT have emerged as key ICT-driven urban development tools (Kim & Kim, 2025). The metaverse is transformative in urban planning, governance, and infrastructure optimisation. The metaverse assists urban planning through advanced simulations that inform real-world smart city designs (Kim & Kim, 2025). A key advantage of metaverse technology is its ability to create virtual urban simulations that support urban planners and decision-makers in designing and managing cities efficiently (Mohammadnejad & Abedini, 2025). For example, Dubai has introduced metaverse-powered urban modelling to visualise infrastructure projects before implementation, ensuring optimised urban development.

The metaverse enhances urban development by optimising resource management, reducing the need for physical infrastructure, and improving service delivery. AI-driven simulations allow urban planners to test urban models before real-world execution, improving efficiency and reducing financial risks. The metaverse also fosters collaboration, as city officials and architects can interact in a shared digital space without requiring physical travel, as seen in Seoul's metaverse city hall initiative. Furthermore, the metaverse improves governance transparency by enabling citizens to participate in digital town halls and policy discussions. Metaverse-based digital services improve accessibility to healthcare and education, while immersive city replicas boost urban tourism, allowing users to experience cultural landmarks virtually (Mohammadnejad & Abedini, 2025).

Integrating the metaverse is crucial for the evolution of smart cities, offering innovative solutions that enhance urban efficiency, sustainability, and digital inclusivity (Chen et al., 2024). The metaverse replicates physical assets through DTs, allowing for optimised maintenance, traffic flow, and city services. Singapore's Digital Twin initiative demonstrates how real-time urban monitoring can enhance city planning and disaster response. Blockchain technology supports decentralised digital economies, facilitating secure transactions in urban services and digital real estate, similar to how Decentraland has revolutionised virtual property transactions. The metaverse also fosters immersive smart governance, providing virtual platforms for citizen engagement, participatory governance, and policy deliberation. For example, China's metaverse-driven e-government services allow users to interact with municipal authorities in digital spaces. Furthermore, AI-powered decision-making enables data-driven urban solutions, improving security, disaster management, and mobility efficiency (Chen et al., 2024). AI-based predictive analytics in cities like Helsinki have helped improve traffic congestion management by integrating smart sensors and digital monitoring.

The smart city and metaverse are not isolated concepts but interconnected elements shaping the future of urban living. A smart city enhances physical urban development through AI, IoT, and data analytics, while the metaverse extends these efforts into the virtual realm, transforming planning, governance, and citizen engagement. These technologies have already been combined in cities like Dubai, where urban development projects integrate smart city frameworks with metaverse applications. Integrating the metaverse becomes essential as cities evolve in future urban ecosystems' sustainable and intelligent development.

1.2 Technological Underpinning of Smart City and Metaverse

The seamless integration of sensor technology with advanced communication systems has opened the way for connecting everyday objects through the IoT. When these sensors are coupled with AI, they give rise to intelligent and responsive environments (Mukhopadhyay et al., 2021). This synergy between sensor technology, IoT, and AI has led to the emergence of various smart ecosystems. Notable examples include smart vehicles that leverage sensor data for efficient navigation (Lucic et al., 2020), smart homes equipped with interconnected devices for automation and convenience (Katuk et al., 2018), and the development of smart cities that utilise these technologies to enhance urban living (Batty et al., 2012). The 21st century has witnessed an unprecedented transformation in urban landscapes, driven by the swift integration of smart technologies into various facets of city life. From intelligent transportation systems to interconnected infrastructure and advanced healthcare services, smart city initiatives promise increased efficiency, sustainability, and an enhanced quality of life for urban dwellers. However, this technological evolution introduces many cybersecurity concerns that demand meticulous consideration and strategic planning (Javed et al., 2022; Katuk et al., 2023).

The International Institute for Management Development's (IMD) 2023 Smart City Observatory report examines 141 cities, highlighting Zurich's leader, trailed by Oslo and Canberra (Lanvin, 2023). Other than that, the United Nations Development Programme (UNDP) and Singapore collaborate on smart city initiatives to enhance urban living that support strategic assessment, project implementation, technical helpdesk, and thematic areas, fostering sustainable development goals (United Nations Development Programme, 2023). Cities worldwide are adopting interconnected systems to optimise services and manage resources effectively, forming the foundation of smart city initiatives. These initiatives encompass diverse applications, such as smart transportation, energy-efficient buildings, intelligent grids, and state-of-the-art healthcare systems (Kumar et al., 2021). These systems heavily rely on ICT, creating a complex network of devices, sensors, and interconnected networks.

Consequently, the expanded attack surface for potential cybersecurity threats in smart cities underscores the critical need for robust security measures (Al-Dosari & Fetais, 2023). Recognising and addressing cybersecurity concerns in developing and operating smart city networks is imperative. The intricate web of interconnected infrastructure means that a security breach in one area can have ripple effects throughout the system (Wright et al., 2022). For example, a cyberattack on a smart transportation system could disrupt traffic management (Ganin et al., 2019) and impact emergency response systems, potentially leading to severe consequences (Ma, 2021). Given the high stakes, understanding and proactively managing the vulnerabilities inherent in smart city networks are crucial for their successful implementation.

Smart cities are characterised by integrating advanced technologies across various domains and incorporating sensors and monitoring systems into foundational elements like roads and bridges to enhance efficiency, sustainability, and resilience (Bibri, 2019). Smart transportation focuses on improving urban mobility through technologies such as intelligent traffic management and real-time public transportation tracking (Mangiaracina et al., 2017). In water and sanitation, sensors and IoT devices are employed to monitor water quality, detect leaks, and optimise water usage (Jan et al., 2021). Smart town planning utilises data-driven insights and technology for more efficient urban design (Bibri, 2022), while smart energy initiatives aim to optimise consumption and incorporate renewable sources (Hoang et al., 2021).

Smart healthcare leverages technology for enhanced healthcare services (Pramanik et al., 2017), while smart security integrates closed-circuit television (CCTV) cameras and AI-driven analytics for improved safety (Jain et al., 2021). Smart buildings use IoT devices to optimise energy usage and enhance occupant comfort (Shah et al., 2019). Smart governance employs technology to improve administrative processes (Pereira et al., 2018), and smart education initiatives transform traditional education through e-learning platforms and interactive tools (Das, 2023). Together, these instances of smart city development underscore a holistic approach to enhancing urban living through

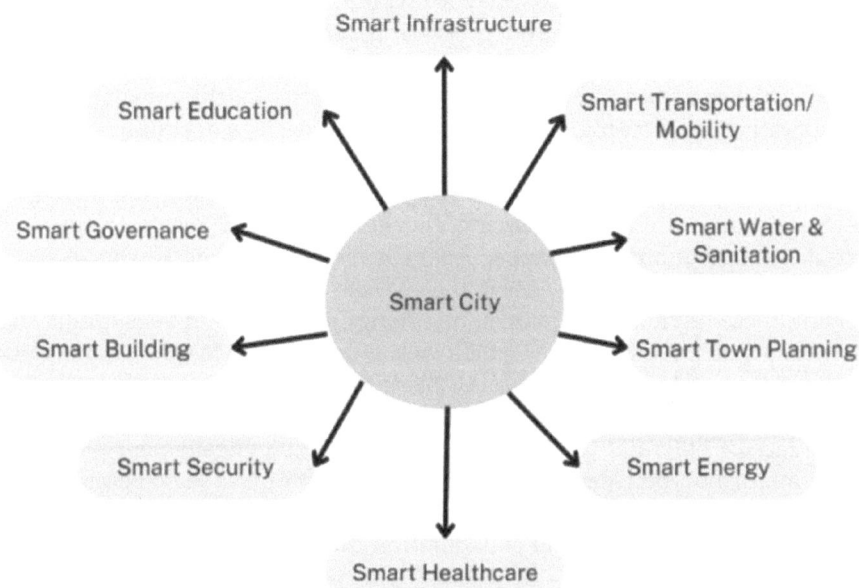

FIGURE 1.1
The smart city instances. (From Dwivedi et al., 2015.)

technological integration. Dwivedi et al. (2015) highlighted that a smart city covers smart transportation or mobility, smart water and sanitation, smart town planning, smart energy, smart healthcare, smart security, smart building, smart governance, and smart education, as illustrated in Figure 1.1.

The communication infrastructure that underpins smart cities is a sophisticated and interconnected system designed to facilitate the seamless operation of diverse technologies, ultimately enhancing urban living conditions. At its core, IoT devices function as sensory inputs, gathering and transmitting data from various sources such as infrastructure, vehicles, and everyday objects (Ullah et al., 2023). Wireless Sensor Networks (WSNs) are crucial in connecting these devices efficiently, enabling flexible and scalable data transmission without physical connections (Mishra & Singh, 2023). This connectivity is maintained through standardised communication protocols like Message Queuing Telemetry Transport (MQTT) and Constrained Application Protocol (CoAP), ensuring interoperability among diverse devices and systems—particularly crucial for resource-constrained IoT devices (Islam et al., 2022). Additionally, the integration of edge computing reduces latency and elevates real-time processing capabilities (Khan et al., 2020). Meanwhile, communication gateways act as intermediaries in managing the flow of information between individual devices and the broader network, contributing to the overall efficiency and effectiveness of the smart city communication ecosystem.

Cloud computing platforms play a pivotal role in smart city settings by providing scalable storage and processing capabilities to handle the vast amounts of data generated by the system (Alam, 2021). This infrastructure facilitates critical functions such as data analytics, machine learning, and collaborative decision-making, contributing to the city's overall intelligence. Simultaneously, the deployment of 5G networks represents a significant leap forward, delivering higher data transfer speeds, lower latency, and increased device density, thereby enhancing the efficiency and responsiveness of smart city operations (Guevara & Auat Cheein, 2020). Robust cybersecurity measures are imperative to ensure the security and integrity of the data traversing these advanced networks, involving implementing encryption and intrusion detection systems (Habibzadeh et al., 2019). Meanwhile, network management systems play a crucial role in overseeing the health and security of communication networks, guaranteeing their reliability and resilience in the face of potential threats. Additionally, citizen engagement platforms foster interaction between residents and city authorities (Viale Pereira et al., 2017). These platforms provide real-time information, creating an avenue for community participation and collaboration that is integral to the success of smart city initiatives.

Within the intricate fabric of smart city networks, data analytics and machine learning algorithms play a pivotal role, extracting valuable insights that significantly contribute to informed decision-making in areas such as traffic management, energy consumption, and optimising public services (Soomro et al., 2019). Geographic Information System (GIS) tools play a crucial role in spatial analysis and mapping, complementing this analytical efficiency (Sharma et al., 2021). It aids not only in the development of infrastructure but also in facilitating more efficient emergency response systems. Moreover, the robustness of smart city communication networks is fortified by redundancy and resilience measures, ensuring uninterrupted operation even in the face of unforeseen challenges (Jha, 2023).

The collaborative synergy between public and private entities further enhances this resilience, with public-private partnerships playing a crucial role in expanding network coverage and ensuring the sustainability of smart city initiatives (Almarri & Boussabaine, 2025). As smart city communication networks evolve, they are intentionally designed with scalability and future-proofing in mind (Yaqoob et al., 2017). This design philosophy allows these networks to seamlessly adapt to increasing device densities and the dynamic landscape of evolving technological standards. A multifaceted approach to security encompasses privacy protection measures, adaptive control systems, open data platforms, interoperability standards, and public awareness and education initiatives (Fabrègue & Bogoni, 2023). These elements collectively contribute to the comprehensive and adaptive nature of the smart city communication infrastructure, fostering a resilient and forward-looking urban ecosystem, as illustrated in Figure 1.2.

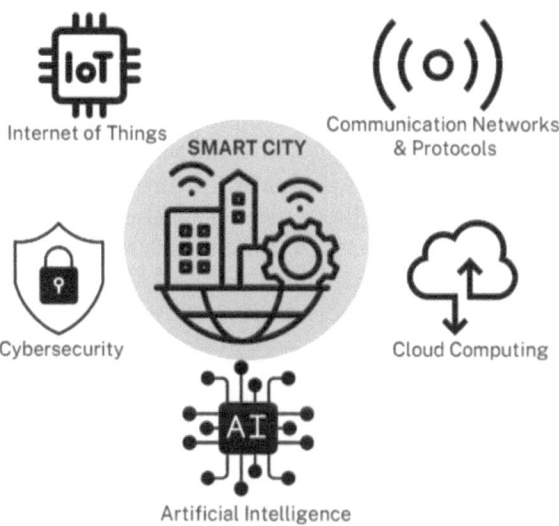

FIGURE 1.2
Elements driving smart cities.

The metaverse is built upon combining digital technologies that enable immersive, interactive, and persistent virtual experiences. At the forefront of this technological foundation is extended reality (XR), which encompasses VR, AR, and mixed reality (MR) (Bibri & Jagatheesaperumal, 2023). These technologies allow users to engage with digital environments in ways that closely mimic real-world experiences, fostering a sense of presence, embodiment, and interaction within the metaverse. VR creates fully immersive digital experiences by completely blocking the physical world and replacing it with a computer-generated environment (Mostajeran et al., 2023). Users access VR through head-mounted displays (HMDs), motion controllers, and haptic feedback devices that allow them to navigate and manipulate objects within a digital space. Advanced VR systems leverage spatial audio, eye tracking, and real-time rendering to create realistic and highly interactive experiences. From gaming to virtual collaboration spaces, VR plays a key role in establishing the spatial dimension of the metaverse. In contrast, AR enhances the physical world by overlaying digital information onto real-world environments (Dargan et al., 2023). Unlike VR, AR does not replace reality but enhances it with digital elements that can be accessed through smartphones, AR glasses, or heads-up displays (HUDs). AR enables applications such as interactive city navigation, virtual furniture placement, and enhanced real-time collaboration by integrating digital information with the user's physical surroundings. Advanced AR applications use computer vision and real-time 3D mapping to ensure digital content aligns with real-world objects, creating an intuitive and natural experience.

MR is a more advanced form of AR that allows digital and physical objects to interact seamlessly. MR enables users to manipulate holographic objects using hand gestures, voice commands, or eye tracking while maintaining real-time awareness of their surroundings (Shvetsov & Alsamhi, 2024). Technologies like Microsoft's HoloLens and Meta's research into full-body tracking and spatial computing push MR towards more lifelike and immersive applications. Breakthroughs in graphical rendering, computing power, and sensor technology drive the continuous advancement of XR technologies. Edge computing and high-speed networks (5G/6G) are essential for reducing latency in XR experiences, ensuring that real-time interactions feel seamless. Additionally, haptic feedback systems, brain-computer interfaces (BCIs), and full-body tracking suits further expand the potential of XR, making the metaverse a more immersive and accessible digital universe.

AI is another metaverse pillar that powers various functions that make virtual environments more intelligent, adaptive, and interactive (Soliman et al., 2024). It is instrumental in enabling real-time natural language processing (NLP), computer vision, behaviour modelling, and automation, all of which contribute to the realism and functionality of digital interactions. One of AI's most visible contributions to the metaverse is the development of AI-driven avatars and digital assistants. These virtual beings can replicate human-like interactions, process natural language, and provide personalised recommendations. AI-powered avatars can serve as virtual guides, customer service agents, or digital companions that adapt to user preferences and behaviours over time. Facial recognition and emotion detection algorithms enhance AI-driven avatars, enabling them to respond to human expressions and emotions with realistic social cues. AI is also crucial in content generation and world-building within the metaverse. Procedural content generation algorithms can create vast, dynamically evolving virtual landscapes without manual intervention. These algorithms are widely used in gaming, architecture, and simulation-based applications, where large-scale environments must be generated efficiently. AI also helps optimise graphics rendering and resource allocation, ensuring complex virtual environments run smoothly across different devices.

Moreover, AI enhances the personalisation of metaverse experiences through data-driven analytics and machine-learning models (Kanade & Batule, 2024). These models analyse user behaviour, preferences, and interactions to create customised content, adaptive learning environments, and real-time recommendation systems. AI can predict user needs, suggest relevant experiences, and optimise virtual interactions to make the metaverse more engaging and user-friendly. Finally, AI revolutionises real-time speech translation and multilingual communication, enabling global connectivity within the metaverse (Sumon et al., 2024). AI-driven translation engines use deep learning to provide seamless cross-language communication, making virtual worlds more inclusive and accessible to users from diverse linguistic backgrounds. As AI technology advances, it will play an increasingly vital role in making the metaverse more dynamic, responsive, and intelligent, ultimately bridging the gap between human cognition and digital interaction.

1.3 Trend and Development in Smart City and Metaverse

The evolution of smart cities and the metaverse is driven by a convergence of advanced technologies, increasing urban demands, and ongoing digital transformation initiatives. The metaverse, as a virtual extension of reality, offers innovative approaches to digitalisation and has the potential to enhance social connectivity among citizens. The metaverse enables virtual engagement in smart cities through immersive and participatory elements in urban planning, governance, and public services, fostering a more inclusive decision-making process. An example of this integration is the German city of Aalen, which plans to hold a virtual town hall meeting to facilitate direct communication between citizens, administrators, and policymakers. Such initiatives exemplify how smart city metaverse applications can streamline urban life by offering virtual citizen services, remote workplaces, real-time transportation insights, and digital access to education and healthcare services (Maier & Weinberger, 2024). These digital enhancements improve accessibility and strengthen community engagement and efficiency within smart cities.

Governments, corporations, and technology innovators are shaping these ecosystems to enhance urban living, improve connectivity, and develop immersive virtual environments seamlessly integrating with physical infrastructures. As the boundaries between digital and physical spaces continue to blur, smart cities are evolving into interconnected, data-driven environments where real-time analytics and automation drive urban efficiency. Several emerging trends define the current landscape of smart cities and the metaverse, reflecting advancements in AI powered urban planning, decentralised economies, 5G connectivity, and sustainability-focused initiatives. These innovations transform how cities operate, how citizens interact with their surroundings, and how digital spaces extend urban experiences. This section explores these key trends and provides real-world examples illustrating their growing impact on urban development, governance, and daily life.

1.3.1 AI and IoT Integration for Urban Intelligence

At the core of smart cities lies the seamless integration of advanced technologies into the urban landscape, leading to the emergence of the Urban Intelligence (UI) paradigm. This paradigm envisions a comprehensive technological ecosystem to enhance urban environments, improve citizen wellbeing, and optimise smart city systems (Silvestri et al., 2024). UI represents a fundamental shift in urban management, leveraging DTs, data analytics, AI, and interconnected networks to create cities that are not only more efficient but also more responsive to the needs of their inhabitants. The implementation of UI relies heavily on DTs, cyber-physical systems (CPS), and IoT-driven data integration, providing a cyber-physical counterpart to real-world city systems. By bridging digital and physical domains, cities can improve resource efficiency, strengthen infrastructure resilience, and foster sustainable urban growth, all while prioritising the well-being and health of their citizens. This fusion of AI, IoT, and real-time analytics enables city administrators to monitor, predict, and respond to urban challenges more precisely, ensuring that public services are more efficient, data-driven, and adaptive to evolving urban dynamics (Bittencourt et al., 2024).

AI and the IoT are the backbone of smart city innovations, enabling real-time decision-making and automation across multiple sectors. Increasingly, cities are adopting AI-powered surveillance systems, predictive traffic management, and smart energy grids to optimise public safety, transportation, and resource distribution. These technologies enhance urban functionality and reduce operational costs and environmental impact by promoting energy efficiency and intelligent infrastructure management. Singapore exemplifies this AI-driven approach by employing intelligent traffic signals powered by AI analytics to manage congestion, significantly reducing travel times and improving road safety (Jagirdar & Pathak, 2025). In addition, IoT sensors deployed across the city continuously monitor air quality, water levels, and waste management processes, enabling proactive governance and sustainable urban planning.

Similarly, Barcelona has pioneered IoT-enabled smart lighting systems, which dynamically adjust brightness based on real-time pedestrian and vehicle movements (Padhiary et al., 2025). This innovation enhances urban safety and reduces energy consumption, contributing to the city's broader sustainability goals. These real-world implementations highlight the transformative potential of AI and IoT in shaping intelligent, sustainable, and citizen-centric urban environments.

1.3.2 Digital Twins and Virtual Urban Planning

One of the most transformative trends in smart city development is the use of DTs—virtual replicas of physical cities that facilitate urban planning and operational efficiency (Ersan et al., 2024). These digital environments simulate real-world conditions, allowing urban developers to test infrastructure projects before implementation. The city of Shanghai, for instance, has developed a comprehensive DT model that mirrors its urban landscape, enabling authorities to optimise emergency response strategies and monitor environmental changes. In the metaverse, companies like NVIDIA's Omniverse provide platforms where architects and urban planners collaborate in a shared digital environment, streamlining the design and execution of smart city projects (Ahmed et al., 2024). These virtual replicas reduce project costs and enhance sustainability by predicting urban impact before construction begins.

1.3.3 5G and Edge Computing for Hyperconnectivity

The rapid deployment of 5G networks accelerates smart city development by enabling high-speed, low-latency connectivity that supports real-time applications. Smart infrastructure, autonomous vehicles, and immersive metaverse experiences rely heavily on ultra-fast data transmission (Hatami et al., 2024). For instance, South Korea has pioneered smart city projects in Songdo, where 5G-enabled autonomous shuttles transport residents while leveraging edge computing for instant data processing (Kumar et al., 2025). In the metaverse, companies like Meta and HTC are developing 5G-powered virtual workspaces, ensuring seamless collaboration between remote users in high-fidelity, interactive environments. The synergy between 5G and smart cities enhances physical and digital interactions, making urban life more efficient and immersive.

1.3.4 Blockchain and Decentralisation in Urban Governance and the Metaverse

Blockchain technology revolutionises smart city governance and metaverse economies by fostering decentralisation, transparency, and security. Cities like Dubai are implementing blockchain-based systems for public services, including land registry, digital identity verification, and secure transactions, reducing bureaucratic inefficiencies and fraud (Shihadeh, 2024). In the metaverse, decentralised platforms like Decentraland and The Sandbox enable users to buy, sell, and trade virtual real estate using blockchain-backed non-fungible tokens (NFTs). These decentralised ecosystems empower individuals by granting them ownership rights and financial control over their digital assets. Adopting blockchain in both domains enhances trust and autonomy, reshaping traditional power structures in governance and virtual economies.

1.3.5 Green and Sustainable Smart Cities

Sustainability is a fundamental priority in smart city initiatives, emphasising reducing carbon footprints, promoting renewable energy, and implementing circular economy practices (Sumra et al., 2025). Cities like Copenhagen have set ambitious carbon neutrality goals, integrating wind energy, electric vehicle (EV) infrastructure, and AI-driven energy optimisation to achieve sustainability targets (Suganya et al., 2025). The metaverse also contributes to green initiatives by reducing the need for physical travel and infrastructure expansion. Virtual conferences, education, and remote workspaces within the metaverse help organisations reduce their environmental impact. Additionally, companies like Microsoft are investing in eco-friendly data centres that power metaverse platforms with renewable energy, ensuring a lower carbon footprint for digital interactions (Hashmi et al., 2025).

1.3.6 Smart Mobility and Autonomous Transportation

Integrating smart mobility solutions, including autonomous vehicles, electric transportation, and AI-driven traffic systems, revolutionises urban commuting. Cities like Helsinki have deployed Mobility-as-a-Service (MaaS) platforms that consolidate various transportation modes—such as buses, e-scooters, and ride-sharing—into a single application, reducing congestion and reliance on private cars (Mubiru & Westerholt, 2024). In parallel, the metaverse influences smart mobility by enabling virtual testbeds for autonomous vehicle simulations. Companies like Tesla and Waymo use metaverse environments to train and refine AI models for self-driving cars, enhancing real-world performance through simulated driving conditions (Ullrich et al., 2024). This interplay between digital and physical mobility solutions is shaping the future of transportation.

1.3.7 Immersive Smart City Engagement through AR and VR

AR and VR technologies are bridging the gap between smart cities and the metaverse by enhancing urban engagement and community participation. Smart cities leverage AR for navigation, cultural tourism, and public service interactions. For example, in Tokyo, AR-powered applications provide real-time translations and virtual guides for tourists, making city navigation more accessible (Jamshed et al., 2024). Meanwhile, the metaverse is revolutionising education, commerce, and social experiences through immersive VR environments. Platforms like VRChat and Horizon Workrooms enable users to engage in lifelike interactions within digital spaces, reshaping how people socialise, learn, and work (Mitchell et al., 2024). The growing adoption of AR and VR technologies fosters an interconnected urban and virtual lifestyle.

1.3.8 Policy and Ethical Considerations in Smart Cities and the Metaverse

As smart cities and the metaverse evolve, regulatory frameworks and ethical considerations are becoming increasingly critical. Data privacy, cybersecurity, and digital inclusivity require proactive governance to ensure fair and secure participation. The European Union's General Data Protection Regulation (GDPR) has set a global benchmark for data protection in smart city applications, ensuring that citizens' data remains safeguarded (Joyce & Javidroozi, 2024). In the metaverse, concerns regarding digital identity protection and virtual harassment are prompting platforms like Meta and Roblox to implement safety measures and content moderation strategies (Zakaria, 2025). Policymakers and technology developers must collaborate to establish guidelines that promote ethical innovation and equitable access to these emerging digital and urban spaces.

1.4 Societal Impact and Benefits of Metaverse within Smart City Context

Integrating the metaverse within smart cities can transform urban life by enhancing connectivity, improving governance, and driving economic growth. Smart cities already leverage advanced digital technologies to optimise infrastructure and public services. With the metaverse, these cities can create interactive, data-driven environments that reshape how residents, businesses, and governments interact. However, alongside its benefits, the metaverse introduces new risks, including digital exclusion, cybersecurity threats, and economic disparities, which must be addressed to ensure inclusive and sustainable development.

1.4.1 Revolutionising Urban Planning but Increasing the Risk of Digital Exclusion

One of the most significant benefits of the metaverse in smart cities is its impact on urban planning and infrastructure development. DTs—virtual replicas of real-world environments—enable city planners to simulate infrastructure projects, optimise energy consumption, and test traffic flows before implementation. For example, Singapore's 3D virtual city model allows planners and citizens to explore, interact with, and provide real-time feedback on urban projects (Mazzetto, 2024). However, over-reliance on digital planning tools may oversimplify real-world complexities and exclude communities lacking digital access, potentially leading to elitist, data-driven governance that does not fully reflect diverse public needs.

1.4.2 Enhancing Education but Widening the Digital Divide

The metaverse revolutionises education and workforce development by offering immersive, interactive learning environments in smart cities. Virtual classrooms provide students access to digital labs, historical simulations, and real-time collaboration. In Dubai, educational institutions are implementing

VR-based classrooms, allowing students to conduct virtual science experiments and interact with 3D learning materials (Zaatar et al., 2024). However, while these innovations enhance education, they may deepen existing inequalities—students without high-speed internet, VR devices, or digital literacy may be left behind, exacerbating educational disparities in urban areas.

1.4.3 Improving Healthcare but Raising Data Privacy and Accessibility Concerns

The metaverse can potentially revolutionise urban healthcare services by facilitating virtual consultations, AI-driven diagnostics, and AR-assisted surgeries (Hatami et al., 2024). In South Korea, VR-based rehabilitation programmes allow stroke patients to undergo guided therapy sessions remotely (Kang et al., 2023). AR-assisted surgeries enhance precision and efficiency by overlaying real-time imaging data. However, these advancements raise concerns about data privacy, misinformation, and digital accessibility. If healthcare systems become overly reliant on metaverse technologies, face-to-face patient care may diminish, negatively impacting those requiring physical examinations and human interaction in medical treatment.

1.4.4 Expanding Civic Engagement but Favouring Digitally Literate Citizens

The metaverse is reshaping civic engagement by offering virtual public forums and immersive policy discussions, increasing public participation in governance. Estonia, a leader in digital democracy, is exploring VR-based urban consultations, enabling citizens to experience proposed city developments before implementation (Akmentina, 2023). However, digital exclusion remains a challenge—low-income groups, older people, and those unfamiliar with virtual platforms may struggle to participate in digital governance, creating a system that privileges the technologically adept while sidelining marginalised communities.

1.4.5 Strengthening Social Connectivity but Contributing to Digital Isolation

The metaverse is helping reduce social isolation in urban environments by providing virtual spaces for cultural events, tourism, and social interactions. Cities like Kyoto in Japan are investing in virtual tourism platforms, allowing residents to experience historical landmarks and festivals remotely (Gadjeva, 2023). However, over-reliance on virtual interactions may erode real-world relationships, leading to digital escapism, increased social isolation, and mental health concerns as individuals substitute physical connections with digital engagement.

1.4.6 Boosting Economic Growth but Encouraging Unregulated Digital Economies

The metaverse unlocks new economic opportunities by enabling virtual marketplaces, AI-powered commerce, and decentralised finance (DeFi) in smart cities. In Shanghai, entrepreneurs are creating virtual shopping districts where customers can interact with AI-driven retail assistants, try on digital fashion, and purchase goods via cryptocurrency (Li, 2024). However, unregulated virtual economies bring risks such as fraud, data privacy violations, and financial instability, particularly as NFTs and cryptocurrencies fluctuate unpredictably, threatening the financial security of digital businesses and consumers.

1.4.7 Optimising Transportation but Increasing Safety Risks in Digital Navigation

The metaverse revolutionises urban mobility by integrating AI-driven traffic models, autonomous vehicle simulations, and AR navigation. In Los Angeles, virtual models help predict traffic congestion patterns and optimise public transit routes (Dikshit et al., 2023). AR-assisted navigation systems embedded in smart glasses provide real-time directions and accessibility features for commuters. However, excessive reliance on digital navigation tools may pose safety risks, as drivers and pedestrians distracted by virtual overlays could increase the likelihood of accidents and injuries.

1.4.8 Promoting Sustainable Practices but Increasing Energy Consumption

The metaverse presents opportunities for sustainability by reducing carbon emissions from commuting and physical infrastructure. Sweden is pioneering sustainable virtual workspaces, allowing businesses to function without relying on large physical offices (Babapour Chafi et al., 2022). However, the metaverse demands massive computational power, leading to higher energy consumption and increased electronic waste. Blockchain transactions, cloud computing, and AI-driven virtual spaces require sustainable energy solutions to offset their environmental impact and ensure that green innovation in smart cities remains viable.

1.4.9 Encouraging Innovation but Deepening Digital Inequality

Despite its potential, the metaverse poses challenges related to digital inclusion and accessibility. Not all citizens have high-speed Internet, advanced computing devices, or access to digital literacy programmes, creating a divide between those who can fully engage in the metaverse and those left behind. Without adequate investment in affordable technology, digital infra-structure, and training programmes, the metaverse risks reinforcing social inequality rather than reducing it in smart cities.

1.4.10 Improving Efficiency but Raising Privacy and Cybersecurity Concerns

The metaverse is built on vast user data, including biometric information, purchasing behaviours, and online interactions. Without proper regulation, this data could be exploited for surveillance, targeted advertising, or cyber-crime. Governments and businesses must establish strict cybersecurity mea-sures, ethical AI policies, and data protection frameworks to safeguard user privacy and prevent exploitation in the digital economy.

1.4.11 Empowering Digital Businesses but Enabling Corporate Monopolisation

As corporations dominate the virtual economy, the risk of economic monop-olisation in the metaverse is growing. Tech giants controlling virtual real estate, digital marketplaces, and financial systems may suppress competi-tion, exploit digital workers, and increase costs for smaller businesses. To prevent monopolisation, governments must enforce fair regulations that promote economic inclusivity and ensure that virtual marketplaces remain competitive and accessible.

1.4.12 Creating Smart Cities but Increasing the Risk of Digital Addiction

As more aspects of daily life move into the metaverse—education, work, entertainment, and social interaction—there is a growing risk of digital addiction and mental health deterioration. Studies show that excessive vir-tual engagement can lead to depression, anxiety, and reduced real-world socialisation. Cities must implement policies to encourage responsible meta-verse usage, ensuring that technology enhances rather than replaces mean-ingful human experiences.

References

Abu-Rayash, A., & Dincer, I. (2025). Development of an integrated model for envi-ronmentally and economically sustainable and smart cities. *Sustainable Energy Technologies and Assessments*, 73, 104096. https://doi.org/10.1016/j.seta.2024.104096

Ahmed, N., Afyouni, I., Dabool, H., & Al Aghbari, Z. (2024). A systemic survey of the omniverse platform and its applications in data generation, simulation and metaverse [Review]. *Frontiers in Computer Science*, 6. https://doi.org/10.3389/fcomp.2024.1423129

Akmentina, L. (2023). E-participation and engagement in urban planning: Experiences from the Baltic cities. *Urban Research & Practice, 16*(4), 624–657. https://doi.org/10.1080/17535069.2022.2068965

Alam, T. (2021). Cloud-based IoT applications and their roles in smart cities. *Smart Cities, 4*(3), 1196–1219. https://doi.org/10.3390/smartcities4030064

Al-Dosari, K., & Fetais, N. (2023). A new shift in implementing unmanned aerial vehicles (UAVs) in the safety and security of smart cities: A systematic literature review. *Safety, 9*(3), 64. https://doi.org/10.3390/safety9030064

Almarri, K., & Boussabaine, H. (2025). Critical success factors for public–private partnerships in smart city infrastructure projects. *Construction Innovation, 25*(2), 224–247. https://doi.org/10.1108/CI-04-2022-0072

Babapour Chafi, M., Hultberg, A., & Bozic Yams, N. (2022). Post-pandemic office work: Perceived challenges and opportunities for a sustainable work environment. *Sustainability, 14*(1), 294. https://doi.org/10.3390/su14010294

Batty, M., Axhausen, K. W., Giannotti, F., Pozdnoukhov, A., Bazzani, A., Wachowicz, M., Ouzounis, G., & Portugali, Y. (2012). Smart cities of the future. *The European Physical Journal Special Topics, 214*(1), 481–518. https://doi.org/10.1140/epjst/e2012-01703-3

Bibri, S. E. (2019). On the sustainability of smart and smarter cities in the era of big data: An interdisciplinary and transdisciplinary literature review. *Journal of Big Data, 6*(1), 25. https://doi.org/10.1186/s40537-019-0182-7

Bibri, S. E. (2022). Eco-districts and data-driven smart eco-cities: Emerging approaches to strategic planning by design and spatial scaling and evaluation by technology. *Land Use Policy, 113*, 105830. https://doi.org/10.1016/j.landusepol.2021.105830

Bibri, S. E., & Jagatheesaperumal, S. K. (2023). Harnessing the potential of the metaverse and artificial intelligence for the internet of city things: Cost-effective XReality and synergistic AIoT technologies. *Smart Cities, 6*(5), 2397–2429. https://doi.org/10.3390/smartcities6050109

Bittencourt, J. C. N., Costa, D. G., Portugal, P., & Vasques, F. (2024). A survey on adaptive smart urban systems. *IEEE Access, 12*, 102826–102850. https://doi.org/10.1109/ACCESS.2024.3433381

Chen, Z., Gan, W., Wu, J., Lin, H., & Chen, C.-M. (2024). Metaverse for smart cities: A survey. *Internet of Things and Cyber-Physical Systems, 4*, 203–216. https://doi.org/10.1016/j.iotcps.2023.12.002

Dargan, S., Bansal, S., Kumar, M., Mittal, A., & Kumar, K. (2023). Augmented reality: A comprehensive review. *Archives of Computational Methods in Engineering, 30*(2), 1057–1080. https://doi.org/10.1007/s11831-022-09831-7

Das, N. (2023). Digital education as an integral part of a smart and intelligent city: A short review. In A. Choudhury, A. Biswas, & S. Chakraborti (Eds.), *Digital learning based education: Transcending physical barriers* (pp. 81–96). Springer Nature. https://doi.org/10.1007/978-981-19-8967-4_5

Dikshit, S., Atiq, A., Shahid, M., Dwivedi, V., & Thusu, A. (2023). The use of artificial intelligence to optimise the routing of vehicles and reduce traffic congestion in urban areas. *EAI Endorsed Transactions on Energy Web, 10*, 1–13.

Dwivedi, M., Uniyal, A., & Mohan, R. (2015). New horizons in planning smart cities using LiDAR technology. *International Journal of Applied Remote Sensing and GIS, 1*(2), 40–50.

Ersan, M., Irmak, E., & Colak, A. M. (2024, May 27–29). Applications, insights and implications of digital twins in smart city management. *2024 12th International Conference on Smart Grid (icSmartGrid)*. https://doi.org/10.1109/icSmartGrid61824.2024.10578291

Fabrègue, B. F. G., & Bogoni, A. (2023). Privacy and security concerns in the smart city. *Smart Cities, 6*(1), 586–613. https://doi.org/10.3390/smartcities6010027

Gadjeva, N. (2023). *Japanese digital cultural promotion: Online experience of Kyoto* (1st ed.). Routledge. https://doi.org/10.4324/9781003373292

Ganin, A. A., Mersky, A. C., Jin, A. S., Kitsak, M., Keisler, J. M., & Linkov, I. (2019). Resilience in intelligent transportation systems (ITS). *Transportation Research Part C: Emerging Technologies, 100*, 318–329. https://doi.org/10.1016/j.trc.2019.01.014

Guevara, L., & Auat Cheein, F. (2020). The role of 5G technologies: Challenges in smart cities and intelligent transportation systems. *Sustainability, 12*(16), 6469. https://doi.org/10.3390/su12166469

Habibzadeh, H., Nussbaum, B. H., Anjomshoa, F., Kantarci, B., & Soyata, T. (2019). A survey on cybersecurity, data privacy, and policy issues in cyber-physical system deployments in smart cities. *Sustainable Cities and Society, 50*, 101660. https://doi.org/10.1016/j.scs.2019.101660

Hashmi, R., Parmar, H., & Murari, U. K. (2025). Exploring carbon neutrality in the metaverse: Opportunities and challenges for business models. In Z. Hussain, A. Khan, M. U. Majeed, & A. Albattat (Eds.), *Metaverse and sustainable business models in SMEs* (pp. 71–102). IGI Global. https://doi.org/10.4018/979-8-3693-9005-4.ch004

Hatami, M., Qu, Q., Chen, Y., Kholidy, H., Blasch, E., & Ardiles-Cruz, E. (2024). A survey of the real-time metaverse: Challenges and opportunities. *Future Internet, 16*(10), 379. https://doi.org/10.3390/fi16100379

Hoang, A. T., Pham, V. V., & Nguyen, X. P. (2021). Integrating renewable sources into energy system for smart city as a sagacious strategy towards clean and sustainable process. *Journal of Cleaner Production, 305*, 127161. https://doi.org/10.1016/j.jclepro.2021.127161

Islam, M. M., Nooruddin, S., Karray, F., & Muhammad, G. (2022). Internet of things: Device capabilities, architectures, protocols, and smart applications in healthcare domain. *IEEE Internet of Things Journal, 10*(4), 3611–3641. https://doi.org/10.1109/JIOT.2022.3228795

Jagirdar, R., & Pathak, C. (2025). AI-driven transportation solutions: Lessons from developed nations for emerging economies. *Journal of Public Transportation, 4*(1). https://doi.org/10.34218/JPTS_04_01_002

Jain, R., Nagrath, P., Thakur, N., Saini, D., Sharma, N., & Hemanth, D. J. (2021). Towards a smarter surveillance solution: The convergence of smart city and energy efficient unmanned aerial vehicle technologies. In R. Krishnamurthi, A. Nayyar, & A. E. Hassanien (Eds.), *Development and future of internet of drones (IoD): Insights, trends and road ahead* (pp. 109–140). Springer International Publishing. https://doi.org/10.1007/978-3-030-63339-4_4

Jamshed, K., Qureshi, M. A., Kishwer, R., & Jamshaid, S. (2024). The benefits and challenges of artificial intelligence applications in tourism industry: How the hospitality industry in Japan is transforming. In A. Alnoor, G. E. Bayram, C. XinYing, & S. H. A. Shah (Eds.), *The role of artificial intelligence in regenerative tourism and green destinations* (pp. 129–147). Emerald Publishing Limited.

Jan, F., Min-Allah, N., & Düştegör, D. (2021). IoT based smart water quality monitoring: Recent techniques, trends and challenges for domestic applications. *Water, 13*(13), 1729. https://doi.org/10.3390/w13131729

Javed, A. R., Shahzad, F., Rehman, S., Zikria, Y. B., Razzak, I., Jalil, Z., & Xu, G. (2022). Future smart cities: Requirements, emerging technologies, applications, challenges, and future aspects. *Cities, 129*, 103794. https://doi.org/10.1016/j.cities.2022.103794

Jha, R. K. (2023). Cybersecurity and confidentiality in smart grid for enhancing sustainability and reliability. *Recent Research Reviews Journal, 2*(2), 215–241. https://doi.org/10.36548/rrrj.2023.2.001

Joyce, A., & Javidroozi, V. (2024). Smart city development: Data sharing vs. data protection legislations. *Cities, 148*, 104859. https://doi.org/10.1016/j.cities.2024.104859

Kanade, T. M., & Batule, R. B. (2024). Artificial intelligence and internet of things with metaverse. In S. Mehta, S. K. Gupta, A. A. Aljohani, & M. Khayyat (Eds.), *Impact and potential of machine learning in the metaverse* (pp. 161–195). IGI Global. https://doi.org/10.4018/979-8-3693-5762-0.ch007

Kang, D., Park, J., & Eun, S.-D. (2023). Home-based virtual reality exergame program after stroke rehabilitation for patients with stroke: A study protocol for a multicenter, randomized controlled trial. *Life, 13*(12), 2256. https://doi.org/10.3390/life13122256

Katuk, N., Abdullah, W. A. N. W., Sugiharto, T., & Ahmad, I. (2023). Smart technology: Ecosystem, impacts, challenges and the path forward. *Information System and Smart City, 1*(1), 1–26. https://doi.org/10.59400/issc.v1i1.63

Katuk, N., Ku-Mahamud, K. R., Zakaria, N. H., & Maarof, M. A. (2018). Implementation and recent progress in cloud-based smart home automation systems. *ISCAIE 2018 – 2018 IEEE Symposium on Computer Applications and Industrial Electronics.* https://doi.org/10.1109/ISCAIE.2018.8405447

Khan, L. U., Yaqoob, I., Tran, N. H., Kazmi, S. A., Dang, T. N., & Hong, C. S. (2020). Edge-computing-enabled smart cities: A comprehensive survey. *IEEE Internet of Things Journal, 7*(10), 10200–10232. https://doi.org/10.1109/JIOT.2020.2987070

Kim, J. H., & Kim, M. J. (2025). Analysis of urban management information technology systems: Ubiquitous city, smart city, metaverse, and digital twin. *International Journal of Urban Sciences*, In-press, 1–21. https://doi.org/10.1080/12265934.2025.2452501

Kumar, A., Sharma, S., Goyal, N., Singh, A., Cheng, X., & Singh, P. (2021). Secure and energy-efficient smart building architecture with emerging technology IoT. *Computer Communications, 176*, 207–217. https://doi.org/10.1016/j.comcom.2021.06.003

Kumar, K., Kaur, R., & Rani, V. (2025). Different methodologies for smart city and urbanization system. In *5G enabled technology for smart city and urbanization system* (pp. 36–55). Chapman and Hall/CRC.

Lanvin, B. (2023). Asian and European citizens see their cities as the 'smartest', finds 2023 IMD Smart City Index. International Institute for Management Development. https://www.imd.org/news/competitiveness/asian-and-european-citizens-see-their-cities-as-the-smartest-finds-2023-imd-smart-city-index/

Li, X. S. (2024). *Building digital twin metaverse cities*. Apress.

Lucic, M. C., Wan, X., Ghazzai, H., & Massoud, Y. (2020). Leveraging intelligent transportation systems and smart vehicles using crowdsourcing: An overview. *Smart Cities, 3*(2), 341–361. https://doi.org/10.3390/smartcities3020018

Ma, C. (2021). Smart city and cyber-security: Technologies used, leading challenges and future recommendations. *Energy Reports, 7*, 7999–8012. https://doi.org/10.1016/j.egyr.2021.08.124

Maier, F., & Weinberger, M. (2024). Metaverse meets smart cities—Applications, benefits, and challenges. *Future Internet, 16*(4), 126. https://doi.org/10.3390/fi16040126

Mangiaracina, R., Perego, A., Salvadori, G., & Tumino, A. (2017). A comprehensive view of intelligent transport systems for urban smart mobility. *International Journal of Logistics Research and Applications, 20*(1), 39–52. https://doi.org/10.1080/13675567.2016.1241220

Mazzetto, S. (2024). A review of urban digital twins integration, challenges, and future directions in smart city development. *Sustainability, 16*(19), 8337. https://doi.org/10.3390/su16198337

Mishra, P., & Singh, G. (2023). Enabling technologies for sustainable smart city. In P. Mishra, & G. Singh (Eds.), *Sustainable smart cities: Enabling technologies, energy trends and potential applications* (pp. 59–73). Springer International Publishing. https://doi.org/10.1007/978-3-031-33354-5_3

Mitchell, A., Owens, D., & Khazanchi, D. (2024). Metaverse research: A 15-year review and research prospectus. *AIS Transactions on Human-Computer Interaction, 16*(4), 396–428.

Mohammadnejad, M., & Abedini, A. (2025). The metaverse: Opportunities and challenges for sustainable future cities. *Sustainable City, 8*(1), 1–16. https://www.jscity.ir/article_215442.html?lang=en

Mostajeran, F., Fischer, M., Steinicke, F., & Kühn, S. (2023). Effects of exposure to immersive computer-generated virtual nature and control environments on affect and cognition. *Scientific Reports, 13*(1), 220. https://doi.org/10.1038/s41598-022-26750-6

Mubiru, I., & Westerholt, R. (2024). A scoping review on the conceptualisation and impacts of new mobility services. *European Transport Research Review, 16*(1), 12. https://doi.org/10.1186/s12544-024-00633-5

Mukhopadhyay, S. C., Tyagi, S. K. S., Suryadevara, N. K., Piuri, V., Scotti, F., & Zeadally, S. (2021). Artificial intelligence-based sensors for next generation IoT applications: A review. *IEEE Sensors Journal, 21*(22), 24920–24932. https://doi.org/10.1109/JSEN.2021.3055618

Padhiary, M., Roy, P., & Roy, D. (2025). The future of urban connectivity: AI and IoT in smart cities. In S. N. S. Al-Humairi, A. I. Hajamydeen, & A. Mahfoudh (Eds.), *Sustainable smart cities and the future of urban development* (pp. 33–66). IGI Global. https://doi.org/10.4018/979-8-3693-6740-7.ch002

Pereira, G. V., Parycek, P., Falco, E., & Kleinhans, R. (2018). Smart governance in the context of smart cities: A literature review. *Information Polity, 23*, 143–162. https://doi.org/10.3233/IP-170067

Pramanik, M. I., Lau, R. Y. K., Demirkan, H., & Azad, M. A. K. (2017). Smart health: Big data enabled health paradigm within smart cities. *Expert Systems with Applications, 87*, 370–383. https://doi.org/10.1016/j.eswa.2017.06.027

Shah, A. S., Nasir, H., Fayaz, M., Lajis, A., & Shah, A. (2019). A review on energy consumption optimization techniques in IoT based smart building environments. *Information, 10*(3), 108. https://doi.org/10.3390/info10030108

Shao, J., & Min, B. (2025). Sustainable development strategies for smart cities: Review and development framework. *Cities, 158*, 105663. https://doi.org/10.1016/j.cities.2024.105663

Sharma, P., Singh, R., & Srivastava, A. (2021). Analysing the role of geospatial technology in smart city development. In P. Sharma (Ed.), *Geospatial technology and smart cities: ICT, geoscience modeling, GIS and remote sensing* (pp. 1–20). Springer International Publishing. https://doi.org/10.1007/978-3-030-71945-6_1

Shihadeh, M. (2024). *Polycentric governance in blockchain based applications: Transforming government services in the UAE.* University of Leicester.

Shvetsov, A. V., & Alsamhi, S. H. (2024). When holographic communication meets metaverse: Applications, challenges, and future trends. *IEEE Access, 12*, 197488–197515. https://doi.org/10.1109/ACCESS.2024.3514576

Silvestri, S., Tricomi, G., Bassolillo, S. R., De Benedictis, R., & Ciampi, M. (2024). An urban intelligence architecture for heterogeneous data and application integration, deployment and orchestration. *Sensors, 24*(7), 2376. https://doi.org/10.3390/s24072376

Soliman, M. M., Ahmed, E., Darwish, A., & Hassanien, A. E. (2024). Artificial intelligence powered metaverse: Analysis, challenges and future perspectives. *Artificial Intelligence Review, 57*(2), 36. https://doi.org/10.1007/s10462-023-10641-x

Soomro, K., Bhutta, M. N. M., Khan, Z., & Tahir, M. A. (2019). Smart city big data analytics: An advanced review. *WIREs Data Mining and Knowledge Discovery, 9*(5), e1319. https://doi.org/10.1002/widm.1319

Suganya, R., Joseph, L. M. I. L., & Kollem, S. (2025). Integrating artificial intelligence in electric vehicles and optimizing logistics for sustainable transportation. In M. U. Tariq, & R. P. Sergio (Eds.), *Cases on AI-driven solutions to environmental challenges* (pp. 385–418). IGI Global. https://doi.org/10.4018/979-8-3693-7483-2.ch014

Sumon, R. I., Uddin, S. M. I., Akter, S., Mozumder, M. A. I., Khan, M. O., & Kim, H.-C. (2024). Natural language processing influence on digital socialization and linguistic interactions in the integration of the metaverse in regular social life. *Electronics, 13*(7), 1331. https://www.mdpi.com/2079-9292/13/7/1331

Sumra, K. B., Siddique, H., Afzal, S., & Qazi, A. (2025). Sustainable smart cities: Promotion of circular economy in urban GCC regions. *Journal of Science and Technology Policy Management (Ahead-of-Print).* https://doi.org/10.1108/JSTPM-01-2024-0025

Ullah, A., Anwar, S. M., Li, J., Nadeem, L., Mahmood, T., Rehman, A., & Saba, T. (2023). Smart cities: The role of internet of things and machine learning in realising a data-centric smart environment. *Complex & Intelligent Systems, 10*, 1607–1637. https://doi.org/10.1007/s40747-023-01175-4

Ullrich, L., Buchholz, M., Dietmayer, K., & Graichen, K. (2024). Expanding the classical V-model for the development of complex systems incorporating AI. *IEEE Transactions on Intelligent Vehicles*, 1–15. https://doi.org/10.1109/TIV.2024.3434515

United Nations Development Programme. (2023). Singapore global centre: Smart cities programme. https://www.undp.org/policy-centre/singapore/smart-cities-programme

Viale Pereira, G., Cunha, M. A., Lampoltshammer, T. J., Parycek, P., & Testa, M. G. (2017). Increasing collaboration and participation in smart city governance: A cross-case analysis of smart city initiatives. *Information Technology for Development, 23*(3), 526–553. https://doi.org/10.1080/02681102.2017.1353946

Wright, M., Chizari, H., & Viana, T. (2022). A systematic review of smart city infrastructure threat modelling methodologies: A Bayesian focused review. *Sustainability*, *14*(16), 10368. https://doi.org/10.3390/su141610368

Yaqoob, I., Hashem, I. A. T., Mehmood, Y., Gani, A., Mokhtar, S., & Guizani, S. (2017). Enabling communication technologies for smart cities. *IEEE Communications Magazine*, *55*(1), 112–120. https://doi.org/10.1109/MCOM.2017.1600232CM

Zaatar, M. T., Masri, N., Alfahel, M., Antar, G., Dayal, A., Khamis, H., Kuruvani, M., & Kachaamy, G. (2024). Exploring the virtual frontier: The impact of virtual reality on undergraduate biology education at the American University in Dubai. *International Journal of Information and Education Technology*, *14*(5), 675–680.

Zakaria, M. G. (2025). Navigating the virtual void: Challenges and solutions in investigating sexual violence in the metaverse. *International Journal of Doctrine, Judiciary and Legislation*, *6*(1), 31–62.

2

Fundamentals of the Metaverse

Noradila Nordin, Bryan Wing Khong Tiew, and Lee Kai Lun

2.1 Introduction to the Metaverse

The metaverse is an emerging concept currently lacking a standardised or universally accepted definition, and the IEEE P2048 standard is still under development. The metaverse gained significant mainstream attention following Mark Zuckerberg's announcement of Facebook's rebranding to Meta (Meta, 2021). This move, alongside advancements in digital technologies, has driven global interest in the metaverse and its potential to transform virtual interactions. Major technology corporations, including Microsoft, Tencent, and NVIDIA, have since launched related ventures (Wang et al., 2022). Neal Stephenson first introduced the term metaverse in his 1992 novel Snow Crash, which is described as a three-dimensional virtual reality (VR) space where users, represented by avatars, can interact with each other and the virtual world. This virtual world, accessed through specialised equipment, is a parallel reality created through advanced computer graphics, enabling global connectivity, and offering immersive experiences and limitless possibilities for interaction and exploration (Stephenson, 1994). The etymology of "metaverse" combines the Greek prefix "meta", meaning "beyond", "after", or "transcendence", and "universe" denotes the physical cosmos, which translates literally to "beyond the universe" (Mystakidis, 2022; Özkan & Özkan, 2024; Rafique & Qadir, 2024; Wang et al., 2022).

Metaverse can be described based on four main criteria derived from existing studies. It is (i) a convergence of physical and virtual worlds, creating a seamless integration of virtual and physical worlds; (ii) an immersive environment where users interact in real-time through avatars to engage in diverse activities; (iii) an evolving concept powered by advanced technologies that enable social, work, and leisure interactions; and (iv) a shared, persistent, and scalable virtual space that supports unlimited interactions and ensures real-time data continuity (Akin & Akin, 2024; Council of the European Union, 2022; Demirci et al., 2024; European Parliament, 2022; Meta, 2021; Ng, 2022; Özkan & Özkan, 2024; Uçgun, 2024; Wang et al., 2022).

The metaverse is envisioned as an integrated space where physical and virtual worlds merge, underpinned by technologies such as augmented reality

DOI: 10.1201/9781003619819-3

(AR), VR, and digital twins that provide precise, real-time updates of physical objects or systems, enhancing the simulation, monitoring, and optimisation capabilities of the virtual world. One of the metaverse's essential aspects is its immersive nature. Users represent themselves using avatars to interact and engage in a wide range of activities that span from leisure and gaming to commerce and healthcare. With advanced tracking and enabler technologies, avatars have more natural interactions that reflect precise physical movements and expressions. These are made possible through artificial intelligence (AI), blockchain, 6G connectivity, extended reality (XR), and other evolving technologies to improve the richness of users' overall experience in the metaverse.

2.2 Key Components and Technologies

The metaverse is described through various terms, including components, elements, characteristics, features, technologies, and enabler technologies that are often used interchangeably. In order to clarify the distinctions among the terms, the descriptions from existing studies are organised into four primary categories as shown in Figure 2.1: (i) key elements, which are the core principles or objectives for an enriched user experience, (ii) key components, which are the foundational structure of the metaverse experience, (iii) metaverse technologies, which are the core technologies facilitating the functionality of the metaverse, and (iv) enabler technologies that support the metaverse but are not exclusive to it (Akin & Akin, 2024; Council of the European Union, 2022; Demirci et al., 2024; Dhillon & Tinmaz, 2024; Dionysopoulos et al., 2024; European Parliament, 2022; Go & Kang, 2023; Meta, 2021; Mystakidis, 2022; Ng, 2022; Özkan & Özkan, 2024; Rafique & Qadir, 2024; Uçgun, 2024; Wang et al., 2022; Xu et al., 2022).

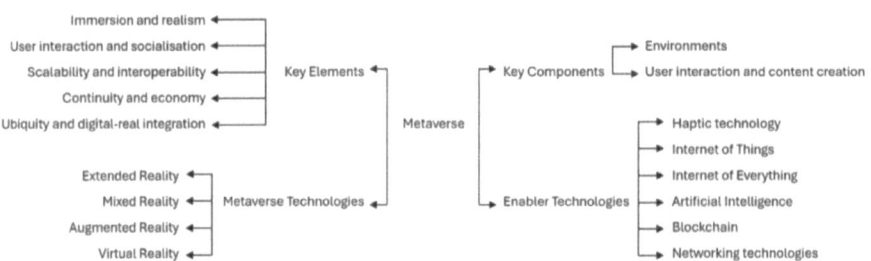

FIGURE 2.1
Metaverse key elements, components, technologies, and enabler technologies.

2.2.1 Key Elements

The metaverse is characterised by various fundamental elements representing its core principles and objectives for a seamless, immersive, and dynamic user experience. These elements can be grouped into five categories: (i) immersion and realism, (ii) user interaction and socialisation, (iii) scalability and interoperability, (iv) continuity and economy, and (v) ubiquity and physical-virtual integration. Immersion and realism are essential elements in the metaverse. They enable user engagement within realistic virtual environments using VR and mixed reality (MR) technologies, which blur the boundaries between physical and virtual worlds. User interaction and socialisation through collaborative activities, virtual gatherings, and social exchanges using avatars have transformed the metaverse into a communal and participatory space.

These interactions are further enhanced by AI, which enables personalised experiences and responsive digital entities for improved immersive experiences. The scalability element in the metaverse refers to its ability to accommodate an increasing number of users and more complex virtual environments without compromising the system's performance. At the same time, interoperability ensures that distinct virtual worlds, platforms, and systems can seamlessly interact. It allows users to move freely across different virtual spaces. Both scalability and interoperability elements rely heavily on advanced technologies, such as cloud and edge computing, and robust networking infrastructure to support high-performance operations and ensure the metaverse's long-term viability and functionality.

In addition, the continuity and persistence of the metaverse are integral to maintaining a cohesive and sustainable virtual space. A persistent virtual environment continues to evolve and remain accessible even when users are not actively engaged, providing the foundation for ongoing interaction and content creation. Central to this persistence is the decentralised economy of the metaverse, which supports the creation, ownership, and exchange of digital assets. Ubiquity and physical-virtual integration ensure the metaverse is accessible across various devices and platforms, making it available to users anytime and from any location. This constant connectivity allows the metaverse to become a pervasive part of users' daily lives. By integrating AR and MR into the user experience, the metaverse allows virtual elements to overlay the real world, creating a richer and more interactive environment that makes the metaverse not just an escape from reality but an extension.

2.2.2 Key Components

The key components in the metaverse are the fundamental core areas of the experience. Existing studies have identified various components categorised into two groups: (i) environment and (ii) user interaction and content creation. The environment consists of mirror worlds, digital twins, and virtual worlds. Mirror worlds are large-scale digital replicas of the physical world, while digital twins are virtual replicas of objects or systems from the physical world. These digital replicas are used to simulate the physical world. Virtual worlds, on the other hand, are computer-generated environments that include digital twins and mirror worlds. Users utilise avatars as an extension of themselves to interact and engage in the virtual world. They can customise their avatars to align with their physical world traits or use them creatively for self-expression. Avatars can be perceived as reflections of users' personalities and identities. At the same time, they can also be perceived as performative entities designed to convey specific aspects of identity.

Another component of the metaverse is user interaction and content creation. User-generated content (UGC) is a driving force behind the metaverse's growth. Users, mainly digital natives proficient in digital technologies, actively contribute to the virtual world. Through the creation of digital assets, experiences, and environments, these contributions play a significant role in the metaverse's dynamic towards the metaverse's vision to evolve into a self-sustaining "surreality" where the distinction between virtual and physical worlds becomes blurred.

2.2.3 Metaverse Technologies

The metaverse is fundamentally enabled by a range of core technologies, with XR serving as the central pillar. XR encompasses VR, AR, and MR, all of which contribute to creating immersive environments that integrate physical and virtual worlds. Users experience enhanced immersion through interaction within XR environments, further enriched by advanced auditory and physical movement tracking. These technologies seamlessly integrate the sensory dimensions of AR and VR into the virtual space. MR employs specialised devices to deliver immersive experiences using advanced technologies that consist of sensors, cameras, and tracking systems. These technologies interpret the user's surroundings to enable real-time interaction between physical and virtual objects. MR devices, such as headsets and glasses, share similarities with those used in AR and VR. By merging the capabilities of AR and VR, MR offers functionalities that surpass each technology individually. Within the metaverse, MR bridges the gap between AR and VR.

AR overlays computer-generated imagery, sounds, or data onto the physical world, typically through devices such as AR glasses, smartphones, tablets and head-mounted displays with computer vision, image processing, and sensors to allow devices to sense and track the user's surroundings, seamlessly integrating digital information into the physical world. This interaction enriches the user's perception of the physical world without fully immersing them in a virtual world, thus creating a hybrid reality. Conversely, VR offers a fully immersive experience by transporting users into a virtual world through specialised equipment such as VR headsets, immersion helmets, and omnidirectional treadmills. VR creates simulations that replicate the physical world or fictional settings, offering experiences that range from realistic to fantastical to provide a convincing and immersive experience. This technology enhances interaction through modalities such as vision, sound, touch, and movement, enabling natural interaction with virtual objects.

2.2.4 Enabler Technologies

In the metaverse, enabler technologies represent the supporting technologies for creating immersive and interactive virtual experiences. These technologies support sensory interaction, such as haptic technology devices that integrate the sense of touch to create a multi-sensory environment. Examples of the devices include haptic gloves, sensors, and XR headsets, which enable users to have physical interaction with virtual objects. The Internet of Things and the Internet of Everything also enhance this experience by connecting people, processes, and data within an interconnected ecosystem. In ensuring seamless interaction and communication between users in both worlds, networking technologies and the emerging Tactile Internet are crucial. The Tactile Internet enhances interactivity by enabling real-time, low-latency data transmission.

Furthermore, technologies such as 6G, edge computing, and cloud computing are vital to ensure efficient, high-bandwidth and low-latency data transmission. It enables seamless interactions across devices, locations, and connectivity between virtual and physical worlds (Zawish et al., 2024). Intelligence in the metaverse is supported through AI to enable personalised services and experiences for its users by facilitating real-time user interactions and non-player characters (NPCs) responses, movement predictions, and avatar and scene generation.

The metaverse blurs the boundaries between the physical and virtual worlds, allowing users to engage in activities similar to those in the real world. Therefore, ensuring a secure environment in the metaverse is essential, which can be achieved through blockchain. Blockchain enhances security, transparency, and trust by facilitating transactions and asset management through its decentralised architecture. It ensures security and authenticity while protecting users' asset ownership of non-fungible tokens (NFTs).

2.2.5 Metaverse Platforms and Applications

Second Life is widely recognised as the pioneer of the virtual world and a precursor to the metaverse. It was launched in 2003 and remains a key reference for the metaverse. Using avatars, Second Life enables users to engage in various activities, from social and gaming to education and commerce. Roblox, founded in 2004, and Decentraland in 2020, are examples of virtual platforms that build on these concepts. However, unlike Second Life, these virtual platforms focus more on gaming, user-created content, and immersive brand experiences (Demirci et al., 2024; Dwivedi et al., 2022). Roblox, in particular, became one of the largest global gaming platforms, with over 214 million active users by 2023.

Decentraland enables users to create, experience, and monetise virtual content, allowing them to purchase and develop virtual land (LAND) represented as NFTs. Additionally, Decentraland enables the creation of diverse virtual environments, such as transportation systems and hotels. Samsung has utilised this feature by expanding its brand engagement through its metaverse on the platform. As Decentraland was built on the Ethereum blockchain and operates on a decentralised model, all content and transactions are recorded. It ensures that users have complete control and ownership of their virtual assets.

Roblox has evolved from a gaming platform into a comprehensive development space that offers avatar creation and teleportation tools and a marketplace for trading assets and code. Brands like Gucci and Nike have leveraged Roblox for immersive virtual experiences, with Gucci launching Gucci Town and Gucci Meta Mansion for brand engagement and digital product sales, while Nike incorporated NFTs and virtual products in NIKELAND through its acquisition of RTFKT. Walmart has similarly integrated virtual and physical retail experiences in the metaverse. It utilised Roblox to introduce Walmart Land and Walmart's Universe of Play (Walmart, 2022). These virtual spaces are designed to engage younger demographics through interactive experiences, including games and virtual renditions of Walmart products. Further advancing this initiative, Walmart partnered with Unity Technologies to develop tools enabling seamless integration of its shopping systems into virtual environments, creating immersive shopping experiences and advancing the convergence of virtual and physical retail spaces (Walmart, 2024).

Cities worldwide are adopting metaverse technologies to enhance urban living and engagement, with the tourism and travel sectors demonstrating the metaverse's transformative potential by expanding access to immersive experiences and distant locations. Seoul, for instance, incorporates metaverse technology into urban governance through its Metaverse Seoul initiative, which is part of the Seoul Vision 2030 plan. This platform features a virtual city hall, tourism destinations, and social service centres to interact with avatar-based officials for civil services and explore virtual replicas of city landmarks and cultural festivals using VR headsets, enhancing civic engagement and tourism.

The impact of metaverse technologies extends into the global travel industry. In Singapore, Singapore's Changi Airport has launched ChangiVerse on Roblox to engage global audiences through a virtual world. First Airlines offers virtual flights in Japan that deliver fully immersive travel experiences from Tokyo to destinations such as Hawaii, New York, Rome, and Paris. In Istanbul, the airport provides Turkish Airlines with a Hezarfen flight experience. The experience allows the users to immerse themselves in wind, motion, and iconic city landmarks through VR technology that simulates a historic flight over Istanbul.

Additionally, various institutions have adopted virtual tours providing global access to cultural and educational heritage, including the Vatican Museums, the New York Botanical Garden, and the Eiffel Tower. Building on this educational focus, universities adopt the metaverse to transform learning environments. The Chinese University of Hong Kong, Shenzhen (CUHKSZ) has created a blockchain-powered virtual replica of its physical campus, offering a hybrid environment where physical world actions influence the virtual space. Similarly, the Hong Kong University of Science and Technology developed MetaHKUST to provide an immersive platform connecting students, faculty, and alums to foster creativity and collaboration across campuses (Uçgun, 2024; Xu et al., 2022).

2.3 Social and Economic Implications

The metaverse extends beyond technology, computers, and the Internet. It further influences the social, economic, and cultural dimensions. It reshapes how individuals connect and interact, transforming experiences and opportunities. In the social realm, the metaverse enhances interaction through real-time multi-sensory communication within immersive virtual environments, where users engage via avatars. These interactions evoke richer emotional responses than traditional 2D Internet experiences (Hennig-Thurau et al., 2023). The metaverse also offers accessibility to approximately 1.3 billion individuals with disabilities, 16% of the global population (WHO, n.d.), enabling engagement in activities otherwise inaccessible in the physical world. Additionally, it offers boundless self-expression, allowing users to represent themselves creatively and authentically.

During its early development, the metaverse has already demonstrated economic potential in education, gaming, and e-commerce. As adoption expands, it could drive the fourth industrial revolution towards a fully digital economy. The metaverse enables a virtual marketplace where users trade, sell, and buy digital goods and services, fostering more efficient cross-border commerce than traditional markets. Rising demand for NFTs and cryptocurrencies will likely make them integral to virtual payment systems (Cantú et al., 2024). This digital economic model will generate new professional roles, including VR designers, AR developers, and digital asset specialists, while reshaping traditional work through increased remote engagement and virtual collaboration.

The metaverse fosters deeper connectivity within the virtual world, influencing society, the economy, and culture. As individuals increasingly integrate into this virtual space, culture, defined as "the way of life for an entire society", may evolve (George et al., 2021). New social norms and behaviours could emerge, challenging traditional values and established lifestyles. The metaverse encourages open and creative expression, allowing users to experiment and interact freely, which may inspire new art forms, music, fashion, language, and social customs. Its borderless structure facilitates real-time cultural exchange, enabling the global sharing and appreciation of diverse traditions through virtual cultural education and events. It provides opportunities to promote global awareness of multiculturalism.

Despite the positive acceptability of the metaverse's adoption, reflected in favourable relationships between social norms, ease of use, and overall behavioural intentions, there are significant concerns, particularly regarding privacy and security (Aburbeian et al., 2022). Even in the current Internet era, society is concerned about privacy during web browsing. This issue is expected to become more invasive and intense with the metaverse, mainly due to the unrestricted and borderless nature of virtual worlds, which may lead to unethical and illegal behaviours, such as the exploitation of users' data by advertisers and marketers to uncover details of their viewing habits, activities, and attention spans through eye-tracking technology in VR headsets and other devices. These risks contribute to scepticism regarding adopting metaverse technologies, particularly considering the ongoing struggle to combat cybercrime on the Internet. Therefore, addressing these issues with robust safeguards and responsible practices is essential to build trust and ensure the metaverse's secure and ethical development.

2.4 Challenges and Opportunities

In order to realise the metaverse's full potential, significant capital investment and technological advancements are required. Challenges such as insufficient computing power, inadequate Internet infrastructure, and high device latency must be addressed (Mosco, 2023). It highlights the necessity for extensive investment in advanced hardware, network improvements, next-generation wireless standards, and cutting-edge technological infrastructure. Beyond technical limitations, critical regulatory and policy challenges must also be addressed. Effective governance should consider social, economic, and cultural dimensions, including establishing ethical guidelines, safeguarding personal privacy, defining criminal law, regulating transactions, and transferring digital assets within virtual marketplaces. Ensuring that users can freely interact while being protected by robust regulatory frameworks is imperative for the responsible growth and widespread adoption of the metaverse.

Looking at the metaverse in the future, it no longer carries the same level of hype as it did in 2021. A survey by the Pew Research Center and Elon University's Imagining the Internet Center found that nearly 46% of 624 technology experts believe the metaverse will not reach the promised level of refinement and immersion by 2040 (Anderson & Rainie, 2022). It highlights significant scepticism regarding its long-term potential. Nevertheless, despite diminished enthusiasm, a more pragmatic and refined resurgence appears possible, driven by lessons learned from past user experiences and feedback. Additionally, the emergence of technologies such as 6G and AI drives the advancement in computer vision, wireless communication, and self-learning systems, which could help the metaverse meet its potential (Zawish et al., 2024). This progress fuels cautious optimism that a more mature and sophisticated version of the metaverse could re-emerge, potentially rekindling excitement and delivering the transformative vision promised initially.

References

Aburbeian, A. M., Owda, A. Y., & Owda, M. (2022). A technology acceptance model survey of the metaverse prospects. *AI*, 3(2), 285–302. https://doi.org/10.3390/ai3020018

Akin, I., & Akin, M. (2024). Valuation, accounting principles, and classification of assets in the metaverse. *Journal of Metaverse*, 4(1), 43–53. https://doi.org/10.57019/jmv.1412352

Anderson, J., & Rainie, L. (2022). *The metaverse in 2040*. Pew Research Center.

Cantú, C., Franco, C., & Frost, J. (2024). The economic implications of services in the metaverse. In *Global perspectives in the metaverse: Law, economics, and finance* (pp. 83–118). Springer Nature Switzerland. https://doi.org/10.1007/978-3-031-54802-4_6

Council of the European Union. (2022). Metaverse – Virtual world, real challenges. Analysis and Research Team. Retrieved December 10, 2024, from https://www.consilium.europa.eu/media/54987/metaverse-paper-9-march-2022.pdf

Demirci, B., Özeltürkay, E. Y., & Gülmez, M. (2024). Metaverse users' purchase intention in second life. *Journal of Metaverse*, 4(1), 84–93. https://doi.org/10.57019/jmv.1423387

Dhillon, P. K. S., & Tinmaz, H. (2024). Academic augmentation: Analysing avatar design in educational metaverse. *Journal of Metaverse*, 4(1), 54–70. https://doi.org/10.57019/jmv.1440122

Dionysopoulos, L., Giaglis, G., Revolidis, I., Arribas, I., Vasiliu-Feltes, I., Mores, I., Slapnik, T., & Lanotte, A. (2024). Blockchain-enabled virtual worlds. *EU Blockchain Observatory and Forum*.

Dwivedi, Y. K., Hughes, L., Baabdullah, A. M., Ribeiro-Navarrete, S., Giannakis, M., Al-Debei, M. M., & Wamba, S. F. (2022). Metaverse beyond the hype: Multidisciplinary perspectives on emerging challenges, opportunities, and agenda for research, practice and policy. *International Journal of Information Management*, 66, 102542. https://doi.org/10.1016/j.ijinfomgt.2022.102542

European Parliament. (2022). Metaverse-opportunities, risks and policy implications. Retrieved December 10, 2024, from https://www.europarl.europa.eu/cmsdata/268589/eprs-briefing-metaverse_EN.pdf

George, A. H., Fernando, M., George, A. S., Baskar, T., & Pandey, D. (2021). Metaverse: The next stage of human culture and the internet. *International Journal of Advanced Research Trends in Engineering and Technology (IJARTET)*, 8(12), 1–10.

Go, H., & Kang, M. (2023). Metaverse tourism for sustainable tourism development: Tourism agenda 2030. *Tourism Review, 78*(2), 381–394. https://doi.org/10.1108/TR-02-2022-0102

Hennig-Thurau, T., Aliman, D. N., Herting, A. M., Cziehso, G. P., Linder, M., & Kübler, R. V. (2023). Social interactions in the metaverse: Framework, initial evidence, and research roadmap. *Journal of the Academy of Marketing Science, 51*(4), 889–913. https://doi.org/10.1007/s11747-022-00908-0

Meta. (2021). Founder's Letters, 2021. Retrieved December 31, 2024, from https://about.fb.com/news/2021/10/founders-letter

Mosco, V. (2023). Into the metaverse: Technical challenges, social problems, utopian visions, and policy principles. *Javnost – The Public, 30*(2), 161–173. https://doi.org/10.1080/13183222.2023.2200688

Mystakidis, S. (2022). Metaverse. *Encyclopedia, 2*(1), 486–497. https://doi.org/10.3390/encyclopedia2010031

Ng, D. T. K. (2022). What is the metaverse? Definitions, technologies and the community of inquiry. *Australasian Journal of Educational Technology, 38*(4), 190–205. https://doi.org/10.14742/ajet.7945

Özkan, A., & Özkan, H. (2024). Meta: XR-AR-MR and mirror world technologies business impact of metaverse. *Journal of Metaverse, 4*(1), 21–32. https://doi.org/10.57019/jmv.1344489

Rafique, W., & Qadir, J. (2024). Internet of everything meets the metaverse: Bridging physical and virtual worlds with blockchain. *Computer Science Review, 54*, 100678. https://doi.org/10.1016/j.cosrev.2024.100678

Stephenson, N. (1994). *Snow crash*. Penguin UK.

Uçgun, G. (2024). The effects of metaverse on the tourism industry. *Journal of Metaverse, 4*(1), 71–83. https://doi.org/10.57019/jmv.1466997

Walmart. (2022, September 26). *Walmart jumps into Roblox with launch of Walmart land and Walmart's universe of play*. Retrieved December 31, 2024, from https://corporate.walmart.com/news/2022/09/26/walmart-jumps-into-roblox-with-launch-of-walmart-land-and-walmarts-universe-of-play

Walmart. (2024, January 4). *Walmart and unity to bring immersive commerce to games, virtual worlds and apps*. Retrieved December 31, 2024, from https://corporate.walmart.com/news/2024/01/04/walmart-and-unity-to-bring-immersive-commerce-to-games-virtual-worlds-and-apps

Wang, Y., Su, Z., Zhang, N., Xing, R., Liu, D., Luan, T. H., & Shen, X. (2022). A survey on metaverse: Fundamentals, security, and privacy. *IEEE Communications Surveys & Tutorials, 25*(1), 319–352. https://doi.org/10.1109/COMST.2022.3202047

World Health Organization (WHO). (n.d.). *Disability*. Retrieved December 31, 2024, from https://www.who.int/health-topics/disability

Xu, M., Ng, W. C., Lim, W. Y. B., Kang, J., Xiong, Z., Niyato, D., Yang, Q., Shen, X., & Miao, C. (2022). A full dive into realising the edge-enabled metaverse: Visions, enabling technologies, and challenges. *IEEE Communications Surveys & Tutorials, 25*(1), 656–700. https://doi.org/10.1109/COMST.2022.3221119

Zawish, M., Dharejo, F. A., Khowaja, S. A., Raza, S., Davy, S., Dev, K., & Bellavista, P. (2024). AI and 6G into the metaverse: Fundamentals, challenges and future research trends. *IEEE Open Journal of the Communications Society, 5*, 730–778. https://doi.org/10.1109/OJCOMS.2024.3349465

3

AI-Powered Smart Cities

Michael Bidollahkhani

3.1 Foundations of AI in Smart Cities

Around 55% of the world's population lives in urban areas, which is expected to increase to 66% by 2030 (United Nations, 2018). Resource management, distribution of services, and optimisation of transportation are becoming difficult due to the lack of adequately modern and smart solutions, and as cities grow, new problems arise (Camero & Alba, 2019). The foundation of any smart city lies in its ability to leverage AI to create intelligent, adaptive, and sustainable systems. This section begins by defining the core principles of AI and its transformative potential in urban environments. It starts with the technological infrastructure that enables AI-driven solutions, including integrating the Internet of Things (IoT), 5G networks, and cloud computing. The discussion extends to the critical relationship between urban and rural areas, emphasising the role of AI in bridging the technological and resource gaps. The evolution of cities is influenced by human progress that has significantly impacted urban life structure, functioning and goals. Table 3.1 summarises the evolution of concepts related to smart cities as synthesised from the literature. As early as 1987, the ecocity concept was used with the latest concept of a generative city.

What is intelligence, and what does it mean at its core? MIT's Dr Alexander Amini (2023) defines intelligence as "the ability to process information and use it to make better decisions or take actions in the future". AI builds on this idea by creating systems and algorithms to do the same. In simple words, AI refers to techniques that allow computers to mimic human behaviour. The most recent definition of AI is "a machine-based system that, for explicit or implicit objectives, infers, from the input it receives, how to generate outputs such as predictions, content, recommendations, or decisions that can influence physical or virtual environments" (The OECD/G20 Inclusive Framework, 2024).

AI is at the centre of smart city innovation, empowering urban systems to analyse, interpret, and act on data in real-time. The capabilities of AI stem from a combination of key components that work together to create dynamic, adaptive, and efficient urban ecosystems. These components – learning,

DOI: 10.1201/9781003619819-4

TABLE 3.1

Evolution of Concepts Related to Smart Cities

Concept	Reference	Definition
Eco City	Register (1987)	A city designed to maintain ecological health, emphasising sustainable living and environmental balance.
Wired City	Dutton et al. (1987)	A digitally connected community where households and businesses have comprehensive access to electronic communication services.
Sustainable City	Haughton and Hunter (1994)	An urban space where communities and businesses work collaboratively to enhance the built, natural, and cultural environment while aligning with global sustainability goals.
Virtual City	Graham and Aurigi (1997)	A digital urban environment where citizens interact in cyberspace, complementing physical urban interactions.
Green City	Hammer et al. (2011)	An urban environment that promotes economic growth while safeguarding natural resources and essential ecosystem services.
Digital City	Ishida (2002)	A regional digital space where individuals interact, exchange knowledge, and foster shared interests within a connected environment.
Ubiquitous City	Shin (2005)	A city where digital infrastructure seamlessly integrates with everyday life, providing pervasive computing and real-time connectivity for services and governance.
Smart City	Giffinger et al. (2007)	A city that utilises ICT, IoT, AI, and data-driven decision-making to enhance urban services, optimise resource use, and improve citizens' quality of life.
Intelligent City	Komninos (2006)	A region characterised by a strong capacity for learning and innovation, leveraging human creativity, institutional knowledge generation, and digital communication networks.
Knowledge City	Edvinsson (2006)	A city strategically designed to cultivate intellectual capital and collective knowledge, driving long-term sustainable welfare and efficiency.
Resilient City	Meerow et al. (2016)	A city designed to withstand and recover from environmental, economic, and social challenges, using adaptive policies and technology-driven risk management.
15-Minute City	Moreno et al. (2021)	The quest for more sustainable and smarter cities, this concept emphasises accessibility, proposing that essential services should be within a 15-minute walk or bike ride from any point in the city. It aims to reduce car dependency and promote sustainable living.
Regenerative City	Wired (2024)	A city that establishes a restorative relationship with the environment, utilising local materials, incorporating green spaces, and leveraging ecosystems to address climate challenges.

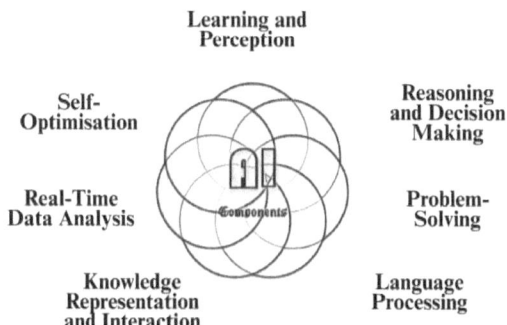

FIGURE 3.1
Transformative core components of AI.

reasoning and decision-making, problem-solving, perception, language processing, knowledge representation, and interaction – enable cities to address challenges, optimise resources, and enhance citizen experiences. Figure 3.1 illustrates these components, highlighting their applications and transformative potential.

Learning is the cornerstone of AI's adaptability, enabling systems to refine operations and improve performance by leveraging new data. It allows AI-driven systems to adapt dynamically to changing conditions and evolving urban demands. Machine learning (ML) algorithms, as the foundation of this component, analyse historical trends and patterns to generate accurate predictions and optimise decision-making processes. Perception equips AI systems with the ability to interpret and understand their environment by processing sensory data, such as images, sounds, and sensor readings. It enables real-time monitoring and interaction with the physical world, forming the basis of many smart city applications. AI systems ensure that urban management is context-aware and capable of timely, informed actions.

Reasoning and decision-making empower AI systems to evaluate complex scenarios, prioritise actions, and implement strategies optimising urban functionality. These capabilities enable AI to transform raw data into actionable solutions that enhance efficiency and responsiveness across city systems. Problem-solving enables AI systems to address complex and evolving challenges, mainly when predefined solutions are insufficient or unavailable. In urban systems' dynamic and interconnected environments, this capability allows AI to devise strategies by analysing multiple variables, such as weather, population density, and resource availability.

Problem-solving AI systems integrate data from diverse sources, identify key constraints, and generate optimal strategies to address multifaceted challenges. This approach is indispensable for managing unpredictable situations and supporting critical decision-making processes. Language processing, powered by Natural Language Processing (NLP) technologies, enables AI systems to understand, interpret, and generate human language. NLP technologies allow AI systems to process natural language data from diverse sources, such as written queries, voice commands, or public feedback, enabling efficient responses and actionable insights. Language processing transforms the interaction between citizens and smart city systems, making communication more efficient, personalised, and accessible.

Knowledge representation and interaction are critical components of AI in smart cities, ensuring that urban systems are both intelligent and user-centric (Wang et al., 2022). Knowledge representation organises complex urban data into structured formats, allowing AI systems to process, understand, and utilise this information effectively. Simultaneously, interaction focuses on designing intuitive interfaces that enable seamless communication between citizens and AI systems, fostering accessibility and trust (Lehtiö et al., 2023). Knowledge representation involves frameworks such as knowledge graphs and ontologies, which establish connections between data points and define their relationships. These structured models enable AI systems to derive insights, identify patterns, and support decision-making processes.

Interaction complements knowledge representation by ensuring that AI systems remain accessible to all citizens, regardless of technical proficiency (Duberry, 2022). It involves designing user-friendly dashboards, voice-activated assistants, and immersive augmented reality (AR) tools. Another vital aspect of interaction is the explainability of AI (xAI) systems. xAI tools and methods provide transparent insights into how AI systems make decisions, building trust between citizens and AI (Manias et al., 2023; Schmager et al., 2024). For instance, when an AI system optimises traffic flow, an explainable interface can display the reasoning behind the changes, such as traffic density analysis or incident reports (Adewopo et al., 2023).

Using effective knowledge representation and intuitive interaction, AI systems in smart cities become more transparent, accessible, and intelligent. These components ensure that urban systems can make complex decisions efficiently and communicate their processes and benefits to the citizens they serve. This dual approach enhances trust, promotes inclusivity, and bridges the gap between AI capabilities and human needs. In a smart city's dynamic and fast-paced environment, processing and analysing large volumes of data in real-time is critical for ensuring efficient and effective urban management. Real-time data analysis allows AI systems to monitor ongoing activities, identify anomalies, and make decisions with immediate impact. It is vital when timely action can significantly affect outcomes, such as energy management, transportation, and public safety.

AI systems with real-time data analysis can integrate inputs from various urban sources, such as IoT sensors, public services, and citizen feedback, transforming raw data into actionable insights (Rathore et al., 2018). This capability creates a cohesive framework that enables urban systems to remain adaptive and responsive. Real-time analysis is the backbone of AI-driven urban management, connecting various aspects of a smart city into a unified and intelligent network (Rathore et al., 2018). It ensures that urban systems can react to changes instantaneously, whether it is optimising resource allocation, managing emergencies, or enhancing service delivery.

Self-optimisation is a critical capability of AI systems that allows them to improve their performance and adapt dynamically without manual intervention (Gausemeier et al., 2014). Self-optimisation ensures that smart city systems operate efficiently, continuously refining their functionality over time. This capability is particularly significant in complex urban environments, where conditions and demands constantly change, and proactive adjustments are essential for sustainable development. AI systems equipped with self-optimisation analyse data, identify inefficiencies, and implement changes to enhance operations autonomously. It improves system reliability and reduces operational costs, resource consumption, and environmental impact.

Beyond lighting, self-optimisation is applied across various urban systems, such as energy grids (Lezhniuk et al., 2019), water management (Zhou et al., 2022), and transportation (Stoilov & Krasimira, 2016). For instance, AI in smart water distribution networks can detect leaks or inefficiencies and adjust pressure levels to minimise water loss. Similarly, AI can reallocate resources like buses or trains in public transport based on real-time passenger demand, improving service reliability and reducing idle time. Self-optimisation transforms urban management by eliminating the need for constant human oversight, allowing city administrators to focus on strategic planning and innovation.

3.2 AI as a Driver for Urban Intelligence

AI is the catalyst for transforming cities into hubs of urban intelligence, redefining how they operate and serve their inhabitants. This section explores how AI supports real-time decision-making systems, enabling cities to address resource allocation, energy efficiency, and disaster preparedness challenges. It examines the role of AI in enhancing citizen services, from personalised healthcare to efficient public transportation, ensuring equitable access under the Universal Service Obligation (USO). Furthermore, the section discusses governance, detailing how AI enables transparent policymaking and adaptive urban management.

3.2.1 AI-Driven Decision Support Systems

AI-driven decision support systems allow cities to process vast amounts of data and generate actionable insights in real-time. These systems enhance urban decision-making by predicting outcomes, optimising resource distribution, and enabling proactive management. AI is a transformative force driving urban intelligence, empowering cities to enhance decision-making, improve citizen services, ensure transparent governance, and align with global sustainability objectives. Cities can address challenges with precision, efficiency, and inclusivity, creating environments that prioritise the well-being of their inhabitants while fostering resilience and sustainability. Through real-world applications and regulatory frameworks, this section demonstrates how AI is redefining the future of urban living.

3.2.2 Enhancing Citizen Services

AI is revolutionising how cities deliver services to their inhabitants by making them more personalised, efficient, and accessible. Cities are bridging the gaps in service delivery, ensuring inclusivity and addressing the diverse needs of their populations. A core strength of AI in enhancing citizen services lies in its ability to process and analyse vast datasets to deliver tailored solutions. For example, in public healthcare, AI-powered platforms analyse patient histories and demographic data to recommend tailored preventive care and treatment plans. Such systems reduce the burden on healthcare providers while ensuring that citizens receive timely and effective care.

AI-driven chatbots and virtual assistants are becoming integral to municipal services, enabling residents to access information and support around the clock. These tools facilitate seamless interactions for tasks such as paying utility bills, scheduling public transport, or applying for permits. With NLP capabilities, these systems can communicate in multiple languages, ensuring accessibility for linguistically diverse populations and those with limited technical skills. AI also enhances the efficiency of public transportation systems, a critical aspect of urban living. Real-time data analysis and predictive algorithms enable AI to optimise bus and train schedules based on commuter demand, reducing wait times and improving reliability. Smart mobility applications powered by AI provide personalised travel suggestions, helping citizens choose the fastest or most sustainable routes. For instance, AI can integrate live traffic data with weather forecasts to recommend alternative routes during disruptions, ensuring smoother commutes.

Beyond urban centres, AI under the USO ensures that rural and marginalised populations benefit from improved services. AI-powered telemedicine platforms bring quality healthcare to remote areas, offering virtual consultations and AI-assisted diagnostics. Similarly, AI systems in education provide rural students with personalised learning experiences through adaptive e-learning platforms, helping bridge the digital divide. AI's ability to manage and allocate resources efficiently transforms essential services like water and energy supply. Smart grids use AI to monitor consumption patterns and predict demand, ensuring a steady and equitable energy distribution while minimising waste. In water management, AI-powered sensors and analytics detect leaks, optimise distribution, and reduce water wastage, ensuring sustainability and consistent access. AI contributes to safety and emergency response services, enhancing cities' overall sense of security. Predictive policing systems analyse crime patterns to allocate resources effectively, while AI-driven surveillance networks monitor public spaces for potential threats. AI systems prioritise calls, recommend evacuation routes, and coordinate resources during emergencies, ensuring rapid and effective responses.

3.2.3 AI-Enabled Governance

AI redefines urban governance by introducing advanced tools that enable data-driven policymaking, adaptive management, and enhanced transparency. City administrations can monitor urban systems comprehensively, identify trends, and respond to challenges quickly and precisely. This transformation enhances the efficiency and accountability of governance structures, fostering trust and collaboration between governments and citizens. One of the primary contributions of AI to governance is its ability to process vast amounts of urban data from diverse sources, including IoT devices, public services, and citizen feedback. AI systems provide actionable insights that inform policy decisions. For example, AI-powered dashboards allow city administrators to visualise real-time data on traffic patterns, energy usage, and environmental quality, enabling them to proactively make informed decisions that address urban challenges.

Adaptive management is another critical benefit of AI-enabled governance. AI systems can model and predict the impact of various policy options, allowing administrators to test scenarios and select the most effective strategies. For instance, during a public health crisis, AI can simulate the outcomes of different containment measures, helping policymakers implement targeted interventions that minimise disruption while maximising public safety. Similarly, AI algorithms can analyse historical data to predict future trends, such as population growth or resource demand, enabling cities to plan for long-term sustainability.

Transparency is a cornerstone of effective governance, and AI plays a pivotal role in enhancing it. For example, AI-driven systems can monitor public procurement processes, ensuring that contracts are awarded fairly and resources are allocated efficiently. Citizen-facing platforms powered by AI enhance transparency by providing accessible information about government activities, budgets, and performance metrics. AI facilitates participatory governance by enabling citizens to engage directly with urban decision-making processes. NLP platforms can analyse public feedback from surveys, social media, and community meetings, helping governments understand citizen priorities and concerns. These insights ensure that policies are aligned with the needs and preferences of the population, fostering a sense of inclusion and shared responsibility.

In addition to its role in policymaking and transparency, AI supports regulatory enforcement and compliance. For example, AI systems can detect anomalies in financial transactions, identify tax evasion, and monitor adherence to environmental regulations. These capabilities ensure that governance systems remain robust and aligned with legal and ethical standards. During emergencies, AI-enabled governance proves indispensable. Real-time data analysis allows city administrations to allocate resources effectively, coordinate responses, and communicate critical information to the public. For instance, AI systems can optimise evacuation plans during natural disasters and ensure that aid reaches affected areas quickly and efficiently.

3.3 Case Studies of AI-Driven Urban Solutions

The practical impact of AI on urban systems is best understood through real-world applications. This section presents a series of case studies that illustrate how AI has been implemented in key areas of urban management. From Singapore's adaptive traffic systems that reduce congestion and emissions to San Francisco's AI-powered waste optimisation programs, each case study provides concrete examples of AI's measurable benefits. The section also highlights Dubai's use of predictive policing for public safety, showcasing how AI contributes to crime prevention and emergency management.

3.3.1 Case Study I: Predictive Traffic Management in Singapore

Singapore, a city-state renowned for its efficient urban systems, has long faced challenges associated with high population density and growing vehicle ownership. Traffic congestion, a common issue in metropolitan regions, posed economic and environmental concerns, such as increased fuel consumption, emissions, and travel delays. Singapore implemented an AI-driven predictive traffic management system to address these challenges and transform its approach to urban mobility (Aloupogianni et al., 2024).

Singapore's intelligent traffic management system integrates advanced AI algorithms with IoT-enabled sensors deployed across the city's transportation network. These sensors continuously monitor traffic flow, vehicle speeds, and congestion levels. AI models analyse this real-time data, predicting congestion patterns and enabling dynamic adjustments to traffic signals. The system optimises the movement of vehicles and minimises bottlenecks. The solution also incorporates ML capabilities, allowing the system to learn from historical data and adapt to evolving traffic behaviours. Additionally, the platform integrates with public transportation systems, ensuring seamless coordination between private vehicles and mass transit options. Commuters benefit from AI-powered navigation apps that provide real-time updates on traffic conditions, suggesting alternate routes to avoid delays.

The implementation of AI-driven traffic management in Singapore has yielded significant benefits. First, it reduced congestion through dynamic signal adjustments, and predictive routing has decreased peak-hour delays, enhancing overall traffic flow. Second, it lowers emissions, which improves traffic efficiency, reduces fuel consumption, and lowers carbon emissions, contributing to Singapore's sustainability goals. Finally, it enhanced the commuter experience. The real-time updates and optimised routes have minimised travel times, increasing commuter satisfaction. Singapore's success highlights the importance of integrating AI with a robust infrastructure. Deploying IoT-enabled sensors and high-speed connectivity was critical in ensuring the system's effectiveness. Stakeholder collaboration, including government agencies, technology providers, and citizens, facilitated seamless implementation.

Singapore's predictive traffic management system is a model for cities worldwide grappling with congestion issues. While the technology requires significant investment in infrastructure, the long-term benefits in efficiency, sustainability, and quality of life outweigh the initial costs. Cities can tailor similar systems to their unique contexts by leveraging available resources and fostering public-private partnerships. Singapore's AI-driven approach demonstrates how intelligent urban solutions can address complex challenges, paving the way for a more efficient, sustainable, and commuter-friendly future. This case study underscores the transformative potential of AI in reimagining urban mobility, offering valuable insights for global urban planners and policymakers.

3.3.2 Case Study II: Disaster Preparedness in Japan

Japan's disaster preparedness framework integrates AI-driven systems with IoT sensors, weather monitoring stations, and seismic activity detectors. These systems continuously collect real-time data on environmental conditions, including weather patterns, oceanic movements, and geological activity. AI algorithms analyse this data to identify anomalies, predict potential disasters, and generate early warnings. One key component of this system is using ML models trained on historical disaster data. These models enable accurate predictions of events' scale, location, and timing, such as earthquakes and typhoons. AI-powered platforms also optimise evacuation plans by analysing population density, road conditions, and available resources, ensuring efficient and safe emergency responses (Balasubramanian & Motoi, 2024).

Additionally, AI supports disseminating critical information through multilingual chatbots and mobile apps, which deliver real-time alerts and instructions to residents. These tools ensure that vulnerable populations, including elderly citizens and non-native speakers, receive timely and comprehensible guidance during crises. Integrating AI into Japan's disaster preparedness system has delivered significant improvements. First, it provides faster response times to disasters. The AI-powered early warning systems provide alerts minutes or hours before disasters occur, allowing citizens and authorities to take preventive actions. Second, it optimised evacuations. The data-driven evacuation plans minimise congestion, reducing risks during large-scale relocations. Finally, it reduces casualties and losses by predicting disaster impacts, and AI helps mitigate the scale of human and economic losses.

Japan's success underscores the importance of integrating AI into national disaster management strategies. A robust infrastructure, including IoT networks and high-speed communication systems, is essential for the seamless operation of AI tools. Collaboration between government agencies, research institutions, and technology providers has also been critical in ensuring the system's reliability and effectiveness. Another key lesson is the value of citizen engagement. Public awareness campaigns and training programs help residents understand and utilise AI-powered tools, enhancing overall disaster preparedness.

Japan's approach to disaster preparedness serves as a model for other disaster-prone regions. While deploying AI technologies requires substantial investment, the potential to save lives and reduce economic losses makes it worthwhile. Governments can adapt Japan's strategies by focusing on scalable solutions, leveraging partnerships, and prioritising data-driven decision-making. Through its innovative use of AI, Japan demonstrates how technology can transform disaster preparedness, offering a blueprint for resilience in the face of environmental challenges. This case study highlights the critical role of AI in safeguarding communities, infrastructure, and economies against the unpredictability of nature.

3.3.3 Case Study III: Public Transport Optimisation in Sweden

Sweden, known for its commitment to sustainability and innovation, faces challenges in managing its public transportation systems to meet the demands of its urban and suburban populations. Stockholm, the nation's capital, experiences significant commuter flow daily, requiring efficient transport systems to minimise delays, reduce congestion, and promote eco-friendly mobility. Sweden has transformed its public transport infrastructure to enhance efficiency, accessibility, and sustainability (Abduljabbar et al., 2019). Stockholm's public transport system integrates AI-powered technologies to optimise schedules, routes, and resource allocation. The system collects and analyses real-time data from various sources, including commuter patterns, GPS-enabled buses and trains, and traffic conditions. ML algorithms process this data to predict peak usage periods and adjust schedules dynamically, ensuring that public transport resources align with demand. AI also enhances route optimisation by analysing traffic congestion and environmental factors such as weather conditions. This real-time adaptability minimises delays, improves commuter satisfaction, and reduces operational costs. In addition, Stockholm employs AI in its ticketing systems, where predictive analytics help forecast revenue, enabling better financial planning for transport authorities.

Another aspect of Sweden's AI-driven approach is its commitment to sustainability. AI optimises energy consumption for electric buses and trains, reducing emissions and supporting the country's goal of achieving carbon neutrality. Real-time passenger information systems powered by AI provide commuters with accurate updates on delays, alternate routes, and arrival times, enhancing the overall user experience. Implementing AI in Sweden's public transport system has delivered measurable benefits. First, it increased efficiency through dynamic scheduling and route optimisation that significantly reduced wait times and improved the reliability of services. Second, it promotes sustainability, in which energy optimisation for electric vehicles has lowered the carbon footprint of Stockholm's transport system. Finally, it enhances the user experience through real-time updates, and personalised travel recommendations have made commuting more convenient and stress-free. Sweden's success underscores the importance of integrating AI with a robust transportation infrastructure. Collaboration between technology providers, government agencies, and transport authorities has improved the system's effectiveness. Public awareness campaigns and user-friendly mobile applications have also facilitated the widespread adoption of these innovations.

Additionally, the scalability of Sweden's model demonstrates the value of starting with pilot projects to test AI solutions before expanding them across broader networks. Continuous monitoring and updates to the system ensure that it evolves alongside changing commuter needs. Sweden's approach to public transport optimisation offers a replicable framework for cities worldwide. While the technologies employed are advanced, the principles of data-driven scheduling, route optimisation, and real-time passenger information can be adapted to varying scales and contexts. Partnerships with private technology firms and investment in digital infrastructure are key factors in replicating this success. Sweden has also showcased how intelligent public transport systems can contribute to sustainable urban mobility. This case study highlights the potential of AI to create efficient, eco-friendly, and user-centric transport networks, providing a roadmap for cities aiming to modernise their public transportation infrastructure.

3.3.4 Case Study IV: Smart Governance in Dubai

Dubai is a global leader in smart city innovation, leveraging technology to enhance governance, urban planning, and service delivery. With a rapidly growing population and ambitious goals for sustainability and economic development, Dubai recognised the need for efficient, data-driven governance systems to ensure responsive and transparent administration. The Smart Dubai Initiative, launched in 2014, exemplifies how AI has been integrated into urban governance to achieve these objectives (Al Batayneh et al., 2021). It employs AI-powered tools and platforms to analyse data collected from urban systems, including transportation, healthcare, utilities, and public services. Dubai Pulse, a centralised data platform at the core of this initiative, aggregates real-time data from various government departments and private organisations. AI models analyse this data to generate actionable insights, enabling city administrators to make informed decisions on resource allocation, urban planning, and policy implementation. AI also powers predictive analytics tools to anticipate and proactively address urban challenges. For instance, AI systems monitor traffic patterns to optimise transportation networks, reducing congestion and emissions. Similarly, energy management systems use AI to predict electricity and water demand, ensuring efficient distribution and minimising waste.

One of the standout features of Dubai's intelligent governance system is its focus on citizen engagement and transparency. AI-driven chatbots and mobile applications provide residents with 24/7 access to government services, from bill payments to permit applications. These platforms streamline processes, reduce wait times, and improve user satisfaction. Additionally, AI tools track the performance of government initiatives, ensuring accountability and fostering public trust. Real-time data analysis and predictive tools have optimised resource management and service delivery. It also enhances transparency by providing citizens with information about government activities, boosting trust and engagement. Automation and AI-driven decision-making have reduced administrative costs while improving service quality.

Dubai's success demonstrates the importance of integrating AI into governance structures with a focus on scalability and inclusivity. A centralised data platform like Dubai Pulse ensures seamless collaboration between departments and stakeholders. Public education campaigns and user-friendly interfaces have been crucial in driving adoption among residents. The initiative also highlights the need for robust data governance policies to protect citizens' privacy and ensure ethical AI usage. Dubai's commitment to regulatory frameworks, such as its Ethical AI Guidelines, has played a key role in maintaining public trust.

Dubai's approach to smart governance offers valuable insights for cities aiming to modernise their administrative systems. While the level of investment in AI infrastructure may not be feasible for all cities, data centralisation, predictive analytics, and citizen engagement principles can be applied at various scales. Collaboration between government agencies, private technology providers, and international organisations is essential for replicating Dubai's model. Dubai has demonstrated how technology can enhance transparency, efficiency, and citizen satisfaction. This case study serves as a benchmark for intelligent urban management, showcasing the transformative potential of AI in creating responsive and inclusive governance systems.

3.4 Challenges in AI Integration and Implementation

Despite its transformative potential, integrating AI into smart cities is fraught with challenges that require careful consideration. This section addresses the technological barriers, including the complexities of integrating legacy systems and the disparities in infrastructure across regions, particularly in less developed countries. Societal concerns, such as data privacy and compliance with regulations like GDPR and the EU AI Act, are critically analysed alongside ethical debates surrounding AI fairness and bias. The discussion extends to regulatory and policy challenges, emphasising the need for adaptive frameworks that balance innovation with oversight. Finally, the section explores economic hurdles, including the high cost of AI deployment and the need for sustainable funding mechanisms.

3.4.1 Technological Challenges

The integration of AI systems into urban infrastructure often encounters significant technological hurdles. A critical challenge lies in the current infrastructure limitations in developed and less developed regions. Many cities, particularly in emerging economies, lack the robust digital infrastructure to support AI technologies, such as high-speed Internet, IoT networks, and data storage capabilities. Without these foundational elements, AI systems cannot operate effectively, widening the gap between technologically advanced cities and those lagging. Another pressing issue is the exponential speed of data generation. Modern urban environments produce data from sensors, cameras, and other sources daily. Processing and analysing this data in real-time often exceeds the capacity of current technologies, leading to delays and inefficiencies. Additionally, AI models are computationally intensive, requiring significant energy and hardware resources. It raises concerns about the environmental impact and sustainability of AI deployment.

3.4.2 Societal and Ethical Concerns

The widespread use of AI in urban systems raises critical societal and ethical concerns. Privacy is a central issue, as AI systems often rely on vast amounts of personal data to operate effectively. The potential misuse of this data, including surveillance and unauthorised sharing, threatens individual freedoms and trust in technology. Regulatory frameworks such as the GDPR in the EU aim to address these concerns by enforcing strict data protection standards. However, ensuring compliance across diverse jurisdictions remains a challenge. Bias and discrimination in AI algorithms also present ethical dilemmas. AI systems trained on biased datasets can perpetuate existing inequalities, leading to unfair outcomes in law enforcement, hiring, and access to public services. Ensuring algorithmic fairness and developing xAI systems are essential to mitigate these risks.

3.4.3 Regulatory and Policy Challenges

The rapid evolution of AI technologies has outpaced the development of regulatory frameworks, leaving significant gaps in governance. Policymakers face the challenge of establishing clear, enforceable guidelines that balance innovation with accountability. The complexity of regulating AI arises from its diverse applications and the difficulty of predicting its long-term societal impact. Frameworks such as the EU Artificial Intelligence Act (AI Act) aim to provide comprehensive regulations for AI systems, categorising them by risk level and imposing stricter requirements on high-risk applications. However, global consensus on AI governance is lacking, leading to fragmented approaches and inconsistent standards across regions. It creates challenges for multinational corporations and hinders the scalability of AI solutions.

3.4.4 Economic Challenges

Implementing AI systems in urban environments requires substantial financial investment. The costs associated with infrastructure upgrades, data collection, algorithm development, and workforce training can strain municipal budgets, particularly in low-income regions. Furthermore, the economic benefits of AI are often distributed unevenly, with large corporations reaping the majority of gains while smaller enterprises struggle to compete. AI adoption also raises concerns about job displacement as automation replaces traditional roles in the manufacturing, transportation, and customer service sectors. While AI creates new opportunities in data science, software engineering, and system management, these roles often require specialised skills that may not be accessible to all workers.

References

Abduljabbar, R., Hussein, D., Sohani, L., & Saeed Asadi, B. (2019). Applications of artificial intelligence in transport: An overview. *Sustainability*, *11*(1), 189. https://doi.org/10.3390/su11010189

Adewopo, V., Elsayed, N., ElSayed, Z., Ozer, M., Wangia-Anderson, V., & Abdelgawad, A. (2023, November). AI on the road: A comprehensive analysis of traffic accidents and autonomous accident detection system in smart cities. In *2023 IEEE 35th International Conference on Tools with Artificial Intelligence (ICTAI)* (pp. 501–506). IEEE.

Al Batayneh, R. M., Taleb, N., Said, R. A., Alshurideh, M. T., Ghazal, T. M., & Alzoubi, H. M. (2021, May). IT governance framework and smart services integration for future development of Dubai infrastructure utilising AI and big data, its reflection on the citizens standard of living. In *The international conference on artificial intelligence and computer vision* (pp. 235–247). Springer International Publishing.

Aloupogianni, E., Doctor, F., Karyotis, C., Maniak, T., Tang, R., & Iqbal, R. (2024, July). An AI-based digital twin framework for intelligent traffic management in Singapore. In 2024 *International Conference on Electrical, Computer and Energy Technologies (ICECET)* (pp. 1–6). IEEE. https://doi.org/10.1109/ICECET61485.2024.10698642

Amini, A. (2023). *Introduction to deep learning*. MIT CS.

Balasubramanian, K., & Motoi, I. (2024, July). Enhancing disaster preparedness in Chiba, Japan: The role of artificial neural networks in flood prediction. In *2024 IEEE/ACIS 9th International Conference on Big Data, Cloud Computing, and Data Science (BCD)* (pp. 199–207). IEEE. https://doi.org/10.1109/BCD61269.2024.10743089

Camero, A., & Alba, E. (2019). Smart city and information technology: A review. *Cities, 93*, 84–94. https://doi.org/10.1016/j.cities.2019.04.014

Duberry, J. (2022). Artificial intelligence and democracy: Risks and promises of AI-mediated citizen–government relations. In *Artificial intelligence and democracy*. Edward Elgar Publishing. https://doi.org/10.4337/9781788977319

Dutton, W. H., Elberse, A., & Hale, M. (1987). *Wired cities: Shaping the future of communications*. GK Hall & Co.

Edvinsson, L. (2006). Aspects on the city as a knowledge tool. *Journal of Knowledge Management, 10*(5), 6–13. https://doi.org/10.1108/13673270610691134

Gausemeier, J., Korf, S., Porrmann, M., Stahl, K., Sudmann, O., & Vaßholz, M. (2014). Development of self-optimising systems. In *Design methodology for intelligent technical systems: Develop intelligent technical systems of the future* (pp. 65–115). Springer. https://doi.org/10.1007/978-3-642-45435-6_3

Giffinger, R., Fertner, C., Kramar, H., Kalasek, R., Pichler Milanovic, N., & Meijers, E. J. (2007). *Smart cities. Ranking of European medium-sized cities*. Final report. Vienna University of Technology.

Graham, S., & Aurigi, A. (1997). Virtual cities, social polarisation, and the crisis in urban public space. *Journal of Urban Technology, 4*(1), 19–52. https://doi.org/10.1080/10630739708724546

Hammer, S., Kamal-Chaoui, L., Robert, A., & Plouin, M. (2011). *Cities and green growth: A conceptual framework*. OECD.

Haughton, G., & Hunter, C. (1994). *Sustainable cities*. Routledge.

Ishida, T. (2002). Digital city Kyoto. *Communications of the ACM, 45*(7), 76–81.

Komninos, N. (2006). The architecture of intelligent cities. *Intelligent Environments, 6*(1), 53–61.

Lehtiö, A., Hartikainen, M., Ala-Luopa, S., Olsson, T., & Väänänen, K. (2023). Understanding citizen perceptions of AI in the smart city. *Ai & Society, 38*(3), 1123–1134. https://doi.org/10.1007/s00146-022-01589-7

Lezhniuk, P., Serhii, K., & Andriy, P. (2019). *Self optimisation local electric systems modes with renewable energy sources.* Przeglad Electrotechniczny.

Manias, G., Apostolopoulos, D., Athanassopoulos, S., Borotis, S., Chatzimallis, C., Chatzipantelis, T., Compagnucci, M. C., Draksler, T. Z., Fournier, F., Goralczyk, M., Gucek, A., Karabetian, A., Kefala, S., Moumtzi, V., Kotios, D., Kovacic, M., Kyrkou, D., Limonad, L., Magopoulou, S., … Kyriazis, D. (2023, June). AI4Gov: Trusted AI for transparent public governance fostering democratic values. In *2023 19th International Conference on Distributed Computing in Smart Systems and the Internet of Things (DCOSS-IoT)* (pp. 548–555). IEEE. https://doi.org/10.1109/DCOSS-IoT58021.2023.00090

Meerow, S., Newell, J. P., & Stults, M. (2016). Defining urban resilience: A review. *Landscape and Urban Planning, 147*, 38–49. https://doi.org/10.1016/j.landurbplan.2015.11.011

Moreno, C., Allam, Z., Chabaud, D., Gall, C., & Pratlong, F. (2021). Introducing the "15-minute City": Sustainability, resilience and place identity in future post-pandemic cities. *Smart Cities, 4*(1), 93–111. https://doi.org/10.3390/smartcities4010006

Rathore, M. M., Paul, A., Hong, W. H., Seo, H., Awan, I., & Saeed, S. (2018). Exploiting IoT and big data analytics: Defining smart digital city using real-time urban data. *Sustainable Cities and Society, 40*, 600–610. https://doi.org/10.1016/j.scs.2017.12.022

Register, R. (1987). *Ecocity Berkeley: Building cities for a healthy future.* North Atlantic Books.

Schmager, S., Gupta, S., Pappas, I., & Vassilakopoulou, P. (2024, June). Designing for AI transparency in public services: A user-centred study of citizens' preferences. In *International Conference on Human-Computer Interaction* (pp. 237–253). https://doi.org/10.1007/978-3-031-61315-9_17

Shin, D.-H. (2005). Design and development of next generation of information infrastructure: Case studies of broadband public network and digital city. *Knowledge, Technology & Policy, 18*, 101–125. https://doi.org/10.1007/s12130-005-1027-6

Stoilov, T., & Krasimira, S. (2016). A self-optimisation traffic model by multilevel formalism. In *Autonomic road transport support systems* (pp. 87–111). Springer International Publishing.

The OECD/G20 Inclusive Framework. (2024). *Report of OECD council.*

United Nations. (2018). *The world's cities in 2018* (p. 34). United Nations. https://doi.org/10.18356/c93f4dc6-en

Wang, R., Wu, S., & Wang, X. (2022). The core of smart cities: Knowledge representation and descriptive framework construction in knowledge-based visual question answering. *Sustainability, 14*(20), 13236. https://doi.org/10.3390/su142013236

Wired. (2024). Here's what the sustainable cities of tomorrow could look like.

Zhou, P., Wang, X., & Chai, T. (2022). Multiobjective operation optimisation of wastewater treatment process based on reinforcement self-learning and knowledge guidance. *IEEE Transactions on Cybernetics, 53*(11), 6896–6909. https://doi.org/10.1109/TCYB.2022.3164476

4

Smart Concrete: IoT-Enabled Smart Materials for Smart Cities

Herry Prabowo, Nurul Qalbi Kurniashally, and Dian Kurnia

4.1 Introduction to Smart Concrete and IoT Integration

Smart concrete is an advanced construction material that attracts considerable attention in civil engineering. Smart concrete is often referred to as self-sensing or self-monitoring concrete. The ability of smart concrete is excellent in adapting structurally to environmental changes. Engineered sensor implants in structures and various smart technologies allow smart concrete to monitor conditions, detect potential problems, and communicate this information to relevant parties. (Ramachandran et al., 2022; Song et al., 2023). The primary ability of smart concrete is to detect and react to environmental changes (Siahkouhi et al., 2021). It also allows combinations with nanomaterials, such as carbon-based nanomaterials (CNMs) or graphene (Figure 4.1),

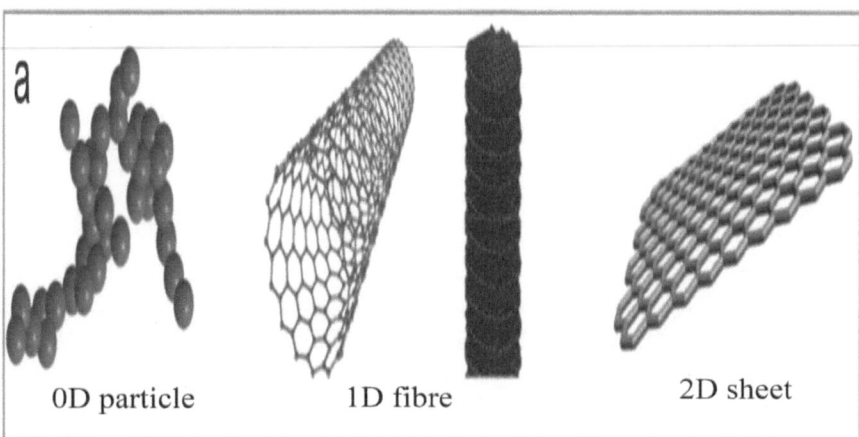

FIGURE 4.1
CNMs used for preparing SSC. (a) Schematic of 0D Nanoparticle, 1D Nanofiber, and 2D Nanosheet. (b) The Appearance of GP (Left) and CB (Right). (c) Single-walled CNT (SCNT) and Multi-walled CNT (MWCNT). (d) The structure of GNP and Graphene. (From Jiang et al., 2024.) *(Continued)*

DOI: 10.1201/9781003619819-5

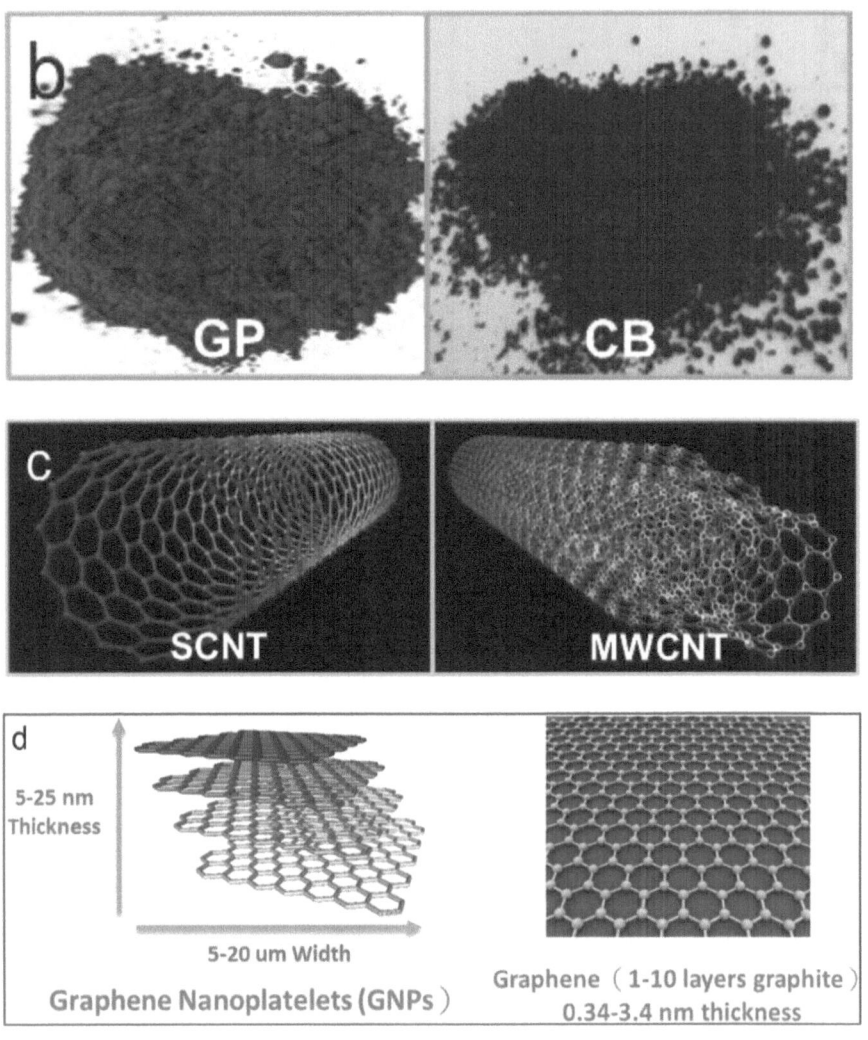

FIGURE 4.1
(Continued)

which are thoroughly dispersed on the concrete to form a sensor network (Jiang et al., 2024; Li et al., 2022). With this sensor, parameters such as strain, voltage, crack development, and damage can be monitored by observing the electrical properties of concrete (Li et al., 2023; Thomoglou et al., 2023).

The capacity to improve the durability, safety, and sustainability of concrete structures is an advantage of smart concrete. It is done by continuously assessing the structural integrity of buildings, bridges, and other infrastructure. Smart concrete offers early detection of potential problems, allowing for quick maintenance and repairs. This capability ultimately results in lower life cycle costs, longer service life, and reduced environmental impact on the construction industry (Makul, 2020; Nilimaa, 2023; Scope et al., 2020). Self-healing properties are one of the many advanced features that smart concrete offers. Smart concrete can repair small cracks and damage through its self-healing properties and mechanisms, such as fibres, shrinkable polymers, or minerals. These properties increase the durability and resistance of concrete structures, minimising the need for extensive repair and maintenance (Berglund et al., 2020; Onyelowe et al., 2022; Shaheen et al., 2022).

The functionality of smart concrete can be improved by combining it with IoT technology. It transforms smart concrete, initially a conventional building material, into a dynamic, responsive, intelligent infrastructure element. Through the implementation of IoT sensors in concrete, various environmental and structural factors such as temperature, humidity, strain, and pressure can be monitored in real-time. With a centralised monitoring system, an engineer or construction manager can monitor the condition of the concrete and detect potential problems before they become critical. Various early signs of damage, such as stress, cracking, or fatigue, can be identified. It is to support proactive maintenance and reduce the risk of significant failures in infrastructure (Mishra et al., 2022; Salehi et al., 2021).

The vision of a smart city in achieving urban development to improve citizens' quality of life, improve operational efficiency, and minimise environmental impact can be realised using technology data-driven solutions. Urban services such as transportation, energy, water, and waste can be appropriately managed through the IoT, artificial intelligence, and big data. These technologies can be integrated into various aspects of a city's infrastructure. The main goal of smart cities is to create a more sustainable, resilient, and efficient environment for an increasing urban population. It can optimise the use of resources, improve security, and improve the well-being of residents while reducing the city's ecological footprint (Bellini et al., 2022; Javed et al., 2022; Syed et al., 2021).

Innovative construction materials that can adapt to dynamic urban environments are the main demands of a smart city. An innovative material that conventional construction materials do not possess is the ability to adapt to changing conditions. Smart materials, such as smart concrete, can cover this gap. Smart concrete, facilitated by sensors and IoT capabilities, can easily monitor and react to temperature changes, humidity, structural stress, and wear. The maintenance and management of urban infrastructure can be easily achieved with the ability of smart materials to provide real-time data and self-monitoring. Early signs of damage can be easily detected, reducing the need for costly repairs and improving safety. Another advantage is that smart materials can improve urban systems' energy efficiency, sustainability, and resilience. By integrating smart materials into urban infrastructure, opportunities open up for a city to be able to better respond to future challenges, optimise resources, and improve the quality of life of its residents (Hui et al., 2023; Matei & Cocoşatu, 2024; Yang et al., 2021).

4.2 Key Technologies behind Smart Concrete

The curing and operational phases require the detection of changes in the internal temperature of the structure. It can be achieved by planting temperature sensors in concrete. The disadvantage of concrete is its sensitivity to temperature variations. Drastic temperature changes can affect its strength, durability, and overall performance. Today, engineers can observe the reaction of concrete to environmental changes by inserting temperature sensors into the concrete mix. Thus, environmental changes, such as seasonal temperature shifts or heat generated during the hydration process, can be observed. So that, in the end, the management of the curing process can be done correctly to achieve the optimal strength of concrete. In addition, with this information, thermal cracking can be prevented, long-term performance evaluations can be carried out, and the structure's life can be predicted (Komary et al., 2024).

Real-time data derived from strain sensors embedded in concrete provides information on changes in the shape of the material due to the influence of various loads and environmental factors. The integrity of the concrete structure depends on the concrete strain indicator. Strain value information determines whether concrete is over-deformed. Excessive deformation may result in cracking, failure, or reduced load-carrying capacity. Strain sensors provide valuable information about stress distribution, load patterns, and early signs of structural problems. It is also valuable for monitoring high-performance or heavily charged structures like bridges, dams, and skyscrapers. Predictive maintenance can be carried out by determining areas that may need to be repaired or strengthened before reaching a critical level, thereby improving the safety and durability of concrete structures (Ferreira et al., 2022). Figure 4.2 illustrates the concept.

Another type of sensor that is very important in understanding the hydration process and regulating the moisture content of the material is the humidity sensor. Moisture content is essential to control in real time because moisture content affects preservation and long-term durability. Moisture levels that are too small or too large result in cracking, shrinkage, reduced strength, and poor frost-thaw resistance. The sensor helps maintain the ideal ratio of cement to water for proper curing. Another function of a humidity sensor is to detect moisture migration over time, detecting problems such as water ingress, corrosion, or alkali-silica reactions. The early warning sensors aid in proactive maintenance and extend the life of concrete structures (Biondi et al., 2020; Zhang et al., 2022). Simultaneously, embedded sensors function in comprehensive monitoring that ensures the health and durability of concrete throughout its life cycle.

Good infrastructure management, especially in terms of security, performance, and maintenance, can be done with a real-time monitoring system supported by an IoT network. The real-time system collects and analyses data

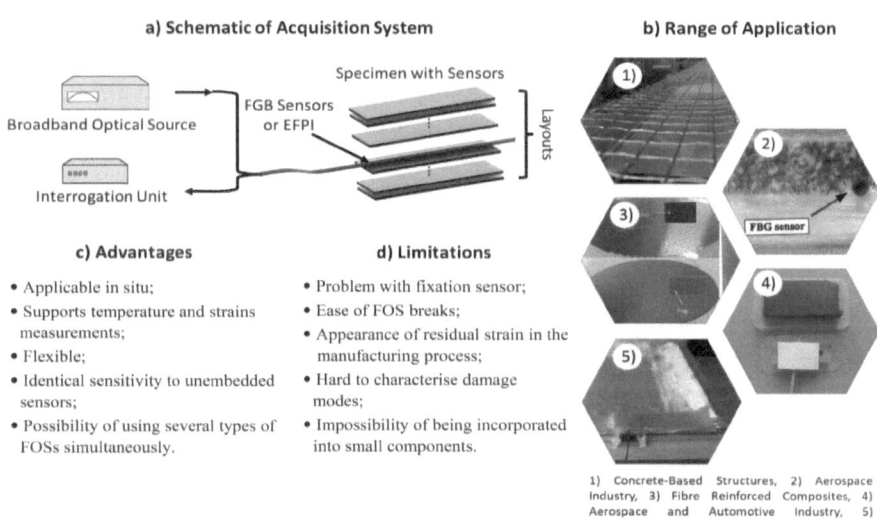

FIGURE 4.2
Fibre optic sensors embedded in composite components. (From Ferreira et al., 2022.)

from various embedded sensors regularly. In addition, the real-time system provides insight into the condition of concrete structures and components of buildings or bridges. The data obtained are processed instantly through a cloud platform or an on-premises server. Real-time monitoring alerts engineers and maintenance teams if strain sensors detect abnormal deformations or temperature sensors record extreme conditions. Thus, problems can be identified early. So that significant failures can be prevented, repair times can be determined, and the structure's life can be extended.

Another benefit of real-time monitoring is that it allows for continuous performance and environmental assessments. Thus, better resource management, better safety, and more efficient supervision of public and private assets can be achieved. It is achieved by integrating these systems into smart cities and smart infrastructure frameworks (Outay et al., 2020; Sarrab et al., 2020). The synergy between IoT communication networks and real-time monitoring systems can improve the effectiveness of smart infrastructure and ensure the long-term sustainability of concrete structures and other critical assets.

One of the latest innovations in the construction industry is self-healing concrete. This concrete functions to increase the durability and longevity of concrete structures. This concrete can minimise the need for costly repairs. Its most important property is to repair cracks that develop over time automatically. The healing process usually uses bacterial media, capsules, or microfibres in a concrete mixture. Water or moisture activates this medium and releases healing substances such as calcium carbonate to fill and close cracks (Figure 4.3) (Jonkers et al., 2009). This capability extends the life of concrete

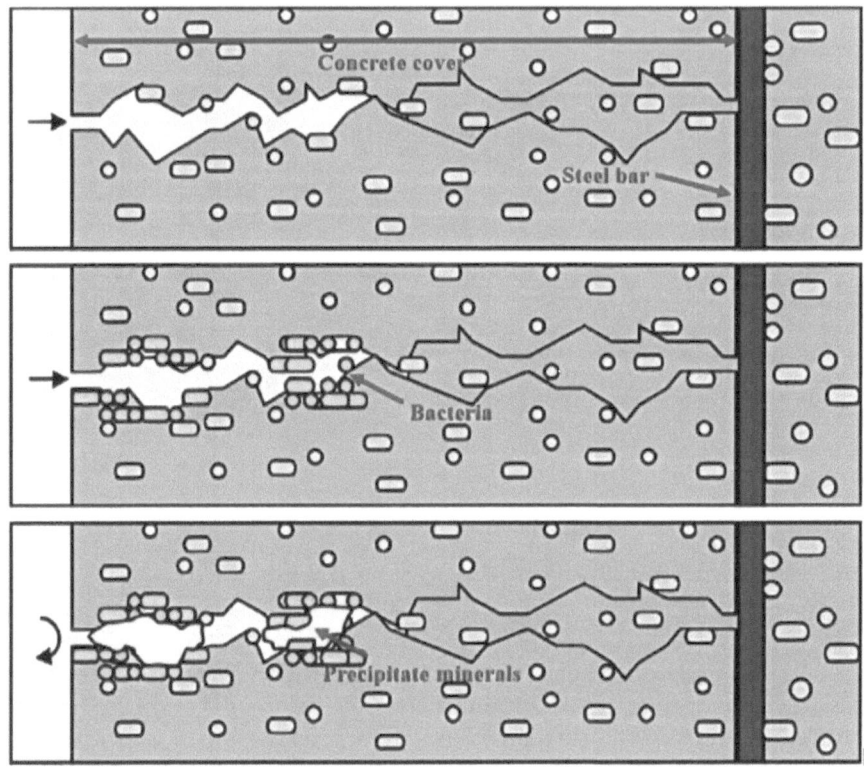

FIGURE 4.3
Typical crack-healing processes via immobilised bacteria in concretes (From Jonkers et al., 2009.)

structures and increases their resistance to common problems such as corrosion, water infiltration, and freeze-thaw damage. In the end, it reduces maintenance costs and improves structural integrity. It solves concrete structures in challenging environments like bridges, tunnels, and high-rise buildings. Efforts to optimise the effectiveness of these materials pave the way for smarter and more sustainable construction practices (Barros et al., 2023; Shah & Huseien, 2020).

Using conductive materials can improve the performance of concrete structures on smart infrastructure and energy-saving design. This conductive material is added to the concrete mixture to provide electrical conductivity. Thus allowing the concrete to interact with embedded sensors and other electronic components. Conductive materials are generally in the form of conductive polymers, carbon fibres, or graphene. The functions of this material include monitoring structural health, regulating temperature, and even offering de-icing capabilities in cold climates (Murtagh et al., 2020; Sargam et al., 2020). Both self-healing concrete and conductive materials significantly contribute to the infrastructure's durability and longevity. Thus, more efficient and environmentally friendly construction practices can be realised.

4.3 Applications of Smart Concrete in Smart Cities

The implementation of sensors connected to IoT networks plays a crucial role in monitoring and managing infrastructure in smart cities. Using temperature, strain, humidity, and crack sensors allows real-time observation of key infrastructure elements such as roads, bridges, buildings, and tunnels. Identifying problems like cracks, deformations, or corrosion in the reinforcement is easy. These sensors provide continuous data on the structural health of concrete components. Engineers and city planners can monitor the condition of smart city infrastructure by observing information in real time. This information is transmitted through an IoT network to a centralised system or cloud platform (Kasznar et al., 2021; Mei et al., 2020).

This system provides the advantage of automatic and continuous monitoring of infrastructure. Engineers can instantly identify the early signs of damage or damage without waiting for routine maintenance. The stress of the concrete structure caused by heavy traffic or bad weather conditions can be immediately detected through sensors embedded in the bridge so that the authorities know of any changes that may require immediate attention. It optimises the allocation of resources for repairs or upgrades. And ultimately improve the security and functionality of the city's infrastructure (Catbas et al., 2022; Sony et al., 2020).

The integration of smart concrete into smart cities facilitates predictive maintenance capabilities. Anticipating maintenance, repairs, or replacements before component or structural failures occur can be achieved with data-driven, predictive maintenance. Dapay engineers easily collect real-time data on stress factors such as load, temperature variation, humidity level, and strain. Machine learning algorithms and predictive analytics can be performed from the data obtained to predict when a structure might face problems like cracks, structural fatigue, or corrosion. Further, sensors can detect abnormal vibrations or strain patterns under certain conditions (for example, on bridges with heavy traffic or seismic activity).

4.4 Challenges and Future of Smart Concrete

The application of smart concrete that can interact with the environment faces various challenges. These challenges include technological aspects, financial aspects, and regulatory aspects. These challenges must be met for the prospects of innovative materials. The following is an overview of the challenges faced (Nilimaa, 2023). Technological challenges faced by smart concrete include the durability of sensors and electronics. The challenge is to ensure that these sensors remain functional throughout the life of the concrete. Technology integration is the main challenge to embedding advanced sensors and technologies into concrete without sacrificing structural integrity or performance. Next, data management and interpretation are other challenges. It ensures the data's accuracy and reliability while minimising false alarms or misinterpretations. Power supply is the technological hurdle to maintaining power for these embedded systems long-term without frequent maintenance or battery replacement. Finally, the advanced material costs are often more expensive than conventional concrete components.

The financial challenges faced by smart concrete include high initial costs. Usually, developing and integrating sensors, actuators, and other smart technologies into real-life concrete is expensive. Further, the uncertain return on investment may take a long time to materialise, especially for small-scale construction projects. Scaling challenges are also present during the production process, may not be optimal for widespread use, and economies of scale are required to reduce costs. Smart concrete faces competition from traditional materials with lower initial costs.

The future of smart concrete is quite promising, even though it still faces various challenges. The successful application of this technology depends on solving problems such as ensuring sensor durability and creating an efficient power system. Financially, the application of smart concrete is quite promising. It considers reduced maintenance costs, improved safety, and longer structural life (Nilimaa, 2023). Regulatory advances are also crucial in making it easier for companies to adopt this technology. Creating standards and frameworks for using smart concrete would be very beneficial, especially in ensuring the fulfilment of safety, environmental, and performance standards. In addition, collaboration between industry stakeholders, researchers, and policymakers is crucial in addressing regulatory issues (Shufrin et al., 2023). Although smart concrete faces various challenges regarding technological advancements and financial benefits, regulatory improvements can be anticipated to drive smart concrete's growth and widespread adoption in the coming years.

References

Barros, L. B., Knockaert, M., & Filho, J. R. T. (2023). Towards a more sustainable construction industry: Bridging the gap between technical progress and commercialisation of self-healing concrete. *Construction and Building Materials, 403,* 133094. https://doi.org/10.1016/j.conbuildmat.2023.133094

Bellini, P., Nesi, P., & Pantaleo, G. (2022). IoT-enabled smart cities: A review of concepts, frameworks and key technologies. *Applied Sciences, 12*(3), 1607. https://doi.org/10.3390/app12031607

Berglund, E. Z., Monroe, J. G., Ahmed, I., Noghabaei, M., Do, J., Pesantez, J. E., Fasaee, M. K., Bardaka, E., Han, K., Proestos, G. T., & Levis, J. (2020). Smart infrastructure: A vision for the role of the civil engineering profession in smart cities. *Journal of Infrastructure Systems, 26*(2). https://doi.org/10.1061/(asce)is.1943-555x.0000549

Biondi, L., Perry, M., McAlorum, J., Vlachakis, C., & Hamilton, A. (2020). Geopolymer-based moisture sensors for reinforced concrete health monitoring. *Sensors and Actuators B Chemical, 309*, 127775. https://doi.org/10.1016/j.snb.2020.127775

Catbas, F. N., Luleci, F., Zakaria, M., Bagci, U., LaViola, J. J., Cruz-Neira, C., & Reiners, D. (2022). Extended reality (XR) for condition assessment of civil engineering structures: A literature review. *Sensors, 22*(23), 9560. https://doi.org/10.3390/s22239560

Ferreira, P. M., Machado, M. A., Carvalho, M. S., & Vidal, C. (2022). Embedded sensors for structural health monitoring: Methodologies and applications review. *Sensors, 22*(21), 8320. https://doi.org/10.3390/s22218320

Hui, C. X., Dan, G., Alamri, S., & Toghraie, D. (2023). Greening smart cities: An investigation of the integration of urban natural resources and smart city technologies for promoting environmental sustainability. *Sustainable Cities and Society, 99*, 104985. https://doi.org/10.1016/j.scs.2023.104985

Javed, A. R., Shahzad, F., Rehman, S. U., Zikria, Y. B., Razzak, I., Jalil, Z., & Xu, G. (2022). Future smart cities: Requirements, emerging technologies, applications, challenges, and future aspects. *Cities, 129*, 103794. https://doi.org/10.1016/j.cities.2022.103794

Jiang, X., Lu, D., Yin, B., & Leng, Z. (2024). Advancing carbon nanomaterials-engineered self-sensing cement composites for structural health monitoring: A state-of-the-art review. *Journal of Building Engineering, 87*, 109129. https://doi.org/10.1016/j.jobe.2024.109129

Jonkers, H. M., Thijssen, A., Muyzer, G., Copuroglu, O., & Schlangen, E. (2009). Application of bacteria as self-healing agent for the development of sustainable concrete. *Ecological Engineering, 36*(2), 230–235. https://doi.org/10.1016/j.ecoleng.2008.12.036

Kasznar, A., Hammad, A., Najjar, M., Qualharini, E. L., Figueiredo, K., Soares, C., & Haddad, A. (2021). Multiple dimensions of smart cities' infrastructure: A review. *Buildings, 11*(2), 73. https://doi.org/10.3390/buildings11020073

Komary, M., Bajić, P., Tošić, N., De La Fuente, A., & Turmo, J. (2024). Development of a low-cost IoT-based sensor for early-stage concrete monitoring. *Procedia Structural Integrity, 64*, 1311–1317. https://doi.org/10.1016/j.prostr.2024.09.202

Li, L., Wei, H., Hao, Y., Li, Y., Cheng, W., Ismail, Y. A., & Liu, Z. (2023). Carbon nanotube (CNT) reinforced cementitious composites for structural self-sensing purpose: A review. *Construction and Building Materials, 392*, 131384. https://doi.org/10.1016/j.conbuildmat.2023.131384

Li, W., Qu, F., Dong, W., Mishra, G., & Shah, S. P. (2022). A comprehensive review on self-sensing graphene/cementitious composites: A pathway toward next-generation smart concrete. *Construction and Building Materials, 331*, 127284. https://doi.org/10.1016/j.conbuildmat.2022.127284

Makul, N. (2020). Advanced smart concrete – A review of current progress, benefits and challenges. *Journal of Cleaner Production, 274*, 122899. https://doi.org/10.1016/j.jclepro.2020.122899

Matei, A., & Cocoşatu, M. (2024). Artificial internet of things, sensor-based digital twin urban computing vision algorithms, and blockchain cloud networks in sustainable smart city administration. *Sustainability, 16*(16), 6749. https://doi.org/10.3390/su16166749

Mei, Q., Gül, M., & Shirzad-Ghaleroudkhani, N. (2020). Towards smart cities: Crowdsensing-based monitoring of transportation infrastructure using in-traffic vehicles. *Journal of Civil Structural Health Monitoring, 10*(4), 653–665. https://doi.org/10.1007/s13349-020-00411-6

Mishra, M., Lourenço, P. B., & Ramana, G. (2022). Structural health monitoring of civil engineering structures by using the internet of things: A review. *Journal of Building Engineering, 48*, 103954. https://doi.org/10.1016/j.jobe.2021.103954

Murtagh, N., Scott, L., & Fan, J. (2020). Sustainable and resilient construction: Current status and future challenges. *Journal of Cleaner Production, 268*, 122264. https://doi.org/10.1016/j.jclepro.2020.122264

Nilimaa, J. (2023). Smart materials and technologies for sustainable concrete construction. *Developments in the Built Environment, 15*, 100177. https://doi.org/10.1016/j.dibe.2023.100177

Onyelowe, K. C., Ebid, A. M., Riofrio, A., Baykara, H., Soleymani, A., Mahdi, H. A., Jahangir, H., & Ibe, K. (2022). Multi-objective prediction of the mechanical properties and environmental impact appraisals of self-healing concrete for sustainable structures. *Sustainability, 14*(15), 9573. https://doi.org/10.3390/su14159573

Outay, F., Mengash, H. A., & Adnan, M. (2020). Applications of unmanned aerial vehicle (UAV) in road safety, traffic and highway infrastructure management: Recent advances and challenges. *Transportation Research Part a Policy and Practice, 141*, 116–129. https://doi.org/10.1016/j.tra.2020.09.018

Ramachandran, K., Vijayan, P., Murali, G., & Vatin, N. I. (2022). A review on principles, theories and materials for self sensing concrete for structural applications. *Materials, 15*(11), 3831. https://doi.org/10.3390/ma15113831

Salehi, H., Burgueño, R., Chakrabartty, S., Lajnef, N., & Alavi, A. H. (2021). A comprehensive review of self-powered sensors in civil infrastructure: State-of-the-art and future research trends. *Engineering Structures, 234*, 111963. https://doi.org/10.1016/j.engstruct.2021.111963

Sargam, Y., Wang, K., & Alleman, J. E. (2020). Effects of modern concrete materials on thermal conductivity. *Journal of Materials in Civil Engineering, 32*(4). https://doi.org/10.1061/(asce)mt.1943-5533.0003026

Sarrab, M., Pulparambil, S., & Awadalla, M. (2020). Development of an IoT based real-time traffic monitoring system for city governance. *Global Transitions, 2*, 230–245. https://doi.org/10.1016/j.glt.2020.09.004

Scope, C., Vogel, M., & Guenther, E. (2020). Greener, cheaper, or more sustainable: Reviewing sustainability assessments of maintenance strategies of concrete structures. *Sustainable Production and Consumption, 26*, 838–858. https://doi.org/10.1016/j.spc.2020.12.022

Shah, K. W., & Huseien, G. F. (2020). Biomimetic self-healing cementitious construction materials for smart buildings. *Biomimetics, 5*(4), 47. https://doi.org/10.3390/biomimetics5040047

Shaheen, N., Khushnood, R. A., Musarat, M. A., & Alaloul, W. S. (2022). Self-healing nano-concrete for futuristic infrastructures: A review. *Arabian Journal for Science and Engineering*, 47(4), 5365–5375. https://doi.org/10.1007/s13369-022-06562-6

Shufrin, I., Pasternak, E., & Dyskin, A. (2023). Environmentally friendly smart construction—Review of recent developments and opportunities. *Applied Sciences*, 13(23), 12891. https://doi.org/10.3390/app132312891

Siahkouhi, M., Razaqpur, G., Hoult, N., Baghban, M. H., & Jing, G. (2021). Utilisation of carbon nanotubes (CNTs) in concrete for structural health monitoring (SHM) purposes: A review *Construction and Building Materials, 309*, 125137. https://doi.org/10.1016/j.conbuildmat.2021.125137

Song, F., Li, Q., & Xu, S. (2023). A review of self-sensing ultra-high performance concrete: Towards next-generation smart structural materials. *Cement and Concrete Composites, 145*, 105350. https://doi.org/10.1016/j.cemconcomp.2023.105350

Sony, S., Dunphy, K., Sadhu, A., & Capretz, M. (2020). A systematic review of convolutional neural network-based structural condition assessment techniques. *Engineering Structures, 226*, 111347. https://doi.org/10.1016/j.engstruct.2020.111347

Syed, A. S., Sierra-Sosa, D., Kumar, A., & Elmaghraby, A. (2021). IoT in smart cities: A survey of technologies, practices and challenges. *Smart Cities, 4*(2), 429–475. https://doi.org/10.3390/smartcities4020024

Thomoglou, A. K., Falara, M. G., Gkountakou, F. I., Elenas, A., & Chalioris, C. E. (2023). Smart cementitious sensors with nano-, micro-, and hybrid-modified reinforcement: Mechanical and electrical properties. *Sensors, 23*(5), 2405. https://doi.org/10.3390/s23052405

Yang, F., Wen, X., Aziz, A., & Luhach, A. K. (2021). The need for local adaptation of smart infrastructure for sustainable economic management. *Environmental Impact Assessment Review, 88*, 106565. https://doi.org/10.1016/j.eiar.2021.106565

Zhang, H., Li, J., & Kang, F. (2022). Real-time monitoring of humidity inside concrete structures utilising embedded smart aggregates. *Construction and Building Materials, 331*, 127317. https://doi.org/10.1016/j.conbuildmat.2022.127317

Section II

Security and Resilience

5

Security Infrastructure and Challenges in Smart Cities

Norliza Katuk, Modhawi Alotaibi, Derar Eleyan, and Amna Eleyan

5.1 Overview of Smart Cities and Security Needs

Smart cities represent the convergence of urban infrastructure with digital technology to enhance efficiency, sustainability, and quality of life. Rapid urbanisation and the proliferation of IoT-driven systems have made security a fundamental pillar of smart city planning (Laufs et al., 2020). A modern smart city is built on interconnected networks of sensors, devices, and cloud-based services that enable seamless automation, predictive analytics, and real-time decision-making. However, as cities integrate artificial intelligence (AI), 5G connectivity, and edge computing into their operational frameworks, cyber-physical security vulnerabilities continue to rise. The need for robust security frameworks that detect, prevent, and respond to threats in real time has never been more critical, mainly as cyberattacks target essential services such as energy grids, transportation, and public safety infrastructure.

The complexity of their digital ecosystems shapes the security landscape of smart cities. Urban centres' primary threats include ransomware attacks on municipal databases, breaches in IoT-enabled surveillance systems, and unauthorised access to biometric authentication networks (Alauthman et al., 2024). Integrating AI-driven facial recognition, intelligent traffic management, and predictive policing mechanisms has significantly improved public safety and raised ethical concerns regarding data privacy and mass surveillance. Furthermore, securing these decentralised platforms from fraud and manipulation has become a pressing challenge with the widespread adoption of blockchain-based digital identity verification and smart contracts. Smart cities require advanced encryption techniques, zero-trust security models, and automated threat response systems to protect sensitive information and ensure resilient urban governance (Desai et al., 2024).

People's lifestyle in a smart city revolves around digital convenience, hyper-connectivity, and seamless interaction with urban infrastructure. Residents rely on AI-driven personal assistants, real-time transportation updates, and automated service delivery to efficiently navigate daily life. However, this reliance on digital platforms also increases the risk of personal data exposure, identity theft, and location-based tracking (Sinimole & Karri, 2024). As contactless payments, biometric authentication, and IoT-powered home automation systems become ubiquitous, security measures must evolve to protect against unauthorised intrusions and data breaches. Governments and technology providers must balance enhancing security and preserving individual freedoms, ensuring that surveillance technologies do not infringe upon fundamental rights.

In response to growing security concerns, cities are deploying cybersecurity frameworks integrating AI-driven threat detection, blockchain-secured data transactions, and multi-factor authentication protocols. Predictive analytics and machine learning (ML) algorithms now play a pivotal role in identifying vulnerabilities before they can be exploited (Ullah et al., 2024). Additionally, public-private partnerships are fostering the development of secure smart city platforms by enforcing stringent cybersecurity regulations and investing in secure-by-design technologies. By embedding security at the foundational level of urban planning, cities can mitigate risks and build trust among residents.

Ultimately, the security needs of smart cities extend beyond technological safeguards to encompass governance, policy, and ethical considerations. Cities must establish transparent cybersecurity policies, strengthen data protection laws, and educate citizens on digital hygiene to foster a resilient security culture. Collaborative efforts among governments, private enterprises, and cybersecurity experts ensure that smart cities remain safe, inclusive, and technologically resilient. Without proactive security measures, the benefits of smart urbanisation could be overshadowed by increasing cyberthreats and systemic vulnerabilities.

5.2 Smart City Infrastructure and Communication

Smart city infrastructure comprises a complex ecosystem of interconnected digital and physical components that enhance urban living, efficiency, and sustainability. This infrastructure's core are Internet of Things (IoT) networks, communication technologies, data management systems, cloud computing, AI analytics, and cybersecurity frameworks. These components ensure real-time data collection, seamless automation, and intelligent decision-making. However, as cities integrate more connected devices and autonomous systems, security vulnerabilities expand, requiring robust protection mechanisms. Integrating secure encryption, access control measures, and continuous monitoring is crucial to safeguarding these infrastructures from cyberthreats and unauthorised intrusions. Without stringent security policies, hackers can exploit vulnerabilities in IoT devices, manipulate data flows, and compromise essential city services.

IoT and sensor networks form the backbone of smart cities by enabling automated data collection and real-time monitoring of urban environments. These sensors are embedded in transportation systems, energy grids, water management, and waste disposal infrastructure, collecting data on traffic congestion, pollution levels, and energy consumption. However, IoT devices are particularly vulnerable to cyberattacks due to their distributed nature and often limited security measures. Threats such as unauthorised access, device spoofing, and Distributed Denial of Service (DDoS) attacks can disrupt city operations, leading to power outages, traffic system failures, and compromised environmental monitoring. Implementing end-to-end encryption, device authentication protocols, and AI-based anomaly detection is essential to securing IoT networks from malicious intrusions and ensuring reliable data integrity.

Communication technologies play a crucial role in ensuring seamless data exchange between smart city components. The deployment of 5G networks, fibre-optic broadband, satellite communication, and Wi-Fi 6 infrastructure facilitates ultra-fast connectivity and low-latency communication, supporting smart transportation, emergency response, and telemedicine services. However, the expanded bandwidth and numerous connected devices increase the risk of data interception, cyber espionage, and network jamming. Secure communication protocols such as quantum encryption, zero-trust network models, and intrusion detection systems must be implemented to prevent unauthorised eavesdropping and ensure secure information transmission. Furthermore, network segmentation can help contain cyberthreats and minimise the impact of potential breaches.

Cloud computing and data management enable cities to store, process, and analyse vast amounts of information generated by smart infrastructure. Smart city platforms rely on centralised cloud servers, edge computing, and AI-driven analytics to facilitate predictive maintenance, emergency response coordination, and intelligent urban planning. However, storing critical city data on centralised cloud platforms creates vulnerabilities such as data breaches, insider threats, and ransomware attacks. Ensuring multi-layered data encryption, blockchain-based data validation, and regulatory compliance with privacy laws is necessary to prevent unauthorised data access and maintain data sovereignty. The adoption of secure edge computing can also reduce reliance on centralised servers, minimising the risk of large-scale cyberattacks by processing data closer to its source.

AI and automated systems optimise decision-making processes in smart cities by analysing data patterns and predicting potential issues before they escalate. AI is widely used in traffic management, law enforcement, waste management, and disaster response, enhancing efficiency and responsiveness. However, AI-driven systems can be exploited if attackers manipulate algorithms, inject biased data, or launch adversarial AI attacks. Securing AI models against data poisoning, ensuring transparency in

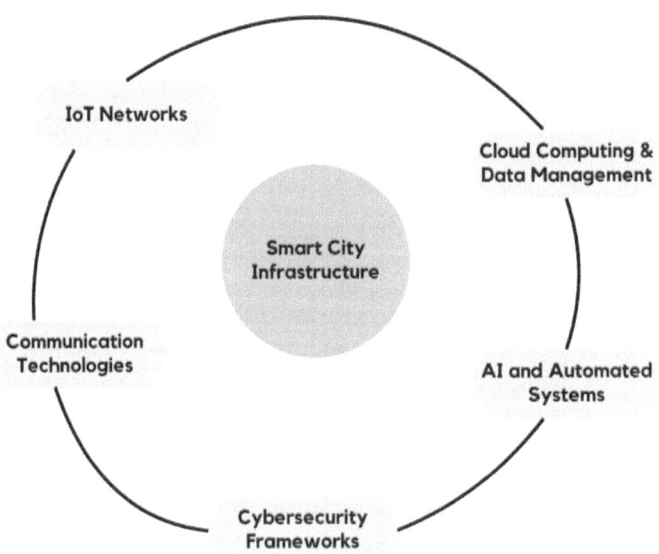

FIGURE 5.1
The smart city infrastructure.

algorithmic decision-making, and establishing ethical AI governance are critical measures to prevent security loopholes in automated city management. Additionally, continuous monitoring and validation of AI-driven decisions can help mitigate biases and maintain trust in smart city operations.

As smart city infrastructure evolves, ensuring comprehensive security across all communication and operational components remains a top priority. Governments and private sector stakeholders must enforce cybersecurity best practices, conduct routine security audits, and implement incident response frameworks to safeguard critical urban infrastructure. By embedding security into the foundational design of smart city technologies, cities can mitigate risks, enhance resilience, and ensure that digital advancements contribute to safer and more efficient urban environments. The top view of smart city infrastructure is illustrated in Figure 5.1.

Security is the cornerstone of smart city infrastructure, ensuring interconnected digital and physical systems' safety, reliability, and resilience. As urban centres increasingly depend on IoT networks, cloud computing, and AI-driven automation, the risk of cyberthreats targeting essential services grows exponentially. Without robust security frameworks, attackers can exploit vulnerabilities in communication networks, manipulate real-time data flows, and disrupt critical operations such as traffic management, energy distribution, and emergency response. The integration of AI in smart cities has been a double-edged sword – while it enhances predictive analytics and automated threat detection, cybercriminals have also weaponised to launch more sophisticated attacks. AI-powered malware, deepfake-based identity fraud, and autonomous hacking bots are emerging threats that can bypass traditional security defences. In this situation, practitioners must understand and be able to identify security threats and attacks within a smart city environment.

5.3 Security Challenges in Smart City Environment

Security in smart cities is essential to address various threats and attacks that target critical urban infrastructure. As cities become increasingly interconnected through IoT networks, communication technologies, cloud computing, AI-driven automation, and cybersecurity frameworks, they also face growing cybersecurity vulnerabilities. Malware threats pose significant risks to IoT devices, leading to unauthorised access, device hijacking, and DDoS attacks that can disrupt essential services. Communication networks are vulnerable to jamming, cyber espionage, and data interception, threatening real-time data exchange and public safety.

Additionally, AI-driven cyberthreats and insider attacks can compromise cloud-based systems, resulting in ransomware attacks, data breaches, and AI algorithm manipulation. The rise of quantum computing further amplifies security risks, potentially breaking traditional encryption methods and exposing sensitive city-data. Privacy concerns also emerge due to unauthorised surveillance access and mass data collection. This diagram highlights the interconnected nature of smart city security risks, reinforcing the urgent need for robust cybersecurity measures, proactive threat detection, and resilient digital infrastructure to safeguard smart urban environments. Figure 5.2 illustrates the threats and potential attacks within a smart city infrastructure.

5.3.1 Quantum Computing Threats

Smart cities, driven by advanced technologies, face an evolving landscape of cybersecurity challenges, with the emergence of quantum computing presenting a particularly formidable threat (Lindsay, 2020). The traditional cryptographic methods relied upon by smart city networks for securing sensitive data are at risk of being compromised by the unprecedented computational capabilities of quantum computers. These quantum machines have the potential to break existing encryption algorithms exponentially faster than classical computers (Althobaiti & Dohler, 2020), raising concerns about the confidentiality and integrity of data within smart city infrastructures.

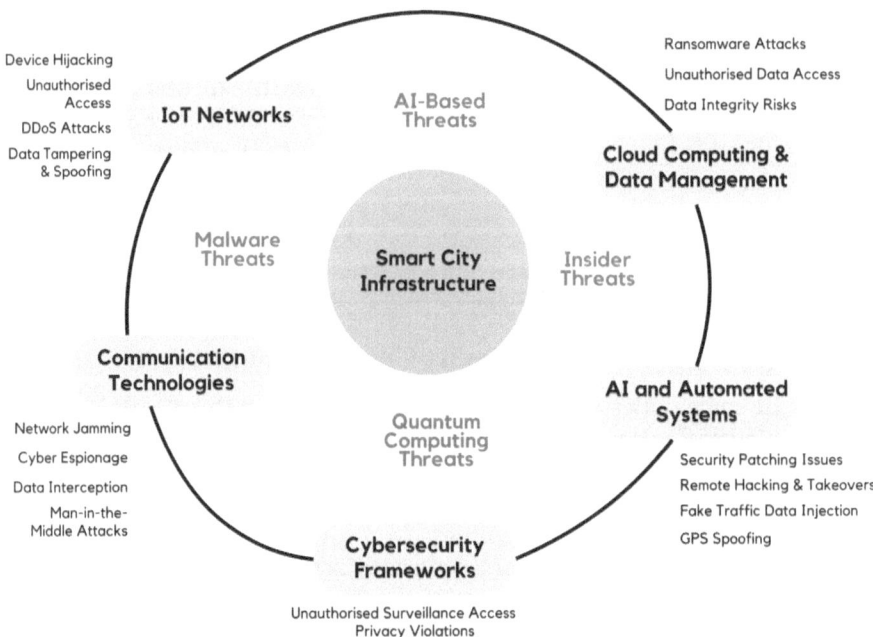

FIGURE 5.2
The threats and attacks within a smart city infrastructure.

5.3.2 Proliferation of IoT Devices

The proliferation of IoT devices in smart cities presents a significant cyber-security challenge, as the sheer number of connected devices expands the potential attack surface for malicious actors. Each IoT device, whether a sensor, smart appliance, or other connected gadget, represents a potential entry point for cybercriminals seeking unauthorised access or exploitation (Samaila et al., 2017). The challenge lies in securing a diverse and ever-growing ecosystem of devices, each with its vulnerabilities that, if exploited, could have far-reaching consequences on the smart city's infrastructure and services.

5.3.3 AI and ML Attacks

Integrating AI and ML in smart city technologies introduces a cybersecurity challenge, as malicious actors can exploit these technologies to devise more sophisticated and evasive attack techniques. The challenge lies in the potential misuse of AI and ML algorithms to enhance the capabilities of cyber-threats, making them more challenging to detect and mitigate by traditional security measures (Kaloudi & Li, 2020). Therefore, at the same time, AI-driven security solutions can detect and prevent attacks that leverage AI and ML.

These advanced security systems employ ML algorithms, constantly adapting and evolving to identify patterns indicative of malicious activities.

5.3.4 5G and Edge Computing Vulnerabilities

The widespread adoption of 5G and edge computing in smart cities brings forth new challenges related to cybersecurity, primarily stemming from the increased speed, low latency, and distributed nature of these technologies. These advancements, while enhancing connectivity and real-time processing capabilities, also introduce novel attack vectors that must be addressed to ensure the security and integrity of smart city systems. Securing the edge devices that form the backbone of edge computing infrastructure is a significant challenge (Khan et al., 2020). These devices, located close to data sources, process information locally before transmitting it to central servers. The distributed nature of edge computing increases the attack surface, as each edge device becomes a potential entry point for cyberthreats.

5.3.5 Integration of Smart City Ecosystems

Integrating diverse smart city components and systems poses a significant cybersecurity challenge due to the potential complexities and interdependencies that arise. As smart cities evolve, various technologies and systems, such as IoT devices, communication networks, and data analytics platforms, are integrated to create a cohesive urban ecosystem. However, this integration introduces vulnerabilities (Tahirkheli et al., 2021), as a compromise in one area can have cascading effects on the entire interconnected system, potentially impacting multiple facets of city operations.

5.3.6 Autonomous Vehicles and Transportation Security

The advent of autonomous vehicles presents a unique set of security challenges in smart cities, particularly concerning vehicle-to-everything (V2X) communication, remote hacking vulnerabilities, and the potential for cyber-physical attacks on transportation systems. As vehicles become increasingly connected and rely on communication with infrastructure, other vehicles, and central networks, the attack surface expands, posing risks to the safety and reliability of transportation in smart cities. One of the primary challenges is securing V2X communication, which encompasses data exchange between vehicles and various elements of the transportation infrastructure, such as traffic lights and road sensors (Soto et al., 2022). The challenge lies in ensuring the confidentiality and integrity of this communication, preventing malicious actors from tampering with data or injecting false information that could lead to traffic disruptions or accidents. Remote hacking possibilities introduce another concern, as autonomous vehicles rely heavily on software and communication systems (Mishra et al., 2023). Cyberattackers could exploit vulnerabilities in the vehicle's software, gain unauthorised access, and potentially take control of the vehicle. This risk not only compromises the safety of passengers but also poses a broader threat to public safety if exploited on a larger scale.

5.3.7 Privacy Concerns and Surveillance

The proliferation of sensors and surveillance technologies in smart cities brings significant challenges, particularly regarding privacy concerns and the potential for unauthorised access to sensitive surveillance data. As smart cities deploy many sensors to monitor various aspects of urban life, from traffic patterns to environmental conditions, the vast amount of data collected raises valid worries about individual privacy rights and the risk of data misuse. The primary challenge lies in finding a delicate balance between leveraging the benefits of surveillance for urban planning and safety while respecting citizens' privacy (Fabrègue & Bogoni, 2023). Unauthorised access to surveillance data can lead to unwarranted invasions of privacy, surveillance abuse, and the potential for misuse by malicious actors.

5.3.8 Cloud Security Risks

The increasing dependence on cloud computing for storage, processing, and analytics in smart cities brings inherent challenges related to cloud security risks. As cities transition towards cloud-based smart services, the data stored in these cloud environments becomes an attractive target for cyberattacks. The challenge lies in safeguarding sensitive information from unauthorised access, data breaches, and other security threats that may compromise the integrity and confidentiality of smart city data (Telo, 2023). One primary concern is the need for robust access controls to regulate who can access, modify, or delete data stored in the cloud. Robust authentication mechanisms and authorisation protocols ensure that only authorised personnel can interact with sensitive information.

5.3.9 Emergence of New Malware and Cyberthreats

The emergence of new malware and cyberthreats presents a significant challenge to the cybersecurity landscape of smart cities. As attackers continually evolve their techniques, introducing more sophisticated tools like polymorphic malware, zero-day exploits, and AI-driven attacks, the potential for disruptive and damaging security incidents escalates. Polymorphic malware, for instance, can change its code signature dynamically, making it difficult for traditional antivirus solutions to detect and mitigate. Zero-day exploits target vulnerabilities unknown to software vendors (Leal & Musgrave, 2023), offering attackers an advantage until the vulnerabilities are discovered and patched. Mitigating these challenges requires smart cities to invest in advanced threat detection and prevention systems that adapt to the evolving dynamic nature of malware.

5.3.10 Smart City Governance and Regulatory Challenges

Navigating the governance and regulatory landscape in smart cities poses a multifaceted challenge. As these cities incorporate advanced technologies, the need for effective governance models and regulatory frameworks becomes paramount. However, the complexity of this task is accentuated by inconsistent regulations across different regions and the ever-evolving legal landscape, which may hinder the enforcement of robust and uniform cybersecurity standards. One significant challenge lies in developing governance models that can keep pace with the rapid evolution of smart city technologies. The interplay between various stakeholders, including government bodies, private enterprises, and citizens, complicates crafting effective regulatory frameworks. Moreover, the dynamic nature of technology often outpaces the ability of regulations to adapt, creating a potential gap in cybersecurity enforcement (Khan et al., 2023). Smart cities must actively collaborate with regulatory bodies to address these challenges and establish standardised cybersecurity guidelines.

5.3.11 Insider Threats in Evolving Work Environments

As smart cities embrace the evolution of work environments, the challenge of insider threats takes on a new dimension, especially with the growing adoption of remote work and digital collaboration tools. The decentralisation of work introduces complexities in safeguarding critical systems, as employees with access to sensitive information may inadvertently or purposefully become sources of security compromise. The remote work paradigm amplifies the challenge of insider threats (Arunprasad et al., 2022), given that employees accessing smart city systems from diverse locations may not continuously operate within the secure confines of a traditional office environment. The potential for security lapses increases as the lines between personal and professional digital spaces blur. It creates a pressing need for smart cities to address the vulnerabilities associated with the human factor in an evolving work landscape.

5.3.12 Economic and Resource Challenges

Smart cities face a significant challenge in cybersecurity due to economic constraints and resource limitations. Not all cities may have the financial means to invest adequately in robust cybersecurity measures, potentially creating disparities in security levels across different urban centres (Kayode-Ajala, 2023). This challenge is crucial as it may compromise smart city initiatives' overall resilience and effectiveness. The economic and resource challenges confronting smart cities underscore the need for innovative approaches to cybersecurity mitigation. Public-private partnerships present a viable solution, fostering collaboration between governmental entities and private sector organisations. Seeking government funding for cybersecurity initiatives is another essential avenue for mitigating economic and resource challenges. Advocating for dedicated budgets or grants aimed at bolstering cybersecurity measures demonstrates a commitment to prioritising the digital security of smart city infrastructure.

5.4 Future Directions and Recommendations

In order to address attacks on smart cities, it is crucial to implement adequate security mitigation techniques and best practices (Habibzadeh et al., 2019). These measures can help safeguard the infrastructure and protect against potential threats. Some key strategies include deploying a multi-layered defence system involving firewalls, intrusion detection and prevention systems (IDPS), antivirus software, and endpoint security solutions. Network segmentation is also essential, as it divides the smart city network into separate segments or zones to limit the impact of a breach. Encryption should be utilised to secure data transmissions and protect sensitive information. Additionally, implementing a robust identity and access management system, conducting regular security audits, and having well-defined incident response and disaster recovery plans are essential. Ongoing cybersecurity training and awareness programmes, along with collaboration and information sharing among stakeholders, further strengthen the security of smart cities. Figure 5.3 demonstrates the potential cybersecurity strategy within a smart city.

5.4.1 Comprehensive Cybersecurity Policy

Comprehensive cybersecurity policies are essential for ensuring the security of smart city environments. They provide a roadmap for maintaining a secure and trustworthy smart city infrastructure, from procuring IoT devices to implementing incident response protocols (Sommestad, 2018). For example, one important aspect covered by comprehensive cybersecurity policies is access control. These policies establish stringent rules and protocols that govern who has access to smart city systems, ensuring that only authorised personnel can interact with critical infrastructure. Implementing robust access controls can prevent unauthorised individuals or entities from compromising sensitive data, manipulating systems, or causing disruptions in smart city systems.

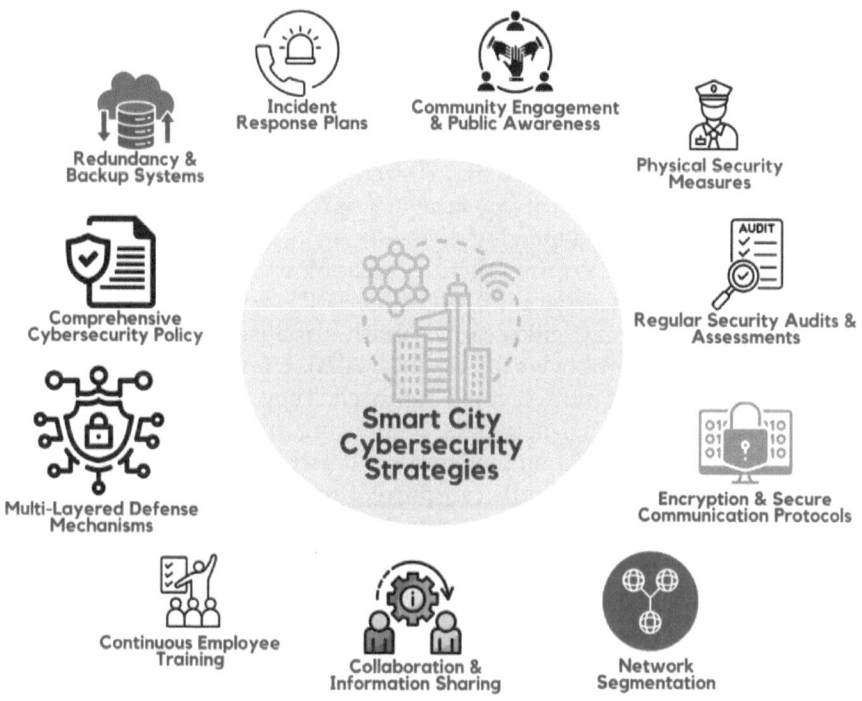

FIGURE 5.3
Smart city cybersecurity strategies.

5.4.2 Regular Security Audits and Assessments

Regular security audits and assessments are indispensable components of a proactive cybersecurity strategy for smart cities (Cissé, 2021). These practices involve systematically evaluating the security infrastructure to identify vulnerabilities, assess the effectiveness of implemented security measures, and address emerging threats. Penetration testing is a crucial aspect of regular security audits, where ethical hackers simulate cyberattacks to identify weaknesses in the smart city's defences. For example, penetration testing in a smart transportation system may involve exploiting vulnerabilities in traffic management software or hacking into the communication network between connected vehicles (Kelarestaghi et al., 2019). Vulnerability scanning is another essential element of regular security assessments (Yu et al., 2020). This process systematically scans smart city systems and networks to detect potential weaknesses or security gaps. In a smart energy grid, vulnerability scanning may involve assessing IoT devices' security protocols to identify exploitable vulnerabilities. Risk assessments are vital in understanding the overall threat landscape that smart cities face. Evaluating potential risks and their impact on the city's operations can prioritise and allocate resources to address the most critical security concerns. For instance, in a smart healthcare system, a risk assessment might consider the potential consequences of a data breach, such as the compromise of patient records.

5.4.3 Multi-Layered Defence Mechanisms

Implementing a multi-layered defence mechanism is a fundamental strategy in fortifying the cybersecurity posture of smart cities (Demertzi et al., 2023). This approach involves deploying diverse security measures across multiple layers of the smart city infrastructure, creating a comprehensive defence-in-depth strategy. Incorporating firewalls, IDPS, antivirus software, and endpoint security, smart cities can establish a robust and resilient defence against a wide range of cyberthreats (Ma, 2021). Firewalls serve as the first line of defence in this multi-layered approach. They act as barriers between the internal and external networks, monitoring and controlling incoming and outgoing traffic based on predetermined security rules. For example, in a smart grid network, firewalls can prevent unauthorised access to critical control systems, protecting against potential cyberattacks that aim to disrupt energy distribution or manipulate grid operations. IDPS enhances security by actively monitoring network and system activities for signs of malicious behaviour. In a smart transportation system, an IDPS might detect anomalous patterns in the communication network, indicating a potential cyberthreat to connected vehicles.

Antivirus software is crucial in safeguarding against malware and other malicious software. As smart cities rely on interconnected systems and IoT devices, antivirus software helps prevent the spread of malware that could compromise data integrity or disrupt essential services (Aslan et al., 2023). For instance, antivirus software scans medical devices and systems in a smart healthcare environment to detect and remove malware that compromises patient data or disrupts healthcare operations (Williams & Woodward, 2015). Endpoint security focuses on securing individual devices connected to the smart city network. This layer of defence is critical in environments where various devices, such as sensors and IoT devices, play a vital role. In a smart building, for example, endpoint security measures would protect individual devices from unauthorised access, ensuring that environmental controls and other automated systems remain secure and operational.

5.4.4 Encryption and Secure Communication Protocols

Implementing robust encryption and secure communication protocols is a fundamental aspect of safeguarding the integrity and confidentiality of data in smart city environments. This mitigation strategy involves employing advanced cryptographic techniques to protect data in transit and at rest, ensuring that sensitive information remains secure and resilient against potential cyberthreats (Zeadally et al., 2021). In a smart transportation system, ensuring secure communication protocols protects real-time data exchanged between connected vehicles and the central traffic management system (Lin et al., 2017). For instance, protocols like Transport Layer Security (TLS) or Secure Socket Layer (SSL) can encrypt communication channels, preventing unauthorised access to information about vehicle locations, routes, and traffic conditions. It only safeguards the privacy of individuals and prevents potential data manipulation that could lead to traffic disruptions or accidents.

Similarly, encryption is pivotal in securing data at rest within smart city databases and storage systems (Sookhak et al., 2018). In a smart energy grid, for example, sensitive information about energy consumption patterns and infrastructure configurations is stored in databases. Employing robust encryption algorithms ensures that the data remains unreadable and protected against tampering even if unauthorised access occurs (Hu & Vasilakos, 2016). It is essential for maintaining the reliability and resilience of energy distribution systems. Furthermore, using secure communication protocols becomes imperative in smart city applications where real-time data exchange is critical. In a smart healthcare system, secure communication between medical devices, wearable technologies, and healthcare servers is vital to protect patient information and maintain the integrity of health monitoring data. Implementing secure protocols for healthcare data exchange ensures that sensitive medical information remains confidential and is only accessible by authorised entities (El Zouka & Hosni, 2021). The mitigation strategy of encryption and secure communication protocols is foundational in smart city cybersecurity.

5.4.5 Continuous Employee Training

Continuous employee training is critical to mitigating cybersecurity risks in smart city environments. This proactive strategy involves providing ongoing education and awareness programmes to empower employees with the knowledge and skills to identify, prevent, and respond to cyberthreats (Trumbach et al., 2023). In the context of smart cities, where human factors can play a significant role in the overall security posture, continuous training is essential for maintaining a vigilant and cybersecurity-aware workforce. Phishing attacks and social engineering tactics are prevalent methods malicious actors employ to gain unauthorised access to sensitive information. Through continuous employee training, individuals within smart city organisations can learn to recognise the signs of phishing emails, malicious links, or deceptive communications. For example, in a smart governance setting, where city officials receive numerous emails related to administrative processes, training can help them identify potential phishing attempts that aim to compromise sensitive government data.

Furthermore, continuous training enables employees to stay informed about the latest cybersecurity threats and best practices (Franchina et al., 2021). In a smart education environment, where digital classrooms and e-learning platforms are integral, educators and administrators can undergo training to understand evolving threats targeting educational technologies. This knowledge equips them to implement effective cybersecurity measures, protect student data, and ensure the uninterrupted operation of digital learning environments. Educated employees also play a crucial role in incident response and reporting. In a smart healthcare system, for instance, healthcare professionals regularly handling sensitive patient information can be trained to recognise and promptly report any suspicious activities or potential breaches. This proactive approach enhances the overall resilience of smart city networks as employees become active contributors to the early detection and mitigation of cybersecurity threats.

5.4.6 Network Segmentation

Network segmentation is a crucial mitigation strategy in fortifying the cybersecurity defences of smart city environments. This approach involves dividing a network into distinct segments or zones, isolating critical infrastructure from less secure areas (Nankya et al., 2023). Smart cities can significantly reduce the potential impact of security breaches, enhancing their interconnected systems' overall resilience and security posture by implementing network segmentation. In the context of smart transportation systems, network segmentation (Jafari et al., 2023) can be applied to isolate the control systems managing traffic lights, intelligent intersections, and autonomous vehicles from less critical networks, such as public Wi-Fi or non-essential services. Even if a security breach occurs in one segment, the impact is contained within that specific zone, preventing unauthorised access to critical transportation infrastructure that could lead to disruptions or safety hazards. Likewise, in a smart energy grid, network segmentation can isolate the control systems managing energy distribution and grid stability from less critical networks, like administrative or public-facing services. If a cyberthreat were to compromise a less secure segment, the integrity of essential energy services would remain intact, minimising the risk of widespread power outages or disruptions.

Network segmentation is crucial in sectors like smart healthcare, where patient data and medical infrastructure must be safeguarded (Javaid et al., 2023). In this context, isolating the network segment that manages electronic health records, medical devices, and communication between healthcare professionals ensures that any potential breach in other areas of the network does not jeopardise patient confidentiality or the integrity of critical healthcare services. Moreover, in a smart governance framework, where administrative processes and citizen services are digitised, network segmentation can isolate the networks handling sensitive government data from those supporting public Wi-Fi or other less secure services. It prevents unauthorised access to critical governmental systems, protecting against potential cyberthreats that could compromise essential civic operations. Network segmentation is a robust mitigation strategy by compartmentalising smart city networks, limiting the lateral movement of cyberthreats, and safeguarding critical infrastructure. This proactive approach enhances the overall cybersecurity resilience of smart cities, ensuring the continued operation of essential services and minimising the potential impact of security breaches on urban environments.

5.4.7 Incident Response Plans

Incident response plans play a pivotal role in fortifying the cybersecurity posture of smart city environments by providing a structured and proactive approach to addressing security incidents (Xia et al., 2023). Developing and regularly testing incident response plans is a critical mitigation strategy, ensuring a swift and coordinated response to potential security breaches. These plans encompass a set of well-defined procedures for identifying, containing, eradicating, recovering from, and analysing security incidents. In the context of a smart transportation system, an incident response plan could involve clear guidelines for responding to a cyberattack that targets traffic management systems. It might include immediate actions to isolate affected segments, implement traffic diversions, and communicate with relevant authorities to minimise disruptions and ensure public safety. Regular testing of this plan through simulated exercises helps smart city stakeholders refine their responses and ensures that the plan remains effective in the face of evolving cyberthreats.

In a smart energy grid, an incident response plan could outline steps for mitigating the impact of a cyberattack on the control systems managing energy distribution (Jha, 2023). It might involve temporarily isolating affected segments, rerouting energy supply, and activating backup systems to maintain uninterrupted power distribution. Regular drills and simulations enable smart city operators to fine-tune their response procedures, ensuring a resilient and adaptive approach to cybersecurity incidents. Incident response plans safeguard patient data and critical medical infrastructure for smart healthcare systems. In the event of a security breach, the plan might dictate actions such as isolating affected network segments, activating backup systems for medical devices, and notifying regulatory authorities about potential data breaches. Regular testing ensures that healthcare professionals are well-prepared to handle cybersecurity incidents without compromising patient care.

In a smart governance context, incident response plans can guide city officials in responding to cyberthreats targeting administrative processes and citizen services (Pereira et al., 2018). These plans may involve procedures for quickly identifying and mitigating the impact of security incidents, notifying the public about potential disruptions, and collaborating with law enforcement agencies for investigation. Regular testing and updates to incident response plans keep smart city administrations agile and responsive in the face of evolving cyberthreats. Developing and regularly testing incident response plans is a crucial mitigation strategy for smart cities. These plans provide a structured framework for responding to security incidents, helping to minimise the impact of breaches, maintain essential services, and enhance overall cybersecurity resilience in the dynamic landscape of urban environments.

5.4.8 Redundancy and Backup Systems

Implementing redundancy and backup systems is a crucial strategy for mitigating cybersecurity risks in smart city environments (Almeida, 2023). This approach involves creating duplicate or backup systems that can seamlessly take over if the primary systems are compromised. In the context of smart cities, where the continuous operation of critical services is paramount, redundancy and backup systems play a pivotal role in ensuring the availability and integrity of essential data and services. For example, redundancy can be applied to traffic management systems in a smart transportation system. If a malicious actor attempts to compromise the primary traffic control infrastructure, redundant systems can quickly take over, preventing disruptions to traffic flow and minimising the impact on public safety. Regular backups of traffic data, such as real-time information on road conditions and traffic patterns, ensure that even in a security incident, the city can quickly recover and restore normal operations. In the smart energy sector, redundancy and backup systems are essential for maintaining a reliable power supply (Yusof et al., 2023). In a cybersecurity incident targeting the control systems of a smart city's energy grid, redundant systems can seamlessly take control, preventing widespread power outages. Regular backups of critical data related to energy distribution, consumption patterns, and grid operations ensure that the city can recover quickly and continue providing uninterrupted power to residents.

In smart healthcare, redundancy and backup systems are critical for safeguarding patient data and maintaining continuous healthcare services (Kumari, 2013). If a cybersecurity incident compromises the primary electronic health records system, redundant systems can ensure that patient information remains accessible and that healthcare services can continue without interruption. Regular backups of patient records and medical data are essential for data recovery in a security breach. Furthermore, redundancy measures can be applied to administrative systems in smart governance. In the event of a cyberattack targeting government databases or administrative processes, redundant systems can prevent service disruptions, ensuring that essential public services continue without interruption. Regular backups of critical government data, such as citizen records and administrative documents, are vital for maintaining the integrity of governance systems. Implementing redundancy and backup systems in smart cities is a proactive measure to enhance resilience against cybersecurity threats.

5.4.9 Physical Security Measures

Physical security measures safeguard critical infrastructure components (Drago, 2015) in smart city environments. These measures are designed to prevent unauthorised physical access to sensitive locations and infrastructure, contributing to the overall resilience of the smart city against various threats, including physical attacks or tampering. For instance, physical security measures can be applied to the control centres managing traffic signals and surveillance cameras in a smart transportation system. Access controls, such as biometric authentication or keycard systems, can only restrict entry to authorised personnel. Surveillance systems, including CCTV cameras and security personnel, can monitor these facilities to detect and deter unauthorised physical access attempts. Secure facilities with reinforced entry points and alarmed perimeters add an extra layer of protection, ensuring the integrity of the transportation infrastructure. Physical security measures are crucial to safeguarding power plants, distribution centres, and control rooms in smart energy grids. Access controls with multi-factor authentication can limit entry to essential personnel, and surveillance systems can monitor these critical areas. Secure facilities with perimeter fencing, motion detectors, and alarms help prevent unauthorised individuals from physically compromising the energy infrastructure.

Physical security measures are essential in smart healthcare environments to protect medical facilities, data centres, and equipment. Access controls and biometric authentication can restrict access to sensitive areas containing patient records and medical equipment. Surveillance systems and security personnel monitor and protect healthcare facilities, ensuring that only authorised individuals have physical access. Secure facilities with controlled entry points further enhance the physical security of the healthcare infrastructure. Smart governance in a city involves securing administrative buildings, data centres, and critical government facilities. Physical security measures, such as access controls and surveillance systems, are implemented to safeguard these locations. Biometric authentication, security personnel, and secure entry points help prevent unauthorised physical access, protecting government data and administrative processes.

5.4.10 Community Engagement and Public Awareness

Community engagement and public awareness play a pivotal role in fortifying the cybersecurity posture of smart cities (Demertzi et al., 2023). Mitigating potential threats involves actively involving citizens through various initiatives, including awareness campaigns, public forums, and educational programmes. Community engagement begins with disseminating information about cybersecurity best practices and potential threats in a smart city context. Awareness campaigns can be conducted through multiple channels, including social media, local newspapers, and community events. These campaigns aim to educate residents about the importance of cybersecurity, the risks associated with various online activities, and the role individuals play in ensuring the overall security of the smart city. Public forums provide open communication between city authorities, cybersecurity experts, and the community. These forums allow residents to voice concerns, seek clarifications, and receive updates on the latest cybersecurity measures implemented in the smart city. Creating a collaborative environment fosters a sense of shared responsibility, empowering citizens to contribute actively to the city's cybersecurity efforts.

Educational initiatives are instrumental in enhancing public awareness and understanding of cybersecurity issues. Workshops, seminars, and training sessions can be organised to educate citizens on recognising potential threats, understanding secure online practices, and reporting suspicious activities. These programmes empower individuals with the knowledge and skills needed to protect themselves and contribute to the collective security of the smart city. For example, community engagement initiatives in smart transportation may focus on educating residents about the potential cybersecurity risks associated with connected vehicles and intelligent transportation systems. In the context of smart healthcare, community engagement may involve informing citizens about the security measures in place to protect their medical data and their role in ensuring the confidentiality of health information. Educational initiatives can cover topics such as recognising phishing attempts and safeguarding personal health records, empowering residents to actively support the cybersecurity resilience of the smart healthcare ecosystem. Community engagement and public awareness are essential mitigation strategies in smart cities.

5.4.11 Collaboration and Information Sharing

Collaboration and information sharing are indispensable to mitigating cybersecurity threats in smart city environments. Establishing partnerships and collaborative frameworks for sharing threat intelligence is pivotal in enhancing the collective defence against evolving cyberthreats (Skopik et al., 2016). Collaboration becomes imperative for bolstering resilience in smart cities, where interconnected systems create a shared cybersecurity landscape. For instance, collaboration could involve sharing information about recent cyberthreats targeting traffic management systems in a smart transportation network. If one city detects a new malware variant affecting its traffic control infrastructure, timely sharing of this threat intelligence with other cities allows them to proactively implement preventive measures, such as updating their security protocols or temporarily isolating vulnerable systems. In the smart energy sector, information sharing could revolve around emerging threats to critical infrastructure control systems. By participating in collaborative initiatives, smart cities can benefit from shared insights and intelligence on potential vulnerabilities and attack vectors. This collective knowledge enables cities to fortify their energy grids against similar threats, ensuring an uninterrupted power supply to residents.

Smart healthcare systems can also reap significant benefits from collaboration and information sharing. If one city experiences a cybersecurity incident targeting its healthcare infrastructure, sharing this information with other smart cities enhances their preparedness. Lessons learned from such incidents, including tactics employed by attackers and successful mitigation strategies, can be disseminated to the broader smart city community. In governance, collaboration can involve sharing information on phishing campaigns or other social engineering tactics targeting city employees. Fostering collaboration with law enforcement agencies and other smart cities, municipal governments can collectively combat these threats, ensuring the security of sensitive data and maintaining the integrity of administrative processes. Collaboration and information sharing serve as proactive measures for smart cities to address cybersecurity challenges collectively (Nova, 2022).

Developing and implementing robust government regulations for smart city cybersecurity is imperative for fostering a secure and resilient urban landscape. As smart cities continue to integrate cutting-edge technologies to enhance efficiency, sustainability, and the quality of life for citizens, the potential risks associated with cyberthreats cannot be overlooked. Government regulations are crucial for guiding smart city stakeholders towards responsible and secure practices, including municipalities, technology vendors, and citizens. The multifaceted nature of these regulations encompasses data protection, network security, incident response, vendor accountability, and public awareness, reflecting the comprehensive approach needed to address the diverse cybersecurity challenges posed by smart city ecosystems.

Establishing clear standards and certifications ensures that smart city technologies adhere to recognised cybersecurity protocols. It safeguards critical infrastructure and fosters a competitive market where security is a priority. By mandating incident response plans and reporting mechanisms, regulations contribute to proactively identifying and mitigating cybersecurity threats, preventing potential disruptions. Collaboration and information sharing at the national and international levels are vital to effective cybersecurity regulations. Cyberthreats often transcend geographical boundaries, and collective efforts enhance the ability to respond to evolving challenges. Furthermore, regulations should be adaptable and designed to future-proof smart cities, considering the dynamic nature of technology and the ever-changing threat landscape.

As smart city initiatives evolve, the emphasis on public awareness and education becomes paramount. Government regulations should encourage transparent communication about cybersecurity measures, educate citizens on digital literacy, and empower them to actively ensure the security of their data and the urban environment. Ultimately, the success of government regulations for smart city cybersecurity hinges on collaboration between government entities, the private sector, academia, and the public. A holistic and inclusive approach that considers the interests and well-being of all stakeholders is essential for creating a secure, resilient, and citizen-centric smart city landscape. Through continuous evaluation, adaptation, and a commitment to innovation, government regulations can pave the way for a future where smart cities thrive securely and sustainably.

References

Alauthman, M., Aldweesh, A., & Al-Qerem, A. (2024, February 26–28). IoT security challenges in modern smart cities. In *2024 2nd International Conference on Cyber Resilience (ICCR)*. https://doi.org/10.1109/ICCR61006.2024.10533174

Almeida, F. (2023). Prospects of cybersecurity in smart cities. *Future Internet, 15*(9), 285. https://doi.org/10.3390/fi15090285

Althobaiti, O. S., & Dohler, M. (2020). Cybersecurity challenges associated with the Internet of Things in a post-quantum world. *IEEE Access, 8*, 157356–157381. https://doi.org/10.1109/ACCESS.2020.3019345

Arunprasad, P., Dey, C., Jebli, F., Manimuthu, A., & El Hathat, Z. (2022). Exploring the remote work challenges in the era of COVID-19 pandemic: Review and application model. *Benchmarking: An International Journal, 29*(10), 3333–3355. https://doi.org/10.1108/BIJ-07-2021-0421

Aslan, Ö., Aktuğ, S. S., Ozkan-Okay, M., Yilmaz, A. A., & Akin, E. (2023). A comprehensive review of cyber security vulnerabilities, threats, attacks, and solutions. *Electronics, 12*(6), 1333. https://doi.org/10.3390/electronics12061333

Cissé, M. (2021). Cyber security for smart cities: End-to-end cyber security strategy for IoT connected services. *Cyber Security: A Peer-Reviewed Journal, 4*(3), 251–266. https://www.ingentaconnect.com/content/hsp/jcs/2021/00000004/00000003/art00007

Demertzi, V., Demertzis, S., & Demertzis, K. (2023). An overview of cyber threats, attacks and countermeasures on the primary domains of smart cities. *Applied Sciences, 13*(2), 790. https://doi.org/10.3390/app13020790

Desai, B., Patil, K., Mehta, I., & Patil, A. (2024). A secure communication framework for smart city infrastructure leveraging encryption, intrusion detection, and blockchain technology. *Advances in Computer Sciences, 7*(1). https://acadexpinnara.com/index.php/acs/article/view/149

Drago, A. (2015). *Methods and techniques for enhancing physical security of critical infrastructures*. University of Naples "Federico II": Naples.

El Zouka, H. A., & Hosni, M. M. (2021). Secure IoT communications for smart healthcare monitoring system. *Internet of Things, 13*, 100036. https://doi.org/10.1016/j.iot.2019.01.003

Fabrègue, B. F. G., & Bogoni, A. (2023). Privacy and security concerns in the smart city. *Smart Cities, 6*(1), 586–613. https://doi.org/10.3390/smartcities6010027

Franchina, L., Inzerilli, G., Scatto, E., Calabrese, A., Lucariello, A., Brutti, G., & Roscioli, P. (2021). Passive and active training approaches for critical infrastructure protection. *International Journal of Disaster Risk Reduction, 63*, 102461. https://doi.org/10.1016/j.ijdrr.2021.102461

Habibzadeh, H., Nussbaum, B. H., Anjomshoa, F., Kantarci, B., & Soyata, T. (2019). A survey on cybersecurity, data privacy, and policy issues in cyber-physical system deployments in smart cities. *Sustainable Cities and Society, 50*, 101660. https://doi.org/10.1016/j.scs.2019.101660

Hu, J., & Vasilakos, A. V. (2016). Energy big data analytics and security: Challenges and opportunities. *IEEE Transactions on Smart Grid, 7*(5), 2423–2436. https://doi.org/10.1109/TSG.2016.2563461

Jafari, M., Kavousi-Fard, A., Chen, T., & Karimi, M. (2023). A review on digital twin technology in smart grid, transportation system and smart city: Challenges and future. *IEEE Access, 11*, 17471–17484. https://doi.org/10.1109/ACCESS.2023.3241588

Javaid, M., Haleem, A., Singh, R. P., & Suman, R. (2023). Towards insighting cybersecurity for healthcare domains: A comprehensive review of recent practices and trends. *Cyber Security and Applications, 1*, 100016. https://doi.org/10.1016/j.csa.2023.100016

Jha, R. K. (2023). Cybersecurity and confidentiality in smart grid for enhancing sustainability and reliability. *Recent Research Reviews Journal, 2*(2), 215–241. https://doi.org/10.36548/rrrj.2023.2.001

Kaloudi, N., & Li, J. L. (2020). The AI-based cyber threat landscape: A survey. *ACM Computer Survey, 53*(1), Article 20. https://doi.org/10.1145/3372823

Kayode-Ajala, O. (2023). Establishing cyber resilience in developing countries: An exploratory investigation into institutional, legal, financial, and social challenges. *International Journal of Sustainable Infrastructure for Cities and Societies, 8*(9), 1–10. https://vectoral.org/index.php/IJSICS/article/view/27

Kelarestaghi, K. B., Foruhandeh, M., Heaslip, K., & Gerdes, R. (2019). Intelligent transportation system security: Impact-oriented risk assessment of in-vehicle networks. *IEEE Intelligent Transportation Systems Magazine, 13*(2), 91–104. https://doi.org/10.1109/MITS.2018.2889714

Khan, L. U., Yaqoob, I., Tran, N. H., Kazmi, S. A., Dang, T. N., & Hong, C. S. (2020). Edge-computing-enabled smart cities: A comprehensive survey. *IEEE Internet of Things Journal, 7*(10), 10200–10232. https://doi.org/10.1109/JIOT.2020.2987070

Khan, S. K., Shiwakoti, N., Stasinopoulos, P., & Warren, M. (2023). Cybersecurity regulatory challenges for connected and automated vehicles – State-of-the-art and future directions. *Transport Policy, 143*, 58–71. https://doi.org/10.1016/j.tranpol.2023.09.001

Kumari, A. (2013). Security aspects of patient's data in a medical diagnostic system. In *Machine learning in healthcare and security* (pp. 195–210). CRC Press.

Laufs, J., Borrion, H., & Bradford, B. (2020). Security and the smart city: A systematic review. *Sustainable Cities and Society, 55*, 102023. https://doi.org/10.1016/j.scs.2020.102023

Leal, M. M., & Musgrave, P. (2023). Backwards from zero: How the U.S. public evaluates the use of zero-day vulnerabilities in cybersecurity. *Contemporary Security Policy, 44*(3), 437–461. https://doi.org/10.1080/13523260.2023.2216112

Lin, J., Yu, W., Zhang, N., Yang, X., Zhang, H., & Zhao, W. (2017). A survey on Internet of Things: Architecture, enabling technologies, security and privacy, and applications. *IEEE Internet of Things Journal, 4*(5), 1125–1142. https://doi.org/10.1109/JIOT.2017.2683200

Lindsay, J. R. (2020). Demystifying the quantum threat: Infrastructure, institutions, and intelligence advantage. *Security Studies, 29*(2), 335–361. https://doi.org/10.1080/09636412.2020.1722853

Ma, C. (2021). Smart city and cyber-security: Technologies used, leading challenges and future recommendations. *Energy Reports*, 7, 7999–8012. https://doi.org/10.1016/j.egyr.2021.08.124

Mishra, D., Pursharthi, K., & Rewal, P. (2023). Development of quantum-enhanced authenticated key agreement protocol for autonomous vehicles. *Vehicular Communications*, 44, 100688. https://doi.org/10.1016/j.vehcom.2023.100688

Nankya, M., Chataut, R., & Akl, R. (2023). Securing industrial control systems: Components, cyber threats, and machine learning-driven defense strategies. *Sensors*, 23(21), 8840. https://doi.org/10.3390/s23218840

Nova, K. (2022). Security and resilience in sustainable smart cities through cyber threat intelligence. *International Journal of Information and Cybersecurity*, 6(1), 21–42.

Pereira, G. V., Parycek, P., Falco, E., & Kleinhans, R. (2018). Smart governance in the context of smart cities: A literature review. *Information Polity*, 23, 143–162. https://doi.org/10.3233/IP-170067

Samaila, M. G., Neto, M., Fernandes, D. A., Freire, M. M., & Inácio, P. R. (2017). Security challenges of the Internet of Things. In: J. Batalla, G. Mastorakis, C. Mavromoustakis, & E. Pallis (Eds.), Beyond *the Internet of Things:* Everything *interconnected* (pp. 53–82). https://doi.org/10.1007/978-3-319-50758-3_3

Sinimole, K., & Karri, S. L. (2024). Security and privacy issues in smart cities. In *Handbook of artificial intelligence for smart city development* (pp. 228–248). CRC Press.

Skopik, F., Settanni, G., & Fiedler, R. (2016). A problem shared is a problem halved: A survey on the dimensions of collective cyber defense through security information sharing. *Computers & Security*, 60, 154–176. https://doi.org/10.1016/j.cose.2016.04.003

Sommestad, T. (2018). Work-related groups and information security policy compliance. *Information & Computer Security*, 26(5), 533–550. https://doi.org/10.1108/ICS-08-2017-0054

Sookhak, M., Tang, H., He, Y., & Yu, F. R. (2018). Security and privacy of smart cities: A survey, research issues and challenges. *IEEE Communications Surveys & Tutorials*, 21(2), 1718–1743. https://doi.org/10.1109/COMST.2018.2867288

Soto, I., Calderon, M., Amador, O., & Urueña, M. (2022). A survey on road safety and traffic efficiency vehicular applications based on C-V2X technologies. *Vehicular Communications*, 33, 100428. https://doi.org/10.1016/j.vehcom.2021.100428

Tahirkheli, A. I., Shiraz, M., Hayat, B., Idrees, M., Sajid, A., Ullah, R., Ayub, N., & Kim, K.-I. (2021). A survey on modern cloud computing security over smart city networks: Threats, vulnerabilities, consequences, countermeasures, and challenges. *Electronics*, 10(15), 1811. https://doi.org/10.3390/electronics10151811

Telo, J. (2023). Smart city security threats and countermeasures in the context of emerging technologies. *International Journal of Intelligent Automation and Computing*, 6(1), 31–45.

Trumbach, C. C., Payne, D. M., & Walsh, K. (2023). Cybersecurity in business education: The 'how to' in incorporating education into practice. *Industry and Higher Education*, 37(1), 35–45. https://doi.org/10.1177/09504222221099389

Ullah, A., Anwar, S. M., Li, J., Nadeem, L., Mahmood, T., Rehman, A., & Saba, T. (2024). Smart cities: The role of Internet of Things and machine learning in realising a data-centric smart environment. *Complex & Intelligent Systems*, 10(1), 1607–1637. https://doi.org/10.1007/s40747-023-01175-4

Williams, P. A. H., & Woodward, A. J. (2015). Cybersecurity vulnerabilities in medical devices: A complex environment and multifaceted problem. *Medical Devices: Evidence and Research, 8*, 305–316. https://doi.org/10.2147/MDER.S50048

Xia, L., Semirumi, D. T., & Rezaei, R. (2023). A thorough examination of smart city applications: Exploring challenges and solutions throughout the life cycle with emphasis on safeguarding citizen privacy. *Sustainable Cities and Society, 98*, 104771. https://doi.org/10.1016/j.scs.2023.104771

Yu, M., Zhuge, J., Cao, M., Shi, Z., & Jiang, L. (2020). A survey of security vulnerability analysis, discovery, detection, and mitigation on IoT devices. *Future Internet, 12*(2), 27. https://doi.org/10.3390/fi12020027

Yusof, Y. B., Ping, T. H., & Isa, F. B. M. (2023). Strengthening smart grids through security measures: A focus on real-time monitoring, redundancy, and cross-sector collaboration. *International Journal of Intelligent Automation and Computing, 6*(3), 14–36.

Zeadally, S., Das, A. K., & Sklavos, N. (2021). Cryptographic technologies and protocol standards for Internet of Things. *Internet of Things, 14*, 100075. https://doi.org/10.1016/j.iot.2019.100075

6

Cybersecurity in a Smart City Environment: Motives and Methods for Launching Attacks

Norliza Katuk, Modhawi Alotaibi, Derar Eleyan, and Amna Eleyan

6.1 Navigating the Cyber Terrain of Smart Cities

The increasing digitalisation of urban spaces has created an intricate cyber terrain where data-driven infrastructure, artificial intelligence (AI), and Internet of Things (IoT) devices form the backbone of smart city functionality. The modern city operates on an interconnected web of intelligent systems, from automated traffic control and public surveillance to energy grids and emergency response networks. While these advancements bring efficiency, sustainability, and convenience, they also introduce new and complex cybersecurity challenges (Hossain & Hasan, 2025). The cyber terrain of smart cities is unique in that it combines digital and physical elements, making it vulnerable to cyber-physical threats capable of disrupting essential services and daily life.

The many IoT-enabled devices deployed in smart cities significantly expand the potential attack surface. These sensors and connected systems are designed to optimise urban living, monitoring everything from environmental conditions to transportation flows and energy consumption. However, their widespread use and decentralised deployment present significant security concerns (Sebestyen et al., 2025). Many IoT devices operate with minimal security protections, making them attractive targets for cybercriminals. Exploiting vulnerabilities in these devices can allow attackers to manipulate data, turn off essential services, or conduct large-scale distributed denial-of-service (DDoS) attacks that can disturb city functions.

Another key aspect of smart city infrastructure is the reliance on high-speed communication networks, particularly 5G. While 5G technology enables ultra-low latency communication and enhances real-time automation, it also increases the number of entry points for cyber intrusions. Cyberattackers can exploit unsecured endpoints in these networks to intercept data, manipulate real-time decision-making processes, or inject malicious commands into automated city functions. Additionally, cloud computing and edge computing solutions, which support the large-scale processing of urban data,

DOI: 10.1201/9781003619819-8

introduce new concerns regarding unauthorised access, data breaches, and insider threats.

The cyber terrain of smart cities is further complicated by its reliance on cyber-physical systems (CPS), which integrate traditional information technology (IT) infrastructure with operational technology that controls critical physical infrastructure. Unlike conventional IT security threats, attacks on CPS can have immediate and tangible consequences, such as power outages, public transportation disruptions, or the compromise of emergency response mechanisms (Alomari et al., 2025). The risk of cascading failures is particularly alarming, as a single cyberattack on one system could trigger a domino effect across multiple services. This interconnectedness makes it imperative to secure not just individual components but also the broader network of integrated city functions.

One of the major challenges in securing the cyber terrain of smart cities lies in the fragmentation of responsibility among various stakeholders. Municipal governments, private technology providers, infrastructure operators, and regulatory agencies all play distinct roles in city management. However, the lack of uniform security standards and governance models creates vulnerabilities that adversaries can exploit (Siddiqui et al., 2024). Ensuring security across this vast digital landscape requires coordination between multiple entities, implementing consistent security policies, and fostering cross-sector collaboration.

The emergence of AI, blockchain, and quantum computing further reshapes the cyber terrain of smart cities. While these technologies offer enhanced security mechanisms, they also introduce new risks. AI-driven cyberattacks, such as deepfake-based social engineering or automated hacking tools, present increasingly sophisticated threats. Though considered a secure data authentication method, blockchain is still susceptible to consensus-based attacks or smart contract vulnerabilities. The potential impact of quantum computing on traditional encryption methods also raises concerns about the long-term resilience of smart city security frameworks. As the cyber terrain evolves, cities must continuously assess their digital landscapes, anticipate emerging threats, and adopt proactive measures to mitigate risks.

6.2 Motives of Attacks in a Smart City Environment

In the dynamic landscape of urban development, smart city networks, conceived to elevate urban living through cutting-edge technologies, grapple with an array of security challenges inherent to their intricate and interconnected nature. These challenges, rooted in the escalating sophistication of cyberthreats, are compounded by the intrinsic vulnerabilities woven into the communication infrastructure of smart cities (Braun et al., 2018). A fundamental

FIGURE 6.1
Security breaches due to human errors.

understanding of the motivations driving these attacks becomes paramount to fortifying these networks against potential threats and upholding the reliability and privacy of smart city infrastructures. Malicious actors exploit vulnerabilities within smart city networks with diverse intentions, from disrupting essential services and gaining unauthorised access to critical components to compromising sensitive data and manipulating sensor information for deceptive purposes (Neshenko et al., 2022). As smart city networks progressively embed themselves into the fabric of urban operations, deciphering the "why" behind security attacks emerges as a critical imperative. This section explains seven motives or reasons that lead to cyberattacks, as illustrated in Figure 6.1. This comprehension is the linchpin for developing comprehensive countermeasures, ensuring the resilience and integrity of smart city infrastructures as they play an increasingly integral role in shaping the urban landscape (Giannaros et al., 2023).

6.2.1 Human Error

Security vulnerabilities can emerge from accidental and deliberate causes, and understanding these triggers is crucial for formulating robust cybersecurity strategies. Human error is a prominent source of accidental security breaches, where misconfigurations, negligence, or the unintentional exposure of sensitive information become entry points for potential attacks (Yeo,

FIGURE 6.2
Statistics on security breaches due to human errors. (From Abraham, 2022.)

2023). Real-world instances reported in various newspapers shed light on the gravity of these issues. For example, in a recent incident, a misconfigured sensor or an inadequately secured IoT device inadvertently provided attackers with exploitable opportunities (Alfandi et al., 2021). Similarly, coding errors, outdated software, and unpatched systems create vulnerabilities that can be accidentally exposed when developers overlook security best practices or fail to apply necessary updates promptly. The IBM Cyber Security Intelligence Index Report reveals that 95% of cyber breaches are human mistakes. Additionally, the 2020 Cost of a Data Breach Report from IBM highlights an average cost of $3.33 million for cybersecurity incidents caused by human error (Abraham, 2022). Further, the statistics revealed that human errors have been the top cause of security breaches in organisations (Abraham, 2022), as illustrated in Figure 6.2.

Furthermore, the absence of comprehensive security measures within smart city networks, including encryption, access controls, and proper authentication protocols, can lead to unintended security lapses. This security deficiency often stems from budget constraints, lack of awareness, or oversights during smart city projects' planning and implementation phases. The intricate interplay of interconnected systems within smart cities magnifies the probability of accidental security incidents (Habibzadeh et al., 2019). A flaw in one system can cascade and affect others, resulting in unforeseen consequences.

6.2.2 Financial Gain

Security attacks on smart city networks often stem from a spectrum of motives, including financial gain, ideological pursuits, and geopolitical objectives. A nuanced understanding of these motivations is the cornerstone for effectively devising targeted security measures to counter potential threats. One prominent motive driving cyberthreats in smart cities is the pursuit of financial gain. Cybercriminals strategically target a smart city network through a sophisticated ransomware attack. The attackers exploited vulnerabilities within the network infrastructure, encrypting critical data and demanding a substantial ransom for its release (Yaqoob et al., 2017). The city faces immense pressure to pay the ransom to restore essential services promptly. Such incidents highlight the tangible risks and consequences of financially motivated cybercriminal activities within smart city environments.

Data theft is another avenue cybercriminals exploit for financial gain (Sarkar & Shukla, 2023) in smart city networks. Malicious actors infiltrate a city's network, exfiltrating sensitive information such as citizen data, financial records, and infrastructure blueprints. The stolen data was later sold on the dark web, underscoring the profit-driven nature of these cyberthreats. The impacted city suffered reputational damage and incurred financial losses in mitigating the aftermath and implementing enhanced security measures. Cybercriminals demanded substantial payments under the threat of disrupting essential services, armed with compromising information about critical infrastructure vulnerabilities (Lehto, 2022). These cases exemplify the multifaceted strategies employed by cybercriminals to exploit smart city networks for financial gain.

6.2.3 Espionage and Cyber Warfare

Security attacks transcend individual actors, extending their reach to encompass nation-states or state-sponsored entities motivated by espionage objectives. Beyond the conventional pursuit of financial gain, these sophisticated entities delve into strategic manoeuvres, seeking unauthorised access to sensitive information and orchestrating disruptions in critical infrastructure to gain geopolitical advantages. Nation-states or state-sponsored entities may strategically target smart city networks, employing cyber warfare techniques to compromise systems and achieve their geopolitical objectives. Instances of infiltrating and extracting sensitive information showcase these attacks' deliberate and calculated nature. The motivation goes beyond mere data breaches; it involves the acquisition of intelligence that can be wielded for manipulation or disruption of essential services, amplifying the stakes involved.

In April 2022, Ukraine's Computer Emergency Response Team (CERT-UA) successfully thwarted a cyberattack orchestrated by Russia's Sandworm group against an energy provider (Lin, 2022). The attackers sought to turn off electrical substations by employing a new variant of Industroyer malware (Page, 2022). Notably, the Industroyer malware had been previously used in 2016 to disrupt power in Ukraine, leading to a widespread blackout just two days before Christmas and impacting hundreds of thousands of customers.

This example underscores the interconnected nature of cyberattacks on critical infrastructure, marking a convergence of cyber warfare and kinetic military actions.

6.2.4 Hacktivism

Hacktivism, a portmanteau of "hack" and "activism," represents a form of cyber activism where individuals or groups leverage hacking techniques to further their ideological or political beliefs (George & Leidner, 2019). Smart city networks have become a focal point for hacktivist activities as these actors aim to champion a cause or express dissent through digital means. The motivations behind hacktivist attacks are diverse, ranging from environmental concerns and social justice issues to political ideologies. Hacktivist attacks on smart city networks take various forms, each designed to convey a powerful message or draw attention to a specific cause. One common tactic involves defacing websites, where hacktivists alter the visual appearance or content of the site to communicate their message (Romagna & van den Hout, 2017). This visual impact is a symbolic gesture highlighting their disagreement with specific policies or practices within the smart city framework. Illustrating this motive, after the conflict in October 2023 between Israelis and Hamas, more than 100 hacktivists launched over 500 web defacement attacks specifically targeting Israeli websites. It mirrors the hacktivist attacks observed in the aftermath of the 2022 Russian invasion of Ukraine (Goodwin, 2023).

Disruption of services is another prevalent method employed by hacktivists. These actors seek to disrupt regular operations, causing inconvenience and drawing attention to their cause by targeting critical components of smart city infrastructure. This disruption may manifest as temporary service outages, system malfunctions, or interference with communication channels. Amid the Ukraine-Russian conflict, Kyiv assembled an "IT Army" of approximately 400,000 individuals who engaged in DDoS attacks, causing disruptions to Russian banks and the Moscow Stock Exchange. It also targeted hospitals and healthcare services, including the Red Cross, to cause disruptions to healthcare services (Schwartz, 2023). Hacktivism in smart city networks represents a dynamic and impactful form of digital activism. It demonstrates the growing intersection between technology, ideology, and civic engagement, with hacktivists utilising their skills to influence and shape the discourse surrounding smart city initiatives.

6.2.5 Competitor and Corporate Espionage

In the competitive arena of both corporate entities and nations, resorting to cyber-attacks has emerged as a strategic choice to gain a significant edge. The motives behind these purposeful attacks are often rooted in pursuing a competitive advantage, where entities seek to outpace rivals through clandestine means. This strategic manoeuvring is multifaceted within the context of smart city networks, highlighting the intricate interplay of technology, economics, and geopolitics. Purposeful attacks may aim to steal intellectual property and proprietary information (Srinivas et al., 2019). Companies and nations invest substantial research, development, and innovation resources to gain a technological edge. Cyber adversaries, whether state-sponsored or corporate competitors, may employ sophisticated tactics to infiltrate smart city systems and abscond with valuable intellectual assets. This stolen information can provide a shortcut to advancements in technology or infrastructure development, enabling the perpetrator to leapfrog ahead in the competitive landscape.

Intentional disruption of competitors' operations is another motive behind purposeful cyber-attacks in the system networks (Huang et al., 2018). The entities aim to hamper the functionality of rival systems by strategically targeting critical components or infrastructure. This disruption could manifest as temporary outages, operational malfunctions, or deliberate manipulation of data, all to undermine the efficiency and reliability of a competitor's smart city initiatives. The landscape of purposeful attacks in smart city networks reflects the evolving dynamics of competition in the digital age. The stakes are higher as technology becomes increasingly integral to economic and national interests.

6.2.6 Terrorism and Sabotage

Integrating technology into the fabric of smart city infrastructure has heralded advancements and introduced new avenues for potential threats, with terrorism and sabotage emerging as ominous considerations. Terrorism, often driven by ideological motives, sees vulnerabilities in the infrastructure as strategic opportunities to instil fear, disrupt public services, and sow widespread chaos (Smith, 2014). The interconnected nature of smart city systems presents a complex challenge, as even minor disruptions can have cascading effects on various essential services. Terrorist organisations, recognising the societal dependence on smart city technologies, may target these vulnerabilities to achieve their objectives. The motivations behind such attacks extend beyond mere disruption; they seek to exploit the pervasive nature of smart city systems to create a sense of vulnerability and insecurity among the populace. For instance, manipulating transportation systems, disrupting emergency services, or compromising communication networks within a smart city can amplify the impact of terrorist actions, both in terms of physical harm and psychological distress.

The potential for sabotage is a significant motivating factor behind purposeful attacks by terrorist entities. Sabotage can take various forms, ranging from causing physical harm to infrastructure to inflicting economic damage by disrupting key services (Lehto, 2022). The severity of this threat is high, with the potential for attacks on power grids, water supply systems, or transportation networks, all of which are critical components of smart city infrastructure. Such acts pose immediate risks to public safety and have long-term consequences, eroding public trust and impeding the socio-economic vitality of the affected smart city.

6.2.7 Personal Vendettas

At an individual level, security attacks can be fuelled by personal vendettas, introducing a dimension of motivation rooted in revenge, disputes, or personal animosities. These attacks are distinctly personal, serving as a means for settling scores or expressing dissatisfaction through digital means. The deeply personal nature that underpins these motives adds a unique layer to the landscape of security threats in smart city networks. Motivations for personal vendettas in smart city attacks can originate from various sources. Individuals harbouring grievances may leverage their understanding of smart city systems to exact revenge or settle disputes covertly. Disgruntled employees, dissatisfied stakeholders, or even residents with personal grievances against the city administration may resort to disrupting smart city operations as a form of retaliation. The methods employed in attacks driven by personal vendettas can vary widely. They may include attempts to compromise critical systems, manipulate data, or disrupt essential services. Such actions, while perhaps not as ideologically charged as other types of cyberthreats, pose a unique challenge due to their individual nature and the potential for unexpected consequences arising from personal vendettas.

6.2.8 Exploration and Curiosity

In some instances, attackers may exploit vulnerabilities in a system driven by a sense of exploration and curiosity (Andress & Winterfeld, 2013). Rather than harbouring specific motives such as financial gain or ideological objectives, these exploratory attacks stem from a desire to test skills, push boundaries, and delve into the intricacies of existing security measures. This motive introduces a unique challenge in comprehensively securing smart city infrastructures, as the attackers may not follow traditional patterns associated with more defined threat motivations. Exploratory attacks often lack a predetermined objective beyond the thrill of discovery. Those behind such attacks might be cybersecurity enthusiasts, ethical hackers, or individuals seeking to understand the vulnerabilities inherent in smart city systems. Their actions may include probing networks, experimenting with potential exploits, or attempting to access restricted areas to gauge the robustness of security protocols.

6.3 Methods for Launching Attacks

Cyberattacks encompass many methods, from traditional unauthorised access to more sophisticated cyber-physical attacks. Unauthorised access and data breaches remain pervasive, where malicious actors exploit system vulnerabilities to gain unauthorised entry, compromising sensitive information and potentially causing significant damage. Ransomware attacks have become a prevalent and financially motivated cyberthreat (Humayun et al., 2021). In these instances, attackers deploy malicious software to encrypt a victim's data, demanding payment for its release. Such attacks have targeted various entities, including individuals, businesses, and critical infrastructure, causing widespread disruptions. DoS and DDoS attacks aim to disrupt the availability of online services. These attacks render systems inaccessible to legitimate users by overwhelming servers or networks with an influx of traffic, causing downtime and potential financial losses (Kautish et al., 2022).

The proliferation of IoT devices has introduced new vulnerabilities. Exploiting these devices has become famous for attackers to gain unauthorised access, manipulate functionalities, or launch larger-scale attacks by compromising interconnected systems (Dos Santos et al., 2021). The deployment of malware and malicious code remains a persistent threat, with attackers continuously evolving tactics to bypass security measures (Chakkaravarthy et al., 2019). Malicious software can infiltrate systems, steal sensitive information, or even enable remote control of compromised devices like remote access Trojan (RAT) (HosseiniNejad et al., 2019). Insider threats pose a unique challenge, as individuals within an organisation may exploit their access maliciously (Saxena et al., 2020). It can include disgruntled employees, unintentional security lapses, or individuals coerced by external forces.

The absence of robust encryption and authentication mechanisms exposes systems to unauthorised access and data compromise (Yang et al., 2020). Inadequate software patching and updating further exacerbate vulnerabilities, as unpatched systems are more susceptible to exploitation by known vulnerabilities (Dissanayake et al., 2022). Social engineering attacks leverage psychological manipulation to deceive individuals into divulging sensitive information or performing actions compromising security (Taib et al., 2019). These attacks often exploit human vulnerabilities rather than technical weaknesses, making them difficult to defend against solely through technical means. These are all methods for launching cyberattacks, as visualised in Figure 6.3.

6.3.1 Cyber-Physical Attacks

CPS seamlessly blend computational and physical processes, fostering a symbiotic relationship between the digital and physical realms. These systems face diverse cyberthreats, like zero-day attacks, eavesdropping attacks,

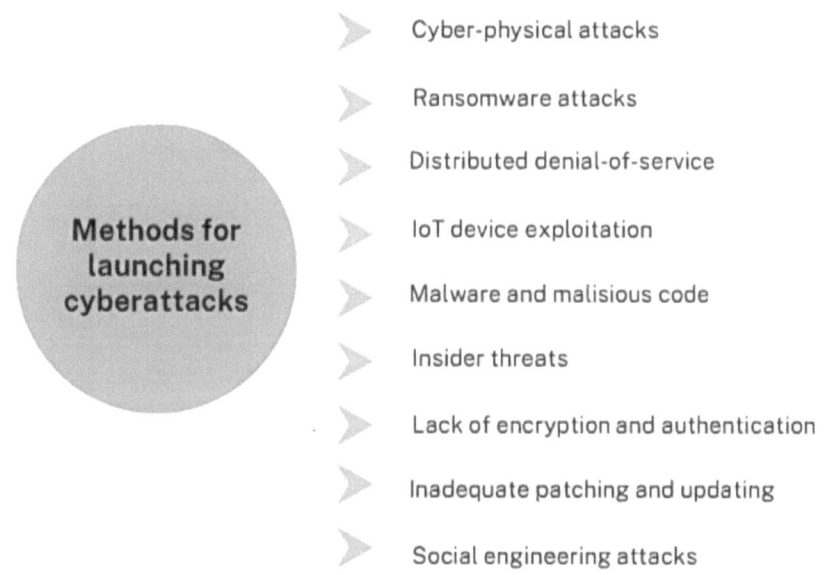

Cyber-physical attacks

Ransomware attacks

Distributed denial-of-service

IoT device exploitation

Malware and malisious code

Insider threats

Lack of encryption and authentication

Inadequate patching and updating

Social engineering attacks

FIGURE 6.3
Methods for launching cyberattacks.

DoS attacks, data injection attacks, side-channel attacks, and replay attacks (Alam & Khan, 2022). Zero-day attacks exploit undiscovered vulnerabilities; eavesdropping attacks aim to intercept and compromise communication channels. DoS attacks disrupt normal operations through overwhelming traffic, and data injection attacks seek to manipulate or insert false data. Additionally, side-channel attacks exploit information leaks from the physical implementation, while replay attacks involve the unauthorised repetition of valid data transmissions. Figure 6.4 illustrates the cyber-physical attacks in IoT, while Table 6.1 describes the attacks.

Cyber-physical attacks represent a sophisticated category of security threats that exploit the integration between digital systems and the tangible smart city infrastructure. In smart cities, where various components are interconnected and digitally controlled, malicious actors may seek to manipulate vulnerabilities to compromise the functionality of crucial physical systems. For instance, consider a scenario where an attacker gains unauthorised access to the control systems governing smart traffic lights. In December 2022, a group of hackers in Germany demonstrated how traffic lights could be manipulated (Teller Report, 2022) to disrupt the normal functioning of traffic lights, leading to chaotic traffic conditions, increased congestion, and elevated risks of accidents.

Cyber-physical attacks could extend to critical systems such as smart grids, water treatment plants, or emergency response mechanisms in the context of smart city infrastructure (Demertzi et al., 2023). An attacker might

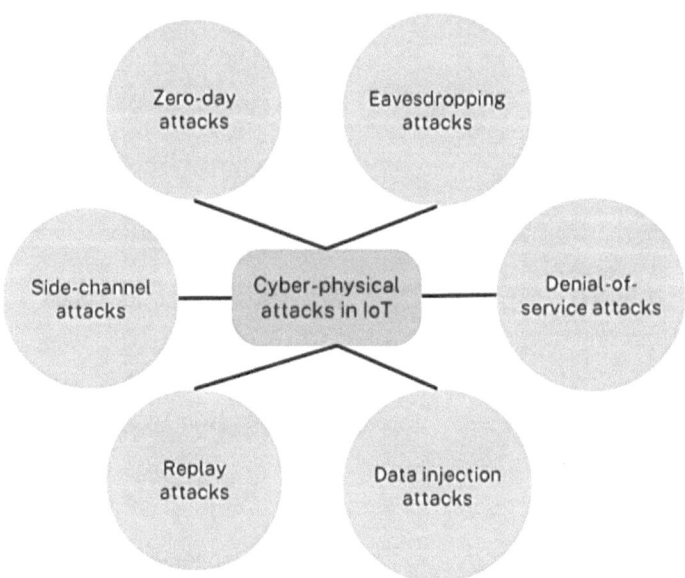

FIGURE 6.4
Types of cyber-physical attacks in IoT.

TABLE 6.1

Description of the Cyber-Physical Attacks in IoT

Attacks	Description
Zero-day attacks	The attacks exploit unknown vulnerabilities of software or applications that make it difficult for developers to create timely fixes (Sharma et al., 2017)
Eavesdropping attacks	Attackers gain access to sensitive information through unauthorised interception of communication between IoT devices (Hasan et al., 2022)
DoS attacks	Attackers overwhelm a network or device with a flood of illegitimate requests, causing it to become unresponsive or unavailable to legitimate users (Lohachab & Karambir, 2018)
Data injection attacks	Unauthorised insertion or modification of data within the system aiming to manipulate the functioning or behaviour of connected devices (Gunduz & Das, 2020)
Replay attacks	Attackers capture and subsequently replay legitimate data or commands to deceive IoT devices or systems (Sadikin et al., 2020)
Side-channel attacks	Attackers exploit unintended information leakage from the physical implementation of devices, such as power consumption, electromagnetic emissions, or timing variations, to extract confidential data or gain unauthorised access (Tsague & Twala, 2018)

compromise the control systems of a smart grid, leading to disruptions in electricity distribution and potential cascading effects on various city services. Recent news claimed that Chinese-origin cyberspies, collectively called APT41, are targeting power in the grid in an Asian country (Greenberg, 2023). Similarly, tampering with the control mechanisms of water treatment plants could jeopardise drinking water quality. In emergency response systems, unauthorised access could hamper the timely and effective deployment of services during crises.

6.3.2 Ransomware Attacks

In 2022, ransomware made up 17% of cyberattacks, while in the first half of 2023, Chainalysis found that ransomware extorted at least $449 million, surpassing the earnings from the same period in 2022 by $176 million (Smith, 2023). Ransomware attacks represent a particularly insidious cyberthreat involving encrypting critical data or systems to extort a ransom for their release. In the context of smart cities, these attacks pose severe risks as they can potentially paralyse essential services integral to urban functionality, including transportation systems, energy grids, and emergency response systems. Cybercriminals typically exploit vulnerabilities in the city's network infrastructure or gain unauthorised access to critical systems in a ransomware attack on a smart city. Once inside, they deploy malicious software that encrypts vital data or takes control of critical components within the city's infrastructure. For example, an attacker might target the control systems of transportation networks, compromising the ability to manage traffic signals, monitor public transportation, or even control autonomous vehicles. Following the encryption or compromise, the attackers demand a ransom, usually in cryptocurrency, to provide the decryption key or restore control of the affected systems. The ransom demand is often accompanied by threats to disrupt services further or expose sensitive data if the ransom is not paid promptly. The consequences of such attacks can be widespread and impactful, affecting residents' daily lives and posing risks to public safety.

The Mumbai Power Grid experienced a ransomware attack, known as "GridLock," that unfolded over three days starting May 12, 2023 (digiAlert, 2023). The sophisticated attack was initiated through a phishing campaign targeting power company employees, who unwittingly introduced the ransomware into the network by clicking on malicious attachments in the deceptive emails. This scenario disrupts electricity distribution to homes, businesses, and critical infrastructure. It could result in widespread power outages, affecting everything from street lighting to essential services like hospitals and emergency response centres. Similarly, a ransomware attack on a smart city's emergency response systems could compromise the city's ability to manage and respond to crises effectively. Attackers may encrypt critical communication channels, making it challenging for emergency services to coordinate and respond to incidents such as natural disasters or public safety threats.

6.3.3 Distributed Denial-of-Service Attacks

DDoS attacks are disruptive cyberthreats that target the normal functioning of a network or system by overwhelming it with a massive influx of traffic (Kaur Chahal et al., 2019). In the specific context of smart cities, these attacks pose substantial risks, as they can render critical services inaccessible, potentially causing chaos in transportation systems, public safety disruptions, or interruptions in utilities. DDoS attacks simultaneously escalate the impact by coordinating multiple sources to inundate the targeted network. Cybercriminals often compromise a network of computers, creating a botnet that can be remotely controlled to launch a synchronised assault. In the context of a smart city, a DDoS attack might target the communication infrastructure supporting emergency response systems.

The attack could hinder the transmission of critical information during emergencies by overwhelming the network with traffic, impacting the city's ability to respond effectively to incidents like natural disasters or public safety threats. Consider a scenario where a smart city's public transportation system becomes the target of a DDoS attack. The attackers overwhelm the system's servers with a flood of traffic, making it impossible for residents to access real-time transportation information or use digital payment systems. It not only inconveniences residents but can also disrupt the smooth functioning of public transportation services. The DDoS attacks on smart cities extend beyond mere inconvenience. Interruptions in transportation systems could lead to public safety concerns, potentially impacting emergency response times. Similarly, utility disruptions, such as water treatment plants or smart grids, could affect urban life.

6.3.4 IoT Device Exploitation

IoT device exploitation attacks refer to the unauthorised manipulation or compromise of IoT devices to gain control, access sensitive data, or disrupt their normal functioning (Chinbat, 2023). These attacks can range from exploiting vulnerabilities in device firmware or software to leveraging insecure communication protocols, potentially leading to privacy breaches, unauthorised access, or disruption of critical services. Malicious actors leverage IoT device exploitation to compromise poorly secured devices, subsequently gaining unauthorised access to the broader smart city networks. This infiltration allows attackers to launch various malicious activities, including eavesdropping on communications and using compromised devices as launchpads for further cyber-attacks. For example, this attack has been found in the IZ1H9 Mirai, discovered by FortiGuard Labs, which quickly updated its exploits, incorporating 13 payloads that targeted vulnerabilities in various IoT devices (Mascellino, 2023). This campaign demonstrated the ability to infect vulnerable devices, expand its botnet, and launch DDoS attacks, highlighting the persistent threat of remote code execution attacks on IoT devices.

In the context of smart cities, the vulnerabilities associated with IoT devices can have far-reaching consequences. One example is the compromise of smart home devices connected to a city's network. If an attacker gains access to a poorly secured smart thermostat or surveillance camera, they can potentially infiltrate the city's communication infrastructure. This unauthorised access may enable the attacker to eavesdrop on sensitive information, such as traffic management data or public safety communications. Another concern is the compromise of environmental sensors within a smart city's infrastructure. If these sensors are exploited, attackers could manipulate their data, leading to inaccurate information about air quality, weather conditions, or other critical environmental factors (Gupta et al., 2020).

6.3.5 Malware and Malicious Code

Malware attacks on IoT devices have seen a significant increase of 400% compared to the previous year, according to a report by Zscaler (Business Insider India, 2023). The report highlights that cyberthreat actors primarily target legacy vulnerabilities, taking advantage of weak security standards and unmanaged and unpatched devices in the IoT ecosystem. Malware and malicious code represent significant cybersecurity threats in the context of smart cities, as they can be employed to disrupt operations, compromise data integrity, and enable unauthorised access to critical systems. The injection of malicious software into smart city networks poses considerable risks, and various forms of malware, including worms, viruses, and other malicious code, can rapidly spread across interconnected systems, causing widespread damage. Malware can be introduced through vectors, such as phishing emails, compromised software updates, or infected IoT devices (Humayun et al., 2021). For example, a phishing attack targeting city employees might deliver malware through seemingly legitimate emails, enticing recipients to click on malicious links or download infected attachments. Once the malware gains access to an employee's device, it can propagate through the network, potentially compromising sensitive data and critical infrastructure.

For example, the IZ1H9 botnet, a variant of Mirai, spreads through HTTP, SSH, and Telnet protocols. Once installed on an IoT device, it checks the network portion of the infected device's IP address, avoids execution for certain IP blocks, and prints 'darknet' to the console (Poireault, 2023). On the other hand, worms, a specific type of malware designed to self-replicate and spread autonomously, can rapidly propagate across interconnected systems. In a smart city, if a worm infects one device or system, it can quickly move to others, potentially disrupting various services. The P2Pinfect botnet, previously known for targeting servers running the Redis system, is now expanding into the IoT ecosystem. Researchers have discovered a variant of the P2Pinfect worm designed to infect Linux devices with MIPS processors, commonly found in routers and IoT devices, indicating a potential shift in focus for the botnet (Constantin, 2023). Worms could infiltrate a smart grid system, compromising the distribution of electricity and causing power outages across the city. Viruses, another form of malware, can be designed to infect files or software within smart city networks. For example, a virus may target the software controlling water treatment plants, manipulating the processes and potentially contaminating the water supply.

6.3.6 Insider Threats

Insider threats pose a significant cybersecurity risk (Georgiadou et al., 2022), involving individuals with authorised access to smart city systems intentionally or unintentionally compromising security. This category of threats encompasses a range of actors, including city employees, contractors, or other trusted entities who may exploit their insider status to compromise the integrity and security of smart city systems. In the context of smart cities, insider threats can manifest in various ways. One example is a disgruntled city employee with access to the smart grid system who intentionally manipulates energy distribution. They could disrupt the electrical supply to specific areas by exploiting their insider knowledge, causing widespread power outages and impacting various services reliant on electricity. Unintentional insider threats may arise from negligence or lack of awareness. For instance, a contractor working on a smart city project may inadvertently expose sensitive information by mishandling data or failing to follow established security protocols. This inadvertent action could create vulnerabilities that malicious actors might exploit for unauthorised access or data manipulation.

Another scenario involves an insider threat exploiting their access to the city's traffic management system. A trusted employee with knowledge of the system's vulnerabilities may intentionally manipulate traffic signals, leading to congestion or gridlock. Such disruptions could have cascading effects on emergency response times and public safety. Insider threats can also involve individuals with privileged access to city databases, compromising sensitive citizen information. For instance, an employee in the city's health department might intentionally leak personal health records, violating privacy and potentially causing reputational damage to the city.

6.3.7 Lack of Encryption and Authentication

The lack of encryption and authentication mechanisms in smart city networks presents a critical vulnerability, exposing these networks to interception, tampering, and potential unauthorised access. Encryption and authentication are fundamental components of cybersecurity that safeguard the confidentiality and integrity of data exchanged between devices and systems within smart cities. In the context of smart cities, inadequate encryption can compromise sensitive information as it traverses the network. For example, if traffic management data or surveillance footage is transmitted without proper encryption, malicious actors could intercept and eavesdrop on the communication, potentially gaining access to real-time information about traffic patterns, public events, or even sensitive security operations. This lack of encryption jeopardises data privacy and risks public safety and the city's overall security.

Weak authentication processes exacerbate the vulnerability of a system (Jaime et al., 2023). If critical infrastructure components, such as control systems for transportation or utilities, lack robust authentication measures, unauthorised entities may exploit these weaknesses to gain illicit access. For instance, a compromised authentication process in a smart water management system could allow unauthorised individuals to manipulate water distribution, leading to potential contamination or disruptions in the water supply. Furthermore, insufficient authentication mechanisms in smart city networks may enable unauthorised access to surveillance systems, compromising public safety. For example, if authentication protocols do not adequately protect surveillance cameras, malicious actors could gain control over these devices, potentially using them for unauthorised surveillance or manipulating footage to create deceptive scenarios.

6.3.8 Inadequate Patching and Updating

The issue of inadequate patching and updating poses a significant cybersecurity risk in the context of smart cities (Habibzadeh et al., 2019). Failure to promptly apply security patches and updates to the software and systems that form the backbone of smart city networks creates vulnerabilities that malicious actors can exploit. According to a report by Bitdefender, at least five models of EZVIZ IoT cameras are vulnerable to multiple vulnerabilities that could allow threat actors to access, decrypt, and download video from the devices (Dark Reading, 2023). The vulnerabilities include a stack-based buffer overflow bug, an insecure direct object reference vulnerability, and a local vulnerability, enabling remote camera control and compromising its integrity. EZVIZ has issued security patches and updates for the affected cameras since June 2023 to address this issue.

As smart city infrastructures are composed of diverse components and devices, each running specialised software, without vigilant maintenance, these systems may become susceptible to various security threats, potentially compromising the integrity and reliability of the entire smart city ecosystem. In practical terms, inadequate patching and updating can expose smart city networks to known vulnerabilities that security updates have addressed. For example, if a smart traffic management system fails to promptly apply a critical security patch, it may remain vulnerable to exploitation. Malicious actors could then potentially manipulate traffic signals, leading to disruptions, accidents, or even a complete breakdown of the traffic management system. Moreover, smart city networks often rely on interconnected devices and sensors to collect and transmit data for various applications, from monitoring air quality to managing energy consumption. Failure to update the software on these devices could expose them to security vulnerabilities. In the case of environmental sensors, for instance, outdated software might allow attackers to manipulate the data, leading to inaccurate readings and potentially impacting public health.

6.3.9 Social Engineering Attacks

Social engineering attacks represent a sophisticated cyberthreat relying on psychological manipulation to exploit human behaviour and compromise security (Wang et al., 2021). In these attacks, malicious actors leverage various tactics to deceive individuals, either within the smart city administration or among the general public, into divulging sensitive information or performing actions that may open vulnerabilities within the city's digital infrastructure. Social engineering attacks could manifest in multiple ways in smart cities. For instance, an attacker might pose as a trusted authority figure or a fellow employee, attempting to manipulate smart city employees into revealing access credentials or sensitive information. It could be achieved through deceptive emails, phone calls, or in-person interactions. If successful, the attacker gains unauthorised access to critical systems or data, potentially disrupting city operations or compromising sensitive information (Ghasemi et al., 2019). For citizens, social engineering attacks may target individuals through deceptive means to extract personal information or access credentials.

For example, fraudulent communication disguised as an official city announcement could prompt residents to provide sensitive information, thinking they comply with legitimate requests. Such attacks could compromise citizens' privacy or enable unauthorised access to their data within the smart city infrastructure. Moreover, social engineering attacks may exploit the increasing integration of smart technologies into daily life. For instance, attackers might create fake mobile applications or websites that mimic legitimate smart city services, tricking users into providing login credentials or personal information. Once obtained, this information can be misused to compromise the security of individual accounts or access associated smart city services.

6.4 Looking Ahead: Implications and Strategies for Smart City Defence

As cyberthreats against smart cities become sophisticated, the focus must shift from reactive security responses to proactive defence strategies ensuring digital urban environments' resilience and sustainability. The increasing complexity of smart city ecosystems demands a security-first approach in urban planning, where cybersecurity is embedded into every stage of infrastructure development, from designing IoT devices to deploying citywide networks. The challenge is protecting digital assets and safeguarding the interconnected services millions of citizens rely on daily. Adopting predictive and AI-driven threat detection systems is one of the most critical steps in enhancing smart city security (Gautam et al., 2025). Traditional cybersecurity models rely on detecting and mitigating attacks after they have occurred. However, given the scale and integration of smart city technologies, a more practical approach involves leveraging machine learning algorithms and behavioural analytics to predict and prevent cyberthreats before they manifest. AI-driven security solutions can monitor vast amounts of data in real-time, identifying anomalies that may indicate potential cyberattacks. By integrating automated threat detection with security orchestration and response (SOAR) platforms, smart cities can rapidly neutralise threats and minimise the impact of cyber incidents.

To future-proof smart cities against evolving cyberthreats, governments and regulatory bodies must enforce standardised cybersecurity policies. Strong regulatory frameworks should mandate regular security audits, enforce compliance with data protection laws, and establish minimum security requirements for IoT manufacturers (Channi et al., 2025). Implementing cybersecurity-by-design principles, where security is an integral part of product development rather than an afterthought, can significantly reduce vulnerabilities in smart city devices and networks. Data privacy regulations must also be strengthened to protect citizens' personal information from unauthorised surveillance, identity theft, and mass data exploitation. Cyber resilience in smart cities also depends on fostering public-private partnerships. Since many smart city infrastructures are managed by private sector entities, close collaboration between governments, technology providers, and cybersecurity firms is necessary to ensure a unified defence strategy. Establishing cross-sector intelligence-sharing initiatives can improve situational awareness and facilitate rapid response to emerging cyberthreats. Additionally, international cooperation is crucial, as cyberthreats transcend national borders. Engaging in global threat intelligence networks can provide cities with real-time information on emerging attack patterns and mitigation techniques.

One of the most significant long-term challenges for smart city security is the threat of quantum computing. Due to quantum-based decryption capabilities, traditional encryption protocols (e.g., RSA and ECC) that safeguard most digital communications eventually become obsolete. Smart cities must invest in post-quantum cryptography (PQC) to mitigate this risk, which involves developing encryption algorithms that can withstand quantum attacks (Oliva delMoral et al., 2024). While large-scale quantum computing threats are not yet imminent, preparing for this shift ensures that smart city infrastructures remain secure in the decades to come. Cybersecurity in smart cities is not solely a technological issue; it also requires community engagement and workforce preparedness. A well-informed public can serve as an additional layer of defence against cyberthreats by recognising phishing attempts, avoiding data breaches, and reporting suspicious activities. Cities should invest in cybersecurity awareness programs, educating residents on best practices for digital safety (Lnenicka et al., 2025). Training municipal employees, emergency responders, and infrastructure operators in cybersecurity protocols can further strengthen the overall security posture of a smart city. Moreover, integrating crowdsourced threat intelligence, where citizens can report cyber anomalies, could provide additional insights into emerging security risks.

Building a cyber-resilient smart city requires a comprehensive, multi-layered approach incorporating predictive security models, regulatory enforcement, public-private collaboration, and ongoing technological advancements. By embedding security into the foundational framework of smart city development, cities can mitigate risks while ensuring that technological progress continues to improve urban life safely. The future of smart city defence depends on continuous innovation, vigilance, and a collective commitment to protecting digital infrastructures from cyberthreats.

References

Abraham, S. (2022). *Top 5 cybersecurity breaches due to human error.* Threatcop Inc. https://threatcop.com/blog/top-5-cyber-attacks-and-security-breaches-due-to-human-error/

Alam, M., & Khan, I. R. (2022). Cyber-physical attacks and IoT. In *Intelligent cyber-physical systems security for industry 4.0* (pp. 79–104). Chapman and Hall/CRC. https://doi.org/10.13140/RG.2.2.28500.73605

Alfandi, O., Khanji, S., Ahmad, L., & Khattak, A. (2021). A survey on boosting IoT security and privacy through blockchain. *Cluster Computing, 24*(1), 37–55. https://doi.org/10.1007/s10586-020-03137-8

Alomari, M. A., Al-Andoli, M. N., Ghaleb, M., Thabit, R., Alkawsi, G., Alsayaydeh, J. A. J., & Gaid, A. S. A. (2025). Security of smart grid: Cybersecurity issues, potential cyberattacks, major incidents, and future directions. *Energies, 18*(1), 141. https://doi.org/10.3390/en18010141

Andress, J., & Winterfeld, S. (2013). *Cyber warfare: Techniques, tactics and tools for security practitioners.* Elsevier.

Braun, T., Fung, B. C. M., Iqbal, F., & Shah, B. (2018). Security and privacy challenges in smart cities. *Sustainable Cities and Society, 39*, 499–507. https://doi.org/10.1016/j.scs.2018.02.039

Business Insider India. (2023). IoT malware attacks up by 400% this year: Report. https://www.businessinsider.in/tech/news/iot-malware-attacks-up-by-400-this-year-report/articleshow/104698771.cms

Chakkaravarthy, S. S., Sangeetha, D., & Vaidehi, V. (2019). A survey on malware analysis and mitigation techniques. *Computer Science Review, 32*, 1–23. https://doi.org/10.1016/j.cosrev.2019.01.002

Channi, H. K., Sandhu, R., Singh, N., Ghai, D., Kumar, P., & Cheema, G. S. (2025). Governance frameworks for smart systems. In S. Mahajan, Á Rocha, A. K. Pandit, & P. Chawla (Eds.), *Smart systems: Engineering and managing information for future success: Navigating the landscape of intelligent technologies* (pp. 157–189). Springer Nature Switzerland. https://doi.org/10.1007/978-3-031-76152-2_11

Chinbat, T. (2023). *Performance evaluation of lightweight cryptographic algorithms for IoT in healthcare.* Auckland University of Technology.

Constantin, L. (2023). *P2Pinfect Redis worm targets IoT with version for MIPS devices.* CSO. https://www.csoonline.com/article/1251159/p2pinfect-redis-worm-targets-iot-with-version-for-mips-devices.html

Dark Reading. (2023). *Popular IoT cameras need patching to fend off catastrophic attacks.* https://www.darkreading.com/cyberattacks-data-breaches/popular-iot-cameras-patching-catastrophic-attacks

Demertzi, V., Demertzis, S., & Demertzis, K. (2023). An overview of cyber threats, attacks and countermeasures on the primary domains of smart cities. *Applied Sciences, 13*(2), 790. https://doi.org/10.3390/app13020790

digiAlert. (2023). Ransomware attack on Mumbai's power grid: Lessons learned. https://www.linkedin.com/pulse/ransomware-attack-mumbais-power-grid-lessons-learned-digialert-17zcc?trk=article-ssr-frontend-pulse_more-articles_related-content-card#:~:text=Mumbais%20Power%20Grid%20Ransomware%20Attack%3A%20A%20Brief%20Overview&text=The%20attack%20unfolded%20over%20a,breach%20the%20power%20grid's%20network

Dissanayake, N., Jayatilaka, A., Zahedi, M., & Babar, M. A. (2022). Software security patch management – A systematic literature review of challenges, approaches, tools and practices. *Information and Software Technology, 144*, 106771. https://doi.org/10.1016/j.infsof.2021.106771

Dos Santos, D. R., Dagrada, M., & Costante, E. (2021). Leveraging operational technology and the internet of things to attack smart buildings. *Journal of Computer Virology and Hacking Techniques, 17*(1), 1–20. https://doi.org/10.1007/s11416-020-00358-8

Gautam, V., Sunidhi, S., & Prasad, S. (2025). AI powered surveillance for smart cities. In *Internet of vehicles and computer vision solutions for smart city transformations* (pp. 245–265). Springer. https://doi.org/10.1007/978-3-031-72959-1_11

George, J. J., & Leidner, D. E. (2019). From clicktivism to hacktivism: Understanding digital activism. *Information and Organization, 29*(3), 100249. https://doi.org/10.1016/j.infoandorg.2019.04.001

Georgiadou, A., Mouzakitis, S., & Askounis, D. (2022). Detecting insider threat via a cyber-security culture framework. *Journal of Computer Information Systems, 62*(4), 706–716. https://doi.org/10.1080/08874417.2021.1903367

Ghasemi, M., Saadaat, M., & Ghollasi, O. (2019). Threats of social engineering attacks against security of internet of things (IoT). In *Fundamental research in electrical engineering: The selected papers of the first international conference on fundamental research in electrical engineering* (pp. 957–968). Springer Singapore. https://doi.org/10.1007/978-981-10-8672-4_73

Giannaros, A., Karras, A., Theodorakopoulos, L., Karras, C., Kranias, P., Schizas, N., Kalogeratos, G., & Tsolis, D. (2023). Autonomous vehicles: Sophisticated attacks, safety issues, challenges, open topics, blockchain, and future directions. *Journal of Cybersecurity and Privacy*, 3(3), 493–543. https://doi.org/10.3390/jcp3030025

Goodwin, B. (2023). Hacktivist attacks against Israeli websites mirror attacks following Russian invasion of Ukraine. *Computer Weekly*. https://www.computerweekly.com/news/366555772/Hacktivist-attacks-against-Israeli-websites-mirror-attacks-following-Russian-invasion-of-Ukraine

Greenberg, A. (2023). China-linked hackers breached a power grid – again. *Wired*. https://www.wired.com/story/china-redfly-power-grid-cyberattack-asia/

Gunduz, M. Z., & Das, R. (2020). Cyber-security on smart grid: Threats and potential solutions. *Computer Networks*, 169, 107094. https://doi.org/10.1016/j.comnet.2019.107094

Gupta, M., Abdelsalam, M., Khorsandroo, S., & Mittal, S. (2020). Security and privacy in smart farming: Challenges and opportunities. *IEEE Access*, 8, 34564–34584. https://doi.org/10.1109/ACCESS.2020.2975142

Habibzadeh, H., Nussbaum, B. H., Anjomshoa, F., Kantarci, B., & Soyata, T. (2019). A survey on cybersecurity, data privacy, and policy issues in cyber-physical system deployments in smart cities. *Sustainable Cities and Society*, 50, 101660. https://doi.org/10.1016/j.scs.2019.101660

Hasan, M. K., Ghazal, T. M., Saeed, R. A., Pandey, B., Gohel, H., Eshmawi, A. A., Abdel-Khalek, S., & Alkhassawneh, H. M. (2022). A review on security threats, vulnerabilities, and counter measures of 5G enabled internet-of-medical-things. *IET Communications*, 16(5), 421–432. https://doi.org/10.1049/cmu2.12301

Hossain, M. I., & Hasan, R. (2025). Smart cities: Cybersecurity concerns. In J. R. Vacca (Ed.), *Computer and information security handbook* (4th ed., pp. 1397–1412). Morgan Kaufmann. https://doi.org/10.1016/B978-0-443-13223-0.00089-8

HosseiniNejad, R., HaddadPajouh, H., Dehghantanha, A., & Parizi, R. M. (2019). A cyber kill chain based analysis of remote access Trojans. In A. Dehghantanha, & K.-K. R. Choo (Eds.), *Handbook of big data and IoT security* (pp. 273–299). Springer International Publishing. http://doi.org/10.1007/978-3-030-10543-3_12

Huang, K., Siegel, M., & Madnick, S. (2018). Systematically understanding the cyber attack business: A survey. *ACM Computing Survey*, 51(4), Article 70. https://doi.org/10.1145/3199674

Humayun, M., Jhanjhi, N. Z., Alsayat, A., & Ponnusamy, V. (2021). Internet of things and ransomware: Evolution, mitigation and prevention. *Egyptian Informatics Journal*, 22(1), 105–117. https://doi.org/10.1016/j.eij.2020.05.003

Jaime, F. J., Muñoz, A., Rodríguez-Gómez, F., & Jerez-Calero, A. (2023). Strengthening privacy and data security in biomedical microelectromechanical systems by IoT communication security and protection in smart healthcare. *Sensors*, 23(21), 8944. https://doi.org/10.3390/s23218944

Kaur Chahal, J., Bhandari, A., & Behal, S. (2019). Distributed denial of service attacks: A threat or challenge. *New Review of Information Networking*, 24(1), 31–103. https://doi.org/10.1080/13614576.2019.1611468

Kautish, S., Reyana, A., & Vidyarthi, A. (2022). SDMTA: Attack detection and mitigation mechanism for DDoS vulnerabilities in hybrid cloud environment. *IEEE Transactions on Industrial Informatics*, 18(9), 6455–6463. https://doi.org/10.1109/TII.2022.3146290

Lehto, M. (2022). Cyber-attacks against critical infrastructure. In M. Lehto, & P. Neittaanmäki (Eds.), *Cyber security: Critical infrastructure protection* (pp. 3–42). Springer International Publishing. https://doi.org/10.1007/978-3-030-91293-2_1

Lin, H. (2022). Russian cyber operations in the invasion of Ukraine. *The Cyber Defense Review*, 7(4), 31–46. https://www.jstor.org/stable/48703290

Lnenicka, M., Kysela, T., & Horák, O. (2025). Building security and resilience: A guide to implementing effective cybersecurity and data protection measures in smart cities. *Smart and Sustainable Built Environment* (ahead-of-print). http://doi.org/10.1108/SASBE-09-2024-0363

Lohachab, A., & Karambir, B. (2018). Critical analysis of DDoS – An emerging security threat over IoT networks. *Journal of Communications and Information Networks*, 3(3), 57–78. https://doi.org/10.1007/s41650-018-0022-5

Mascellino, A. (2023). *IZ1H9 botnet targets IoT devices with new exploits*. Reed Exhibitions Ltd. https://www.infosecurity-magazine.com/news/iz1h9-botnet-targets-iot-devices/

Neshenko, N., Bou-Harb, E., & Furht, B. (2022). Cyber brittleness of smart cities. In *Smart cities: Cyber situational awareness to support decision making* (pp. 19–40). Springer International Publishing. https://doi.org/10.1007/978-3-031-18464-2_2

Oliva delMoral, J., deMarti iOlius, A., Vidal, G., Crespo, P. M., & Martinez, J. E. (2024). Cybersecurity in critical infrastructures: A post-quantum cryptography perspective. *IEEE Internet of Things Journal*, 11(18), 30217–30244. https://doi.org/10.1109/JIOT.2024.3410702

Page, C. (2022). Ukraine disrupts attempt by Russian hackers to take down energy provider. *TechCrunch*. https://techcrunch.com/2022/04/12/ukraine-disrupts-attempt-by-russian-hackers-to-take-down-energy-provider/

Poireault, K. (2023). *New Mirai variant campaigns are targeting IoT devices*. Reed Exhibitions Ltd. https://www.infosecurity-magazine.com/news/new-mirai-variant-campaigns/

Romagna, M., & van den Hout, N. J. (2017). Hacktivism and website defacement: motivations, capabilities and potential threats. In *27th Virus Bulletin International Conference* (Vol. 1, pp. 1–10).

Sadikin, F., Deursen, T., & Kumar, S. (2020). A ZigBee intrusion detection system for IoT using secure and efficient data collection. *Internet of Things*, 12, 100306. https://doi.org/10.1016/j.iot.2020.100306

Sarkar, G., & Shukla, S. K. (2023). Behavioral analysis of cybercrime: Paving the way for effective policing strategies. *Journal of Economic Criminology*, 2, 100034. https://doi.org/10.1016/j.jeconc.2023.100034

Saxena, N., Hayes, E., Bertino, E., Ojo, P., Choo, K.-K. R., & Burnap, P. (2020). Impact and key challenges of insider threats on organizations and critical businesses. *Electronics*, 9(9), 1460. https://doi.org/10.3390/electronics9091460

Schwartz, M. J. (2023). *Red cross tells hacktivists: Stop targeting hospitals*. Information Security Media Group, Corp. https://www.bankinfosecurity.com/blogs/red-cross-tells-hacktivists-stop-targeting-hospitals-p-3524

Sebestyen, H., Popescu, D. E., & Zmaranda, R. D. (2025). A literature review on security in the internet of things: Identifying and analysing critical categories. *Computers*, 14(2), 61. https://doi.org/10.3390/computers14020061

Sharma, V., Lee, K., Kwon, S., Kim, J., Park, H., Yim, K., & Lee, S.-Y. (2017). A consensus framework for reliability and mitigation of zero-day attacks in IoT. *Security and Communication Networks*, 2017, 4749085. https://doi.org/10.1155/2017/4749085

Siddiqui, S., Hameed, S., Shah, S. A., Arshad, J., Ahmed, Y., & Draheim, D. (2024). A smart-contract-based adaptive security governance architecture for smart city service interoperations, *Sustainable Cities and Society*, *113*, 105717. https://doi.org/10.1016/j.scs.2024.105717

Smith, G. (2023). Ransomware statistics for 2023: Latest trends and attack methods. StationX Ltd. https://www.stationx.net/ransomware-statistics/#:~:text=5.,the%20same%20period%20in%202022

Smith, R. (2014). The cyber terrorism threat to critical infrastructure. Utica College.

Srinivas, J., Das, A. K., & Kumar, N. (2019). Government regulations in cyber security: Framework, standards and recommendations. *Future Generation Computer Systems*, *92*, 178–188. https://doi.org/10.1016/j.future.2018.09.063

Taib, R., Yu, K., Berkovsky, S., Wiggins, M., & Bayl-Smith, P. (2019). Social engineering and organisational dependencies in phishing attacks. In D. Lamas, F. Loizides, L. Nacke, H. Petrie, M. Winckler, & P. Zaphiris (Eds.), *Human-Computer Interaction – INTERACT 2019 Cham* (pp. 564–584). Springer. https://doi.org/10.1007/978-3-030-29381-9_35

Teller Report. (2022). *Hackers manage to hack traffic lights in Germany.* https://www.tellerreport.com/news/2022-12-20-hackers-manage-to-hack-traffic-lights-in-germany.S1dNKvJYo.html

Tsague, H. D., & Twala, B. (2018). Practical techniques for securing the internet of things (IoT) against side channel attacks. In N. Dey, A. E. Hassanien, C. Bhatt, A. S. Ashour, & S. C. Satapathy (Eds.), *Internet of things and big data analytics toward next-generation intelligence* (pp. 439–481). Springer International Publishing. https://doi.org/10.1007/978-3-319-60435-0_18

Wang, Z., Zhu, H., & Sun, L. (2021). Social engineering in cybersecurity: Effect mechanisms, human vulnerabilities and attack methods. *IEEE Access*, *9*, 11895–11910. https://doi.org/10.1109/ACCESS.2021.3051633

Yang, P., Xiong, N., & Ren, J. (2020). Data security and privacy protection for cloud storage: A survey. *IEEE Access*, *8*, 131723–131740. https://doi.org/10.1109/ACCESS.2020.3009876

Yaqoob, I., Ahmed, E., Rehman, M. H., Ahmed, A. I. A., Al-Garadi, M. A., Imran, M., & Guizani, M. (2017). The rise of ransomware and emerging security challenges in the internet of things. *Computer Networks*, *129*, 444–458. https://doi.org/10.1016/j.comnet.2017.09.003

Yeo, L. H. (2023). Unintentional insider threat assessment framework: Examining the human security indicators in healthcare cybersecurity. Eastern Michigan University.

7

Governance and Ethics in the Metaverse

Elif Calik

7.1 Introduction

The rapid evolution of digital technologies has led to transformative innovations, with the metaverse emerging as a groundbreaking concept that pushes the boundaries of our virtual experiences. As a dynamic, immersive, and decentralised digital space, the metaverse has the potential to revolutionise various sectors, including entertainment, education, healthcare, and the development of smart cities. By integrating cutting-edge examples in the digital realm, the metaverse offers unprecedented opportunities to improve the quality of life in a human-centric approach through a universe where urban infrastructure, energy resources, public transportation, and all conceivable digitalisable environments can interact with each other in the context of smart cities.

However, their transformative potential, interactivity technologies, artificial intelligence (AI), the Internet of Things (IoT), edge computation, blockchain (refer to Figure 7.1), and others have intensified the need for sustainable solutions. It addresses the complex governance and ethical challenges inherent in the fields in which they are applied and the impact of all the defects encountered during the maturation process (e.g., algorithmic bias, privacy, security, and data leakage). It should also be noted that the metaverse, unlike traditional digital spaces, operates in a decentralised and borderless environment that transcends physical, social, cultural, and legal frameworks. How to ensure privacy, transparency, accountability, security, and equality in this rapidly expanding metaverse is a matter of debate in the scientific community. Moreover, ethical and governance challenges such as privacy concerns, algorithmic bias, surveillance capitalism, and interoperability pose significant obstacles to creating an inclusive and sustainable metaverse.

According to Maier and Weinberger (2024), metaverse technology is built upon a multi-layered technology stack that ensures functionality and scalability. At the foundational level, infrastructure and hardware provide the necessary computational power and network connectivity to support virtual environments. Network and communication technologies enable low-latency data transmission, which is essential for seamless interactions. Cloud

DOI: 10.1201/9781003619819-9

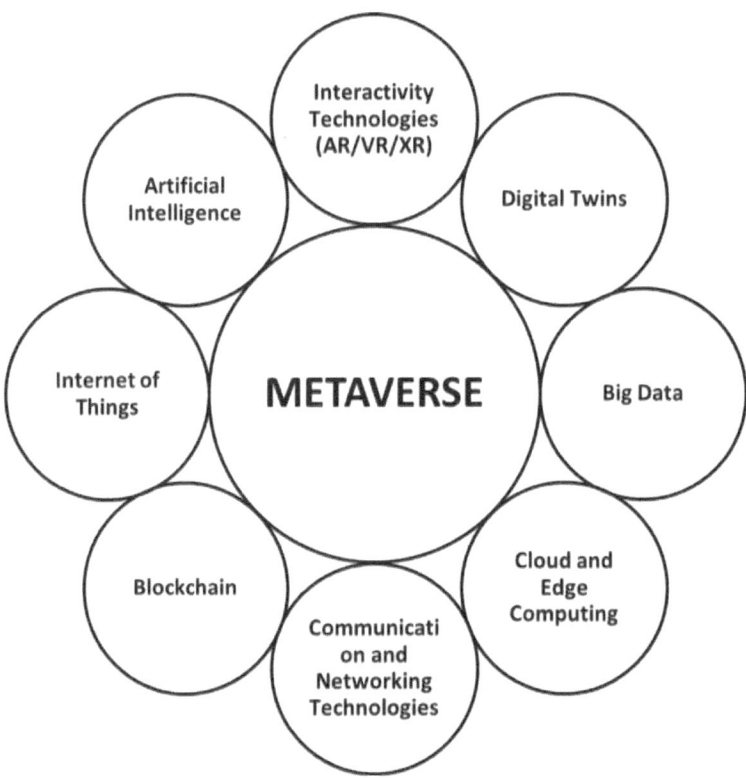

FIGURE 7.1
Technological components of the metaverse. (From Kuru, 2023; Truong et al., 2023.)

computing and distributed ledger technology (DLT), including blockchain, offer secure and decentralised data management solutions. AI, machine learning (ML), and the IoT facilitate interactive and personalised user experiences, while extended reality (XR) technologies enhance engagement with virtual environments through intuitive devices. These interconnected layers create a secure, scalable, and immersive metaverse experience.

In the context of smart cities, the metaverse highlights the integration of key technologies such as AI, big data, blockchain, IoT, digital twins (DT), and edge computing or 5G or 6G. AI, including ML and deep learning (DL), has been identified as a fundamental component in all reviewed studies. It plays a crucial role in enabling intelligent automation and decision-making within metaverse-based smart city applications (Allam et al., 2022; Bibri, 2023; Bibri & Jagatheesaperumal, 2023; Chen et al., 2024; Huynh-The et al., 2023; Maier & Weinberger, 2024; Sarwatt et al., 2024; Wang et al., 2024; Yaqoob et al., 2023). DT is particularly significant for transportation systems (Sarwatt et al., 2024), urban planning (Yaqoob et al., 2023), and smart city modelling (Chen et al., 2024), as they provide real-time simulations and predictive insights for urban development. Blockchain technology is primarily used to verify digital asset ownership and maintain transparent transaction records within the metaverse (Chen et al., 2024; Sarwatt et al., 2024; Yaqoob et al., 2023), while IoT is critical for managing connected infrastructure and data flow (Chen et al., 2024; Huynh-The et al., 2023; Sarwatt et al., 2024; Yaqoob et al., 2023).

Though explored in a limited number of studies, big data is considered a key enabler for smart city design and advanced data analytics (Chen et al., 2024). Edge computing, 5G, and 6G technologies facilitate real-time interactions in the metaverse by providing low-latency connections, which is particularly beneficial for smart city and IoT applications (Chen et al., 2024; Huynh-The et al., 2023). A study by Lifelo et al. (2024) highlights the transformative role of AI in enhancing the functionality and sustainability of smart cities through its integration with the metaverse. The study particularly emphasises the impact of generative AI models such as transformers, diffusion models, autoencoders, autoregressive models, and Generative Adversarial Networks (GANs) in creating more dynamic and adaptive virtual environments. Additionally, the findings indicate that incorporating big data analytics, natural language processing (NLP), computer vision, DT, IoT, edge AI, and 5G/6G networks can further enhance smart city applications' efficiency, sustainability, and interactivity. However, the research also identifies key challenges that need to be addressed, including data collection complexities, achieving higher levels of realism, establishing ethical standards, improving computational efficiency, ensuring data privacy, and enhancing interoperability (Bibri, 2022).

Integrating metaverse technologies reshapes urban management by blurring the boundaries between physical and digital spaces. Cities are leveraging these advancements to digitise public services, enhance citizen engagement, and drive economic and social transformations. The metaverse is redefining urban infrastructure, administrative functions, and cultural ecosystems by utilising data-driven simulations, immersive social interactions, and digitalised economic activities. This shift fosters the development of DT of cities, ultimately contributing to the emergence of a new digital city paradigm that enhances public participation, optimises urban services, and strengthens global connectivity.

Several real-world examples illustrate the diverse applications of metaverse technology in urban environments. One of the most notable implementations is Metaverse Seoul, South Korea's ambitious initiative, which is being developed in three phases. The first phase, which includes digital administrative services and virtual city tours, has already been launched. On the other hand, the project set for completion by 2030 expands to include services related to economy, education, communication, culture, urban development, governance, and taxation. Similarly, Zoan in Helsinki, Finland, initially launched in 2018 as a digital twin of the city, has since evolved into a comprehensive metaverse supporting urban planning, digital administration, virtual events and exhibitions, city tours, and virtual shopping experiences. Another example is CatVers, a metaverse explicitly developed for the Catalan region of Spain, which primarily focuses on preserving and promoting Catalan culture. However, access to this platform is currently limited due to its exclusive use of the Catalan language.

Beyond administrative applications, some cities are exploring innovative diplomatic and economic use cases. Barbados pioneered the metaverse-based diplomacy concept by establishing the first virtual embassy. Additionally, the country has introduced a project enabling avatars, called "teleporters," to navigate between different virtual spaces, thus fostering a new cultural and diplomatic engagement model. Santa Monica has developed a metaverse experience inspired by Pokémon Go in the United States. This platform allows citizens to collect digital tokens through augmented reality (AR) while exploring the city using smartphone cameras, promoting local businesses and the digital economy. Lastly, BenidormLand, an award-winning digital tourism initiative, has positioned Benidorm, Spain, as a leader in metaverse-driven tourism experiences (Maier & Weinberger, 2024).

Recent research has analysed blockchain-based governance systems in the metaverse, highlighting that decentralised governance may, in practice, be more centralised than anticipated. Goldberg and Schär (2023) found that they are insufficient, while blockchain-based management frameworks and ownership structures are essential for establishing a neutral metaverse infrastructure. The study cautions against perceiving blockchain and decentralised autonomous organisation (DAO)-based governance as guarantees of a fully decentralised decision-making process. Similarly, Uzun (2023) defines metaverse governance as a multi-layered and complex process requiring comprehensive policies and strategic frameworks to regulate interactions between virtual and physical environments. While decentralised technologies foster autonomous structures within the metaverse, they also introduce regulatory challenges for central authorities. User rights, security, data privacy, and digital ownership are critical for ensuring an open and secure virtual space. The study underscores governments' need to formulate national strategies, invest in metaverse-related initiatives, establish regulatory frameworks, and implement flexible governance mechanisms that promote innovation.

Further analysis by Duggal et al. (2024) examines the governance structure of Decentraland DAO, revealing its limitations due to its nearly fully automated decision-making system. The study points out that while streamlining governance, smart contracts impose functional constraints that limit decision-making flexibility. Modifying governance procedures can be time-consuming and challenging, while broad participation in decision-making may slow progress and hinder development. Additionally, automated governance mechanisms lack the interpretative and reasoning abilities of traditional human-led voting processes, potentially diminishing critical thinking in governance. Moreover, voting power and token distribution disparities may lead to decision-making authority becoming concentrated in the hands of a few stakeholders, raising concerns about equitable governance. As the metaverse continues to evolve, there is an urgent need to develop robust governance and ethical frameworks that balance innovation with human-centric values. Addressing these governance challenges ensures that the metaverse drives digital transformation and serves as a force for social well-being, equity, and sustainability.

7.2 Metaverse Applications and Governance

The metaverse rapidly evolves into an ecosystem where users can create digital identities, interact with virtual assets, and participate in decentralised economies. In this context, major technology companies and brands establish their presence within the metaverse to enhance customer engagement, develop new business models, and implement governance strategies. This section provides an overview of well-known metaverse applications to better understand their contributions to the evolution of this digital environment.

One notable example is Nikeland, a virtual space created by Nike on the Roblox platform. Nikeland allows users to engage with the brand through interactive experiences. Governance in such platforms involves monitoring user behaviour, enforcing content moderation, and implementing data privacy policies. Nike integrates NFTs and Web3 technologies to personalise user experiences, offering blockchain-based digital asset ownership and transfer solutions. This decentralised governance model enhances users' control over their virtual assets. Another significant application is Microsoft Mesh, a platform that enables shared holographic experiences among users in different locations. Governance in Mesh revolves around identity verification, data security, and user interaction monitoring. Microsoft employs stringent security protocols and policies to protect user privacy and ensure a safe virtual experience.

Amazon AR View, Walmart Land, and Walmart's Universe of Play are additional examples of metaverse applications. Amazon's AR View allows users to interact with products through AR, while Walmart's virtual platforms on Roblox provide gamified shopping experiences. Governance mechanisms in these platforms focus on user data collection and usage, content moderation, and monitoring user interactions to ensure compliance with digital safety standards. Decentraland, built on the Ethereum blockchain, offers a decentralised platform where users can purchase virtual land and create digital content. It operates using MANA, its native cryptocurrency. Unlike traditional platforms, Decentraland follows a community-driven governance model, where users have a say in the platform's development and regulations. Governance is facilitated through smart contracts and DAOs, ensuring a more democratic decision-making process.

Similarly, Roblox Studio allows users to design their games and virtual worlds. From a governance perspective, this platform must address issues such as content moderation, copyright protection, and user behaviour monitoring to maintain a secure and ethical environment. Horizon Worlds, developed by Meta (formerly Facebook), enables users to create and interact within virtual spaces. Governance structures in Horizon Worlds focus on identity authentication, data privacy, content moderation, and user interaction management. Meta implements security protocols to ensure a safe and privacy-conscious user experience.

Governance frameworks play a crucial role in shaping user experiences within metaverse platforms. Key governance concerns include decentralisation, data security, user rights, and economic sustainability. Companies like Nike, Microsoft, Amazon, Walmart, Decentraland, Roblox, and Meta actively develop strategies to address regulatory requirements, content management, and digital economy frameworks within this rapidly evolving landscape. For instance, Meta created an autonomous organisation (i.e., Oversight Board) to assess content moderation decisions on Facebook and Instagram (Duggal et al., 2024; Park & Kim, 2022).

7.3 The Need for Governance and Ethics in the Metaverse

Addressing governance and ethical challenges is crucial for the long-term sustainability of the metaverse. Although legality and ethics are often discussed together, they are distinct concepts. Legality refers to compliance with rules and regulations established by governmental authorities, whereas ethics involves making decisions based on universal values, social norms, and moral principles. While specific ethical concerns in the metaverse can be addressed through legal frameworks such as the General Data Protection Regulation (GDPR), the absence of a comprehensive ethical framework limits how these measures effectively serve human well-being.

7.3.1 Ethical Considerations

While various researchers have acknowledged the ethical challenges associated with the metaverse, a limited number of studies still provide a comprehensive framework for addressing these issues. Some scholars argue that developing standardised ethical guidelines can mitigate these ethical concerns. Key focus areas include content moderation and digital identity management (Duggal et al., 2024). Ethics, as a branch of philosophy, provides a framework for evaluating actions as right or wrong. Four fundamental ethical principles are respect for autonomy, non-maleficence (do-no-harm), justice, and explicability. They can be used to categorise ethical challenges in the metaverse (High-Level Expert Group on Artificial Intelligence, 2019).

A primary concern regarding autonomy in the metaverse is informed consent. While users are typically required to agree to extensive terms and conditions before accessing platforms, the nature of these agreements raises ethical concerns. The extensive and complex nature of the information provided often makes it difficult for users to understand what they consent to fully. Furthermore, since access to these platforms is conditional on accepting such agreements, users may face an ethical dilemma where their autonomy is seemingly respected but effectively constrained. Another critical issue is surveillance risks. Many metaverse platforms collect vast amounts of data through immersive technologies such as VR, AR, XR, and mixed-reality tools (Kourtesis, 2024). Even if this data is not explicitly personal, aggregating various datasets can lead to identifying unique behavioural patterns, effectively compromising user privacy. This raises concerns about excessive data collection and the potential misuse of personal information, constituting another ethical dilemma.

The immersive nature of the metaverse presents risks that can negatively impact users' physical and mental well-being. Extended engagement in virtual environments may contribute to addiction, leading to social isolation, weakened interpersonal relationships, and psychological distress. Users who spend excessive time in the metaverse may experience a diminished ability to engage with real-world experiences, which can alter cognitive functions such as memory retention and critical thinking. Since digital environments store and retrieve vast amounts of data, users may increasingly rely on algorithmically curated information rather than independent reasoning, affecting their decision-making processes. Furthermore, physical health concerns arise from prolonged engagement with virtual environments. Extended screen exposure may cause vision impairments, while remaining in static postures for extended periods can contribute to musculoskeletal disorders. These risks highlight the need for guidelines that promote responsible usage and mitigate health-related consequences. Another serious concern is psychological harm caused by negative social interactions in the metaverse. Instances of cyberbullying, harassment, violent behaviour, and harmful discourse can significantly impact users' emotional well-being. Effective content moderation mechanisms and policies are essential to create a safe and inclusive digital environment (Munn & Weijers, 2023).

The principle of justice emphasises equity and non-discrimination, ensuring that all users, regardless of socio-economic status, ability, or cultural background, have fair access to metaverse platforms. However, in practice, access to metaverse technologies is often restricted by economic barriers. High-cost VR headsets, digital assets, and subscription fees limit participation to individuals from privileged socio-economic backgrounds. This economic divide restricts access and reinforces existing inequalities, as revenue generated within the metaverse primarily benefits those with the means to engage in these digital spaces. Moreover, inclusivity concerns extend to vulnerable groups such as children, older people, and individuals with disabilities. Platforms should implement accessibility features, such as colour contrast adjustments for users with visual impairments or advanced safety measures to prevent child exploitation in virtual environments. Addressing these disparities is essential for ensuring that the metaverse remains inclusive for all users (Benjamins et al., 2023).

The increasing reliance on AI-driven decision-making in the metaverse raises concerns regarding transparency, accountability, and explainability. Many platforms incorporate blockchain-based smart contracts to automate transactions and interactions, enhancing security and posing ethical risks. Since smart contracts operate based on predefined conditions, developers must ensure that these automated processes align with ethical principles and do not contribute to unintended consequences. Moreover, the immutability of blockchain technology raises concerns regarding the right to be forgotten. Users may struggle to remove or modify past digital actions, posing long-term privacy risks. Ethical design approaches, such as "design by ethics," should be integrated into the development of metaverse platforms to ensure that these technologies remain adaptable to ethical considerations while maintaining their intended functionalities (High-Level Expert Group on Artificial Intelligence, 2019; Yasuda, 2024; Zhuk, 2024).

7.3.2 Governance Considerations

Governance in the metaverse can generally be categorised into three models: centralised, decentralised, and hybrid. Centralised governance involves regulatory frameworks established by national governments to align metaverse operations with country-specific policies and legal structures. A universally accepted governance model would prioritise human-centred approaches, protecting fundamental rights and freedoms while maintaining regulatory standards for sustainability and security. Decentralised governance emerges from the metaverse's unique nature as a virtual world that interacts with real-world assets and extends beyond traditional geographical boundaries. DAO represents a key mechanism for decentralised governance, leveraging blockchain technology to distribute decision-making power. However, it is essential to acknowledge that blockchain technology, which underpins DAOs, is still in its early stages of development. Although theoretically designed to offer democratic, borderless, and decentralised experiences, the growth of decentralised governance structures remains influenced mainly by major market players' financial and strategic interests.

Hybrid governance seeks to balance centralised and decentralised governance approaches by integrating oversight from both governmental and independent international organisations. This approach acknowledges the metaverse's expansion beyond national borders and emphasises a cooperative regulatory framework that combines the strengths of centralised policies with the innovative potential of decentralised governance.

7.4 Frameworks for Responsible Governance

The metaverse, as a combination of virtual worlds, is evolving beyond the mere integration with our physical world, giving rise to a new digital universe where digital interactions, identities, economies, and communities coexist. However, this digital space's rapid development and expansive potential raise essential responsibilities and ethical considerations. Establishing a robust framework for the metaverse's responsible governance is critical in this context. Such governance should not only be shaped by legal frameworks but also by core principles such as ethics, data security, transparency, and sustainability.

These are central to ensuring justice within the digital realm. In platforms like the metaverse, users' digital identities and interactions form a distinct structure from those in the physical world, yet the underlying sensitivities remain the same. Therefore, the ethical governance of the metaverse should be grounded in fundamental human rights and ethical norms. Initially, ensuring that the platform does not infringe upon basic rights and freedoms is essential. Moreover, ethical principles such as autonomy, non-maleficence, justice, and transparency must be prioritised. Autonomy requires users to manage their digital identities and data freely, while the principle of non-maleficence protects users from both physical and psychological harm within the digital experience. The principle of justice aims to ensure equitable treatment for all users, preventing negative interactions such as discrimination and exclusion. Additionally, transparency and accountability are crucial, necessitating that decisions made within the platform be understandable and auditable by its users. The practical implementation of these principles contributes to establishing an ethical framework for the metaverse, fostering trust at both the individual and societal levels.

At its core, this pertains to the protection of digital privacy. Metaverse platforms collect and process users' private and personal data, transforming it into large pools of information. Ensuring data security and privacy should be one of the primary responsibilities of the metaverse. Special attention must be given to the sensitivity of personal data collected during users' creation of digital identities or their interactions within the virtual environment, including data such as eye movement, heart rate, breathing patterns, physical movements, facial expressions, and gestures. This data must be safeguarded against misuse and external attacks. Protecting privacy allows users to retain control over their digital identities in the virtual space. Furthermore, personal data should only be utilised with the explicit consent of users and in a limited and transparent manner. Any form of misuse must be strictly prevented. The security of users' digital assets can be ensured in an environment that mitigates risks such as fraud and data theft. In this regard, metaverse platforms must comply with local and global data protection laws and maintain the highest standards of security protocols (Fernandez & Hui, 2022; Keeney & Patra, 2024).

The governance of the metaverse necessitates a structure in which every user actively participates in the development of the platform and the establishment of its rules. This requirement applies not only to centrally controlled platforms but also to decentralised structures, which must be ensured comprehensively. While decentralised governance models, such as DAOs, theoretically enable direct and democratic participation by users in decision-making processes, previous studies have highlighted instances where these systems fail to realise this ideal fully. However, democratic governance entails more than user participation; it also demands accountability and transparency. Users must understand how platform administrators and algorithms influence them and have clear access to information regarding these interactions. Metaverse platforms must ensure the transparency of decision-making processes and implement accountability mechanisms when necessary. This approach not only fosters trust among users but also promotes confidence within society at large.

Another critical aspect of responsible governance within the metaverse is the establishment of digital equality. The metaverse offers a digital space where diverse communities and cultures can coexist. Responsible management of this space aims to create an environment where everyone can participate equally and fairly. Ensuring accessibility requires the design of features that allow individuals with disabilities or vulnerable groups to engage with the virtual world. Additionally, the principle of inclusivity should foster an environment where users from different languages and cultural backgrounds can express themselves without fear of exclusion. Social equality plays a vital role in bridging the divide between the digital and physical worlds. The metaverse should provide opportunities for those with limited access to technology and promote educational initiatives such as digital literacy programmes. In doing so, all individuals within the virtual space can have equal opportunities and rights.

Establishing a framework for the responsible governance of the metaverse is a technological necessity and a societal imperative. Elements such as ethical principles, data security, democratic governance, accessibility, inclusivity, and sustainability ensure the metaverse's current success and contribute to the long-term development of a healthy digital ecosystem. This responsible governance framework forms a critical foundation for the security, rights, and well-being of metaverse users and all stakeholders within the broader digital world.

7.5 Towards a Sustainable and Inclusive Metaverse

The development of the metaverse should be shaped not only by technological innovation but also by social, economic, and environmental sustainability principles. A sustainable and inclusive metaverse should provide a virtual world that serves the interests of a broad spectrum of users rather than being designed to benefit a specific group or corporate entities. It should be accessible, equitable, and environmentally responsible. In this context, the sustainability of the metaverse can be approached along three key dimensions: environmental sustainability, social inclusivity, and economic sustainability.

The infrastructure supporting the metaverse relies on energy-intensive technologies such as large-scale data centres, blockchain systems, AR, and VR devices. These technologies contribute to significant environmental challenges, including high energy consumption and carbon footprints. Implementing green computing strategies, promoting data centres powered by renewable energy sources, and optimising coding practices and computational resource management are essential. Furthermore, the virtual economy could encourage carbon offset mechanisms to reduce the environmental impact.

For the metaverse to be an inclusive ecosystem, it must ensure that users from diverse socio-economic backgrounds, ethnicities, genders, and individuals with disabilities have equal opportunities to participate. The existing digital divide remains a significant barrier to access, thus necessitating the development of affordable hardware solutions, open-source software, and accessibility policies that governments can support. Additionally, mechanisms that foster linguistic and cultural diversity within the metaverse should be implemented, along with regulatory frameworks, to combat misinformation, disinformation, hate speech, and discrimination.

While the metaverse introduces new business models and revenue streams within the digital economy, it also carries the risk of exacerbating economic inequalities. Virtual spaces controlled by large technology corporations could reinforce centralisation, making it difficult for independent content creators to compete. Adopting fair economic models and providing more opportunities for independent developers and content creators is critical. Additionally, protecting virtual property rights, creating mechanisms that ensure users can earn fair revenue from the content they generate, and promoting community-driven governance models such as DAOs are essential for promoting economic sustainability. The governance sustainability of the metaverse should not be limited solely to establishing regulatory and legal frameworks; it must also be supported by community participation, transparent governance processes, ethical principles, and the long-term sustainability of technological infrastructure. A governance model that safeguards individual rights ensures fair and inclusive economic activities and prioritises security, enabling the metaverse to maintain a stable ecosystem over time.

In this context, hybrid governance models can combine the strengths of both centralised and decentralised approaches to balance the needs of various stakeholders. Centralised structures can provide effective regulatory compliance, user safety, and content moderation mechanisms, while decentralised systems can promote individual freedoms and community-driven decision-making. Smart contracts, DAOs, and blockchain-based governance models can empower users, creating a transparent and auditable management system. Additionally, the establishment of "transnational independent oversight organisations" contributes to the creation of a sustainable, ethical governance framework for the metaverse (Duggal et al., 2024; Rodríguez de las Heras & López-Tarruella, 2024). However, for governance mechanisms to be effective, they must be transparent, accountable, and fair. Transparency allows users to understand the platform's rules, the operation of algorithms, and data management policies. Accountability ensures decision-making processes are conducted within clearly defined ethical and legal frameworks. The principle of justice requires adopting a governance model in which all users possess equal rights, free from censorship, discrimination, or monopolisation.

Finally, ensuring the sustainability of the metaverse's technological infrastructure is a fundamental component of its long-term success. Enhancing platform interoperability, strengthening data security protocols, and adopting energy-efficient technologies contribute to the technical sustainability of the metaverse. Moreover, continuously reviewing governance models and adapting them to evolving technological and societal needs foster the development of a dynamic and flexible governance structure. This comprehensive approach ensures that the metaverse remains a viable digital space aligned with current technological and economic conditions and guarantees its evolution into a sustainable digital ecosystem.

References

Allam, Z., Sharifi, A., Bibri, S. E., Jones, D. S., & Krogstie, J. (2022). The metaverse as a virtual form of smart cities: Opportunities and challenges for environmental, economic, and social sustainability in urban futures. *Smart Cities, 5,* 771–801. https://doi.org/10.3390/smartcities5030040

Benjamins, R., Rubio Viñuela, Y., & Alonso, C. (2023). Social and ethical challenges of the metaverse. *AI Ethics, 3,* 689–697. https://doi.org/10.1007/s43681-023-00278-5

Bibri, S. E. (2022). The social shaping of the metaverse as an alternative to the imaginaries of data-driven smart cities: A study in science, technology, and society. *Smart Cities, 5*(3), 832–874. https://doi.org/10.3390/smartcities5030043

Bibri, S. E. (2023). The metaverse as a virtual model of platform urbanism: Its converging AIoT, XReality, neurotech, and nanobiotech and their applications, challenges, and risks. *Smart Cities, 6,* 1345–1384. https://doi.org/10.3390/smartcities6030065

Bibri, S. E., & Jagatheesaperumal, S. K. (2023). Harnessing the potential of the metaverse and artificial intelligence for the internet of city things: Cost-effective XReality and synergistic AIoT technologies. *Smart Cities, 6,* 2397–2429. https://doi.org/10.3390/smartcities6050109

Chen, Z., Gan, W., Wu, J., Lin, H., & Chen, C. M. (2024). Metaverse for smart cities: A survey. *Internet of Things and Cyber-Physical Systems, 4,* 203–216. https://doi.org/10.1016/j.iotcps.2023.12.002

Duggal, G., Garg, M., & Nigam, A. (2024). Good governance and implementation. In C. Krishnan, A. Behl, S. Dash, & P. D. Yadav (Eds.), *The metaverse dilemma: Challenges and opportunities for business and society* (pp. 249–267). Emerald Publishing Limited. https://doi.org/10.1108/978-1-83797-524-220241015

Fernandez, C. B., & Hui, P. (2022). Life, the metaverse and everything: An overview of privacy, ethics, and governance in metaverse. arXiv. https://arxiv.org/abs/2204.01480

Goldberg, M., & Schär, F. (2023). Metaverse governance: An empirical analysis of voting within decentralised autonomous organisations. *Journal of Business Research, 160,* 113764. https://doi.org/10.1016/j.jbusres.2023.113764

High-Level Expert Group on Artificial Intelligence. (2019, April). *Ethics guidelines for trustworthy AI.* European Commission. Retrieved January 11, 2025, from https://digital-strategy.ec.europa.eu/en/library/ethics-guidelines-trustworthy-ai

Huynh-The, T., Pham, Q.-V., Pham, X.-Q., Nguyen, T. T., Han, Z., & Kim, D.-S. (2023). Artificial intelligence for the metaverse: A survey. *Engineering Applications of Artificial Intelligence, 117*(Part A), 105581. https://doi.org/10.1016/j.engappai.2022.105581

Keeney, B., & Patra, A. N. (2024). Towards a secured, interoperable, and ethical metaverse. In *Proceedings of SoutheastCon 2024* (pp. 260–268). IEEE. https://doi.org/10.1109/SoutheastCon52093.2024.10500270

Kourtesis, P. (2024). A comprehensive review of multimodal XR applications, risks, and ethical challenges in the metaverse. *Multimodal Technologies and Interaction, 8*(11), 98. https://doi.org/10.3390/mti8110098

Kuru, K. (2023). MetaOmniCity: Toward immersive urban metaverse cyberspaces using smart city digital twins. *IEEE Access, 11,* 43844–43868. https://doi.org/10.1109/ACCESS.2023.3272890

Lifelo, Z., Ding, J., Ning, H., & Dhelim, Q.-U.-A. (2024). Artificial intelligence-enabled metaverse for sustainable smart cities: Technologies, applications, challenges, and future directions. *Electronics, 13,* 4874. https://doi.org/10.3390/electronics13244874

Maier, F., & Weinberger, M. (2024). Metaverse meets smart cities—Applications, benefits, and challenges. *Future Internet, 16,* 126. https://doi.org/10.3390/fi16040126

Munn, N., & Weijers, D. (2023). The real ethical problem with metaverses. *Frontiers in Human Dynamics, 5,* 1226848. https://doi.org/10.3389/fhumd.2023.1226848.

Park, S.-M., & Kim, Y.-G. (2022). A metaverse: Taxonomy, components, applications, and open challenges. *IEEE Access, 10,* 4209–4251. https://doi.org/10.1109/ACCESS.2021.3140175

Rodríguez de las Heras, T., & López-Tarruella, A. (2024). A European regulatory framework for the metaverse. MetaverseUA Research Paper #1. https://metaversechair.ua.es/working-papers/

Sarwatt, D. S., Lin, Y., Ding, J., Sun, Y., & Ning, H. (2024). Metaverse for intelligent transportation systems (ITS): A comprehensive review of technologies, applications, implications, challenges and future directions. *IEEE Transactions on Intelligent Transportation Systems, 27,* 6290–6308. https://doi.org/10.1109/TITS.2023.3347280

Truong, V. T., Le, L., & Niyato, D. (2023). Blockchain meets metaverse and digital asset management: A comprehensive survey. *IEEE Access, 11,* 26258–26288. https://doi.org/10.1109/ACCESS.2023.3257029

Uzun, M. M. (2023). Metaverse governance. In *Metaverse: Technologies, opportunities and threats* (pp. 231–244). Springer Nature Singapore. https://doi.org/10.1007/978-981-99-4641-9_16

Wang, X., Huang, J., Tian, Y. L., & Wang, F. Y. (2024). AGI in metaverse for smart cities and societies: A cyber-physical-social approach. In *Proceedings of the 2024 Australian and New Zealand Control Conference* (pp. 61–66). Gold Coast. https://doi.org/10.1109/ANZCC59813.2024.10432879

Yaqoob, I., Salah, K., Jayaraman, R., & Omar, M. (2023). Metaverse applications in smart cities: Enabling technologies, opportunities, challenges, and future directions. *Internet of Things, 23,* 100884. https://doi.org/10.1016/j.iot.2023.100884

Yasuda, A. (2024). Metaverse ethics: Exploring the social implications of the metaverse. *AI Ethics.* https://doi.org/10.1007/s43681-024-00507-5

Zhuk, A. (2024). Ethical implications of AI in the metaverse. *AI Ethics.* https://doi.org/10.1007/s43681-024-00450-5

Section III

Innovations and Applications

8

Metaverse for Smart Cities

Feras Zen Alden and Abdulaziz Al-Nahari

8.1 Foundations of the Metaverse and Smart Cities

Adopting the metaverse in current and future applications pushes up urban development, offering transformative opportunities to enhance the quality of life, sustainability, and efficiency of the smart cities' services. By implementing more modern technologies such as virtual reality (VR), augmented reality (AR), Internet of Things (IoT), blockchain, and digital twins, the metaverse enables the creation of interconnected, data-driven environments that bridge the physical and virtual worlds. The metaverse can be identified as a collective virtual shared space shaped by the convergence of virtually augmented physical reality and persistent virtual spaces. Neal Stephenson created the Snow Crash in 1992, and the term has gained prominence with developments in future technologies and the rise of platforms like Meta (formerly Facebook) (Lv et al., 2022; Yaqoob et al., 2023).

The integration between VR, AR, AI, blockchain, and digital ecosystems in the metaverse creates a multi-dimensional space which allows users to interact, handle, and collaborate in different types of applications such as virtual meetings, immersive gaming, and e-commerce (Yaqoob et al., 2023). Smart cities are urban environments where users can entertain using various types of technical services, from simple sensors to advanced technology, to improve their lives in terms of efficiency and sustainable solutions. To achieve smart city goals, integrating IoT, AI, and big data helps optimise energy, water, and transportation (Allam et al., 2022; Lv et al., 2022). Implementing metaverse into smart cities exposes a new path of urban innovation. Metaverse enhances urban planning, public service delivery, and citizen participation by creating immersive and interactive environments (Allam et al., 2022; Yaqoob et al., 2023).

For instance, digital twins allow organisers to simulate infrastructure projects, reducing costs and risks. Furthermore, the metaverse supports sustainable development by providing virtual experiments for various applications, such as energy-efficient designs and green infrastructure (Lv et al., 2022). In this development, economic growth through virtual marketplaces, e-governance, and fintech (Allam et al., 2022; Yaqoob et al., 2023).

DOI: 10.1201/9781003619819-11

FIGURE 8.1
An example of a metaverse architecture.

Employing virtuality in the metaverse aims to merge physical and digital spaces by offering immersive and interactive experiences. On the other hand, smart cities aim to adopt all types of technologies to enhance infrastructure, governance, and urban services. This integration improves urban living, improves sustainability, and enhances economic and social interactions (Wang et al., 2023; Yaqoob et al., 2023). Figure 8.1 illustrates a visual of metaverse architecture in a smart city environment.

The integration of the metaverse with smart cities introduces a dynamic platform for urban simulations, citizen engagement, and sustainable city planning (Lv et al., 2022; Wang et al., 2023; Yaqoob et al., 2023). This ecosystem combines multiple advanced technologies, including the IoT, artificial intelligence (AI), blockchain, VR/AR, cloud computing, and high-speed connectivity through 5G/6G networks. The metaverse overcomes traditional geographical and temporal limitations by enabling real-time interactions across digital and physical spaces. A key feature of the metaverse is its decentralised infrastructure, which leverages blockchain for identity verification, asset ownership, and secure digital transactions. Unlike conventional digital environments, the metaverse is persistent—its virtual spaces continue to exist even when users are offline. Through immersive virtual spaces, interconnected digital economies, and enhanced social interactions, the metaverse fosters a seamless and engaging experience, redefining how people interact with urban and digital landscapes.

Smart cities leverage digital technologies and data-driven solutions to enhance infrastructure, governance, and overall quality of life. Their primary objectives include reducing environmental impact through energy-efficient buildings, smart grids, and green transportation (Lv et al., 2022;

Wang et al., 2023; Yaqoob et al., 2023). Digital platforms facilitate governance by enabling smart contracts, virtual consultations, and streamlined administrative processes. AI and digital twins enhance urban resilience by predicting and mitigating challenges such as natural disasters and cyber threats. Digital economies and smart mobility solutions also drive sustainable economic growth, fostering a more connected, efficient, and environmentally conscious urban landscape.

Integrating the metaverse and smart cities is driven by a convergence of advanced technologies, each playing a crucial role in enhancing urban development and digital experiences. IoT forms the backbone of smart city infrastructure, enabling real-time connectivity and monitoring essential systems such as transportation, energy management, and environmental tracking. AI enhances predictive capabilities and automation, making it a key component in metaverse applications for efficient urban management. Meanwhile, blockchain and cryptocurrencies ensure secure digital identities, enable smart contracts, and facilitate decentralised transactions, fostering trust and transparency within the metaverse ecosystem. VR and AR further enrich urban planning and citizen engagement by providing immersive experiences, allowing stakeholders to visualise infrastructure projects before implementation. Additionally, digital twins create real-time, data-driven simulations of physical cities, supporting predictive maintenance, disaster response, and optimised urban planning. Together, these technologies drive the seamless integration of smart cities and the metaverse, transforming urban living through innovation and efficiency.

Integrating the metaverse with smart cities unlocks transformative possibilities, enhancing urban efficiency, governance, and citizen engagement. Urban planning and simulation benefit significantly from digital twins, which enable real-time city modelling, allowing planners to optimise infrastructure, sustainability efforts, and resource allocation. In governance, advanced public services leverage virtual city halls and blockchain-based smart contracts to enhance transparency, improve accessibility, and streamline administrative processes. Meanwhile, modern transportation systems are revolutionised through AI-powered traffic simulations in the metaverse, optimising public transport networks, reducing congestion, and improving overall mobility. The seamless convergence of these technologies marks a significant step towards creating more resilient, efficient, and inclusive urban environments, fundamentally redefining how cities operate and interact with their residents.

8.2 Applications of the Metaverse in Smart Cities

Adopting virtualisation technologies such as VR and AR allows improved urban planners where city officials can try different approaches, optimise traffic, and develop better transportation systems that are incorporated into the development of smart cities (Maier & Weinberger, 2024). For example, the transport systems that use VR to replicate traffic congestion can enhance effectiveness and reduce congestion in urban areas (Wu et al., 2025). Metaverse applications are the solutions to the growing challenges of the urban environment as cities develop and innovate with the help of digital transformation to achieve sustainable development and improve citizens' quality of life.

8.2.1 Urban Planning and Design

Integrating metaverse into urban planning and design brings about new and novel applications that can enhance the development and management of smart cities. In the metaverse, urban planners create an environment that imitates the real-world urban environment in VR. The city officials and community members can visualise and interact with the proposed urban development and transformation. Glickman (2022) explored how cities in the United States used a metaverse platform to hold virtual meetings of the town hall and engage and how the metaverse helps in the development of cities and how technologies impact urban governments in the future. For instance, in the form of digital twins, Orlando, Boston, and Las Vegas have already constructed virtual versions of their cities that enable local governments to simulate the outcomes of speculative scenarios, including new construction, street modifications, and other land use choices. Austin, Miami, and Chandler, AZ, are using blockchain to secure medical records and do voting on mobile. They are getting ready for the smooth, transparent exchange of information in the metaverse.

Metaverse can enhance digital twins due to the virtual replication of physical assets, where the application enables city planners and managers to monitor and manage city infrastructure in real-time (Ritterbusch & Teichmann, 2023). For instance, a digital twin in Singapore has been adopted where the planners simulate real-time traffic flows, environmental effects, and infrastructure requirements. The decision-making has enhanced and utilised resources for sustainable urban development. The development of smart cities shows that the metaverse can be an innovative technique for infrastructure management, community engagement, and urban planning and design improvement. The effects of the decisions made by urban planners can be seen before the implementation of building a more resilient and flexible urban environment. The visualisation in the metaverse creates planned developments in immersive 3D models and shows the effects on the community before the execution.

8.2.2 Visualisation of 3D Urban Infrastructure

Visualising the 3D urban infrastructure helps stakeholders in urban planning and development to sort and interpret massive data more effectively and generate realistic depictions of urban settings, significantly benefiting decision-making processes. Also, it helps planners and the public to under-stand the ramifications of proposed developments to a greater extent. So, it can depict how new structures look in the surrounding environment con-cerning size, attractiveness, and space relationships (van Leeuwen et al., 2018). In addition, it can assist in sharing information with various stakehold-ers to enhance engagement towards better decision-making, which provides better feedback and decision-making processes. The simulation of various urban scenarios can reveal potential problems before they occur in differ-ent situations, such as traffic flow, environmental impact, and emergency response strategies, which assist in making better decisions on how to plan (Isaacs et al., 2011).

Integrating 3D visualisation with GIS technology gives a deeper context for analysis and planning and, therefore, offers excellent value by combining different data sets such as demographic information, land use, and environ-mental factors (Dasgupta et al., 2021). In transportation projects, 3D mod-els can identify where routes can be optimised to improve connectivity by simulating traffic patterns and public transit systems. Disaster situations can be modelled using 3D visualisations to limit flooding or earthquakes and develop proper emergency response measures (Lee & Zlatanova, 2008). The comprehensive view of urban environments that 3D models help planners and the general public understand the effects of proposed developments on the scale, aesthetics, and spatial linkages. These include AR and VR, which are gradually emerging as new technologies that can provide a more immersive experience that can enhance stakeholder engagement and under-standing (Wu et al., 2025). Furthermore, integrating real-time data into 3D models provides dynamic visualisations of current conditions and trends, thus enhancing the ability of urban planners to design proactive and adap-tive planning processes.

8.2.3 Enhancing the Participation of Citizens through Immersive Platforms

Allowing citizens to engage in smart city platforms moves to an impres-sive stage through the metaverse by facilitating creative interactions between citizens and their urban environments and can improve user experience, as shown in Figure 8.2, which gives the local governments the ability to hold virtual Town Halls where people can engage with repre-sentatives and have easy and accessible conversations about local matters wherever they are while respecting the scheduling difficulties or mobility issues for citizens. In construction projects, metaverse allows having inter-active models to let people discover how the neighbourhood might look in the future and provide valuable input regarding the use and design of the space. Furthermore, immersion platforms support group workshops where local people can come up with solutions to challenges such as traffic congestion or environmental issues. The VR tools enable the participants

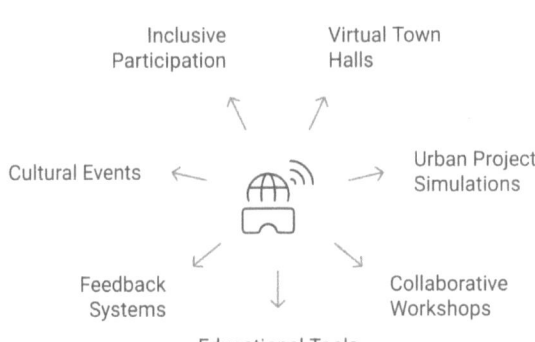

Enhancing Civic Engagement through Immersive Technologies

FIGURE 8.2
Enhancing user engagement through immersive technologies.

to visualise their concepts in 3D, enhancing the discussion's understanding and effectiveness.

Also, the metaverse can be used as an educational tool by providing immersive experiences that help people learn about their civic rights, responsibilities, and the governance of the local area. It is a particularly effective way of engaging young audiences with gamified learning modules highlighting the importance of participatory community action. Immersive platforms can be used so that smart cities can develop user-friendly feedback systems that allow citizens to instantly report problems such as a broken lamp or a pothole. These platforms can assist local officials in understanding and addressing issues by providing a 3D visual representation of the problem areas. Immersion platforms can guarantee the inclusion of the disempowered in public affairs by removing the barriers. Features like translations, sign language avatars, and personalised experiences enable every resident to engage fully, regardless of background or disability. The metaverse can enhance community, togetherness, and a shared identity through social events, cultural events, and online art exhibitions. This feature is vital in multicultural urban environments where social capital is built on the principle of inclusion and the formation of social ties (Mozumder et al., 2022).

8.3 Real-Time City Management with Digital Twins

The increasing complexity in city management is due to the rapid urbanisation of the 21st century. The digital twins, or virtual replicas of physical entities, have revolutionised how we monitor, manage, and maintain urban environments. Digital twins improve the decision-making process due to the combination of real-time data and advanced analytics. Advanced technologies such as IoT, AI, and big data analytics create digital twins that give a dynamic view of urban systems, including infrastructure, transportation networks, utilities, and public services. Also, the digital twins improve operational efficiency, service delivery, and sustainable development of cities.

8.3.1 Monitoring and Predictive Maintenance

Digital twins allow real-time monitoring and offer a better consideration of city operations by collecting and analysing information from different sources, including sensors, cameras, and social media feeds. For instance, digital twins monitor traffic flows in real-time using intelligent traffic management systems, where city traffic sensors collect information on vehicle movements in cities like Barcelona. This information improves general mobility, optimises traffic signals, and decreases congestion.

Maintenance strategy can be predicted using data analysis to determine the expected failure or requirement for maintenance of infrastructure components. In contrast, digital twins predict possible problems by analysing past trends and present situations to notify administrators who can act before the problems become failures. For instance, a digital twin water distribution system could discover leaks or pipe breaks and fix them before they become service-disrupting breaks. Another example is that in Singapore, digital twins monitor the condition of public infrastructure, including bridges and roads, where sensors gather information on stress, strain, and environmental conditions to use this data to determine when maintenance is required, thus extending the life of the infrastructure and cutting on repair costs. On the other hand, the 'Digital Twin London' initiative project aims to develop a comprehensive digital copy of the city from various data sources, including transport, energy, and environmental systems. For instance, the London Underground has digital twins to monitor train performance and track conditions to avoid future breakdowns and enhance commuters' safety.

Integrating digital twins in monitoring and predictive maintenance could reduce costs, enhance public safety and optimise resources. Thus, real-time monitoring reduces threats to the public, enhances their safety by detecting safety risks early, cuts the cost of emergency repair, and lengthens the useful life of assets by predicting failures before they occur. Furthermore, predictive maintenance uses resources effectively by performing when needed, not scheduled.

8.3.2 Emergency Response Systems

Response time is essential in emergency states, and the correct information is life. The emergency responders using digital twins enhance situational awareness by fusing real-time data from different sources, including surveillance cameras, social media, and sensor networks. It gives the responders a quick understanding of the situation and the likely use of resources. In disaster situations such as floods or earthquakes, digital twins can simulate different possible scenarios to determine possible effects and recommend appropriate responses, where they can evaluate the effectiveness of the response protocols and potential weaknesses in the plans (Alam, 2024). Developing more robust emergency response protocols helps cities prepare for the unexpected. For example, during Hurricane Harvey in 2017, Houston used digital twin technology to simulate flood scenarios based on real-time rainfall data that helped emergency responders identify potential problems and target resources accordingly. Combining IoT and AI with digital twins improves the emergency response, where IoT devices (like drones and sensors) can provide real-time information on environmental conditions. AI algorithms can work on this data to predict the possible evolution of emergencies.

8.4 Sustainable Development in the Metaverse Smart City

The importance of sustainable development of cities and towns with the world's cities continues to engage with issues such as climate change, resource competition and social inequality. Addressing these issues showed the importance of integration with metaverse to hold a promise of encouraging sustainable practices.

8.4.1 Energy Efficiency and Carbon Footprint Reduction

Sustainability aims to increase energy efficiency and decrease carbon emissions that lead to climate change. In smart cities, the metaverse can become an indispensable and significant tool to achieve these goals. Visualisation can be used effectively to model and analyse energy consumption and the utilisation of the resources within the urban environment. Metaverse monitors energy consumption by integrating IoT devices in real-time mode. So, smart cities can collect and analyse data on energy consumption patterns to design smart grids that regulate energy distribution according to actual demand, reducing energy waste and losses. Virtual simulations test different renewable energy sources, such as solar panels and wind turbines, in different urban configurations without actual installation, which can be costly and time-consuming (Lifelo et al., 2024).

Moreover, the metaverse can be used as a marketing tool to promote behavioural changes among residents through engaging and immersive experiences that remind people about the effects of energy consumption on the environment and the planet. VR apps can replicate the actual outcomes connected with high energy consumption and, therefore, make people change their behaviour and actions in their daily lives (Spais et al., 2024).

8.4.2 Green Infrastructure Simulations

Green infrastructure is a natural and semi-natural system that offers environmental functions such as stormwater management, heat island effect reduction, and biodiversity. Metaverse can assist in designing and implementing green infrastructure so that urban planners can develop virtual copies of proposed green spaces, parks, green roofs, and urban forests. These simulations help stakeholders to understand the potential impact of green infrastructure. According to Balayev et al. (2024), the application of digital simulation tools to evaluate the sustainability outcomes of green infrastructure thus increases the planning accuracy and the continuity between the urban and suburban areas, which is in line with the concept of virtual modelling for stakeholder engagement and decision-making in urban planning. By allowing residents to interact with virtual copies of their neighbourhoods, cities can collect feedback and create a sense of inclusion among community members. Shared virtual spaces make it easier to develop sustainable urban solutions by collaborating between all stakeholders, making the sustainable development of the urban environment vital (Allam et al., 2022). Figure 8.3 illustrates the examples of a metaverse in a smart city setting.

8.5 Case Studies and Real-World Examples of Smart Cities and the Metaverse

8.5.1 Seoul

Seoul is considered the first city in the world to embrace the metaverse with the 'Soul of City' project. The Seoul city government has taken this initiative in collaboration with technology companies like Samsung and Naver. The project aims to develop a three-dimensional virtual world of the actual city where people can move around, interact with buildings and other people, and access public administration (de Almeida, 2023; Park & Kim, 2022). Seoul has started a multiple strategy to become a metaverse city. It establishes leadership in the metaverse space and fits with marketing strategies that emphasise being the first in a new category. Furthermore, it promotes technological advancement and urban revitalisation and thus makes itself a hub for digital infrastructure. Also, it promotes immersive

Transformative Technologies for Smart Cities and Metaverse Integration

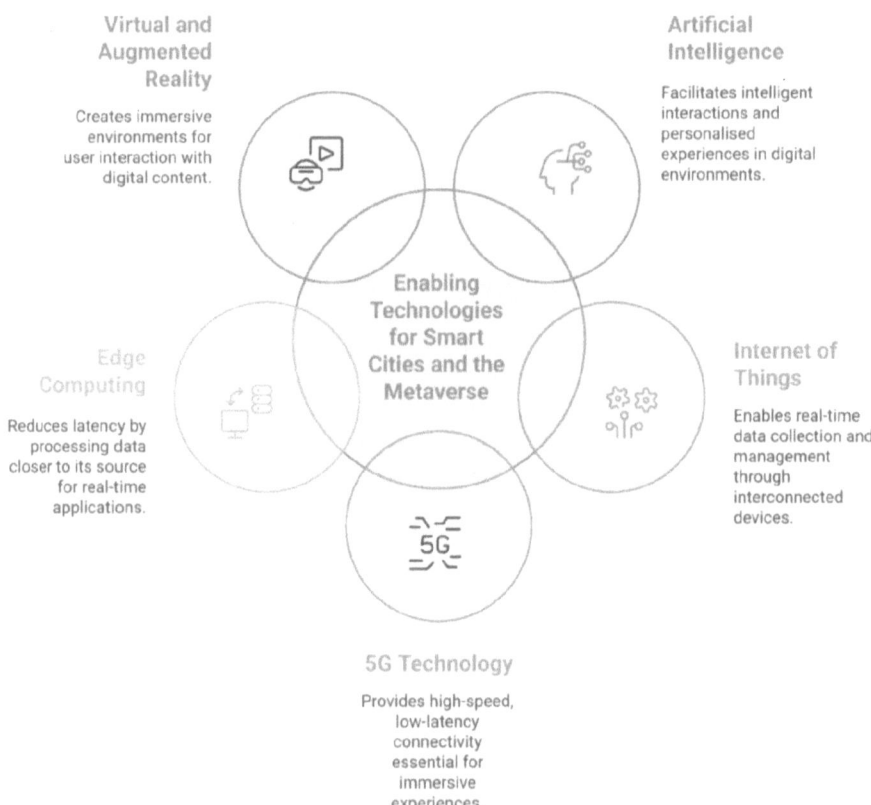

Virtual and Augmented Reality

Creates immersive environments for user interaction with digital content.

Artificial Intelligence

Facilitates intelligent interactions and personalised experiences in digital environments.

Enabling Technologies for Smart Cities and the Metaverse

Edge Computing

Reduces latency by processing data closer to its source for real-time applications.

Internet of Things

Enables real-time data collection and management through interconnected devices.

5G Technology

Provides high-speed, low-latency connectivity essential for immersive experiences.

FIGURE 8.3
Transformative technologies for smart cities and metaverse integration.

virtual inclusion of the physical and virtual urban environment. In addition, it provides a context for urban planning and experimentation and promotes variety and collaboration (de Almeida, 2023).

The 3D virtual environment of Seoul allows users to tour the city virtually and navigate through different city elements. The project aims to improve the bureaucratic processes, provide actual public services, and create virtual business and education environments. Its users can also share their experiences, preserve culture and integrate decentralised technologies into the urban fabric. Figure 8.4 presents the initiatives of Seoul's Metaverse.

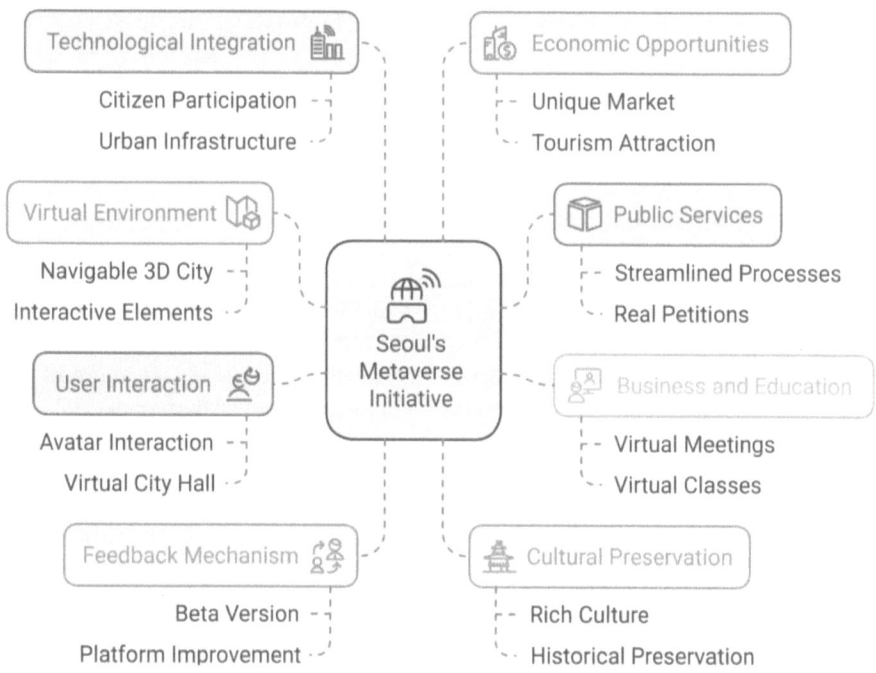

FIGURE 8.4
Seoul's metaverse initiative: Components and objectives.

8.5.2 Singapore

Due to the high engagement of the public sector and investment, Singapore is at the top of the list of smart city development and is better than neighbouring cities like Hong Kong. Using metaverse technologies in Singapore's smart city plans is essential to improve citizens' experience and sustainability (Verma, 2024). The metaverse enables the construction of virtual communities, which aligns with Singapore's goals of enhancing the modernisation of government operations and expanding economic growth. The city's smart city development strategy includes digital twins and the metaverse to model human behaviour and performance in digital environments and promote sustainable urban living (Markopoulos et al., 2024).

8.5.3 Dubai

Metaverse technologies are also being integrated into Dubai's smart city framework. The metaverse can help Dubai grow its tourism sector by offering visitors new and unique virtual experiences (Suanpang et al., 2022). The city's focus on digital transformation and innovation is in harmony with the metaverse, which can potentially change the way urban experiences and services are delivered (Allam et al., 2022). Dubai's smart city initiatives are powered by technologies like AI, IoT, and digital twins, on which the metaverse depends (Zainab & Bawanay, 2023).

8.5.4 Hong Kong

Hong Kong is a leading smart city, but challenges arise from its political and economic linkage with mainland China (Cole & Tran, 2022). Nonetheless, Hong Kong is keen on implementing smart city strategies, emphasising the public sector and the engagement of citizens. The metaverse could be useful for Hong Kong in improving its spatial planning and provision of services in virtual cities. Nevertheless, the city has to consider the metaverse's ethical, social, and cultural effects on people's behaviour and the urban environment (Allam et al., 2022).

Expanding on Hong Kong's smart city landscape, a comparative analysis, as shown in Figure 8.5, indicates that it lacks both technological integration and innovation support in its smart city initiatives (Ang-Tan & Ang, 2022). Unlike Singapore, which leads in innovation and technological advancement, and South Korea, which balances strong innovation with emerging technological integration, Hong Kong faces significant gaps in these areas. Dubai, on the other hand, integrates advanced technologies but has only moderate innovation support. It suggests that while Hong Kong is committed to smart city strategies, its progress is hindered by insufficient technological advancements and innovation frameworks.

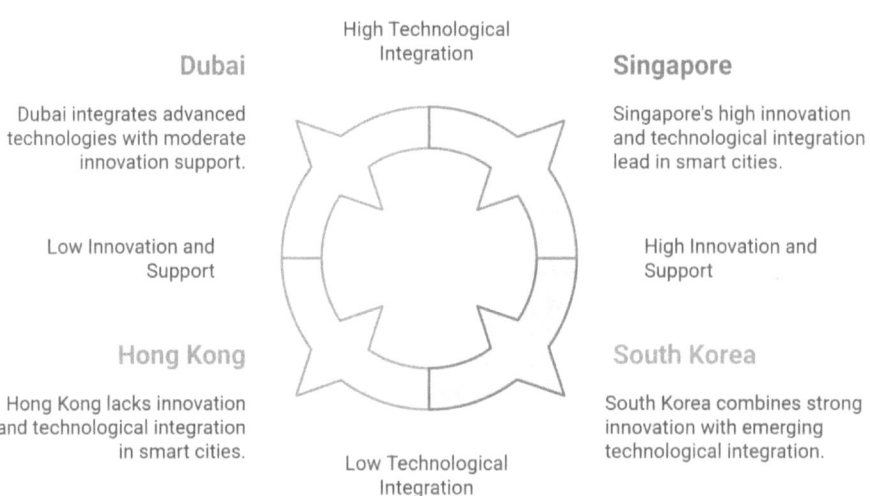

FIGURE 8.5
Comparison between Dubai, Singapore, South Korea, and Hong Kong.

References

Alam, T. (2024). Metaverse of things (MoT) applications for revolutionizing urban living in smart cities. *Smart Cities, 7*(5), 2466–2494. https://doi.org/10.3390/smartcities7050096

Allam, Z., Sharifi, A., Bibri, S. E., Jones, D. S., & Krogstie, J. (2022). The metaverse as a virtual form of smart cities: Opportunities and challenges for environmental, economic, and social sustainability in urban futures. *Smart Cities, 5*(3), 771–801. https://doi.org/10.3390/smartcities5030040

Ang-Tan, R., & Ang, S. (2022). Understanding the smart city race between Hong Kong and Singapore. *Public Money & Management, 42*(4), 231–240. https://doi.org/10.1080/09540962.2021.1903752

Balayev, R., Rzayeva, U., Ahmadzadeh, E., & Mirzammadova, K. (2024). Enhancing sustainable urban areas through digital green infrastructure: Achieving tangible outcomes. *Eastern-European Journal of Enterprise Technologies, 132*(13). https://doi.org/10.15587/1729-4061.2024.317100

Cole, A., & Tran, É. (2022). Trust and the smart city: The Hong Kong paradox. *China Perspectives, 2022*(3), 9–20. https://doi.org/10.4000/chinaperspectives.14024

Dasgupta, S., Rahman, M., Lidbe, A. D., Lu, W., & Jones, S. (2021). A transportation digital-twin approach for adaptive traffic control systems. arXiv Preprint arXiv:2109.10863. https://doi.org/10.48550/arXiv.2109.10863

de Almeida, G. G. F. (2023). Cities and territorial brand in the metaverse: The metaverse Seoul case. *Sustainability, 15*(13), 10116. https://doi.org/10.3390/su151310116

Glickman, J. (2022). How cities are engaging in the metaverse—National league of cities. https://www.nlc.org/article/2022/04/18/how-cities-are-engaging-in-the-metaverse/

Isaacs, J. P., Falconer, R. E., Gilmour, D. J., & Blackwood, D. J. (2011). Enhancing urban sustainability using 3D visualisation. *Proceedings of the Institution of Civil Engineers-Urban Design and Planning, 164*(3), 163–173. https://doi.org/10.1680/udap.900034

Lee, J., & Zlatanova, S. (2008). A 3D data model and topological analyses for emergency response in urban areas. In S. Zlatanova & M. M. Holweg (Eds.), Geospatial information technology for emergency response (pp. 1–20). CRC Press.

Lifelo, Z., Ding, J., Ning, H., & Dhelim, Q.-U.-A. (2024). Artificial intelligence-enabled metaverse for sustainable smart cities: Technologies, applications, challenges, and future directions. *Electronics, 13*(24), 4874. https://doi.org/10.3390/electronics13244874

Lv, Z., Shang, W. L., & Guizani, M. (2022). Impact of digital twins and metaverse on cities: History, current situation, and application perspectives. *Applied Sciences, 12*(24), 12820. https://doi.org/10.3390/app122412820

Maier, F., & Weinberger, M. (2024). Metaverse meets smart cities—Applications, benefits, and challenges. *Future Internet, 16*(4), 126. https://doi.org/10.3390/fi16040126

Markopoulos, E., Markopoulos, P., Nandi, A., Zhao, K., Samkova, M., Wu, T., & Kantola, J. (2024). Aligning digital twins and metaverse with the UN SDGs and applying them to understand human behaviour in smart and virtual cities. *Accessibility, Assistive Technology and Digital Environments, 121*, 36–45. https://doi.org/10.54941/ahfe1004612

Mozumder, M. A. I., Sheeraz, M. M., Athar, A., Aich, S., & Kim, H. C. (2022, February). Overview: Technology roadmap of the future trend of metaverse based on IoT, blockchain, AI technique, and medical domain metaverse activity. In *2022 24th International Conference on Advanced Communication Technology (ICACT)* (pp. 256–261). https://doi.org/10.23919/ICACT53585.2022.9728808

Park, S. M., & Kim, Y. G. (2022). A metaverse: Taxonomy, components, applications, and open challenges. *IEEE Access, 10,* 4209–4251. https://doi.org/10.1109/ACCESS.2021.3140175

Ritterbusch, G. D., & Teichmann, M. R. (2023). Defining the metaverse: A systematic literature review. *IEEE Access, 11,* 12368–12377. https://doi.org/10.1109/ACCESS.2023.3241809

Spais, G., Jain, V., Dwivedi, Y. K., Viglia, G., & Carlson, J. (2024). A new walk in the future of the metaverse: Marketing implications for consumer behavior. *Journal of Consumer Behaviour, 24*(2), 1–6. https://doi.org/10.1002/cb.2446

Suanpang, P., Niamsorn, C., Pothipassa, P., Chunhapataragul, T., Netwong, T., & Jermsittiparsert, K. (2022). Extensible metaverse implication for a smart tourism city. *Sustainability, 14*(21), 14027. https://doi.org/10.3390/su142114027

van Leeuwen, J. P., Hermans, K., Jylhä, A., Quanjer, A. J., & Nijman, H. (2018). Effectiveness of virtual reality in participatory urban planning: A case study. *Proceedings of the 4th Media Architecture Biennale Conference,* 128–136. https://doi.org/10.1145/3284389.3284491

Verma, A. (2024). Application of metaverse technologies and artificial intelligence in smart cities. *The Scientific Temper, 15*(02), 2410–2415. https://doi.org/10.58414/scientifictemper.2024.15.2.60

Wang, H., Ning, H., Lin, Y., Wang, W., Dhelim, S., Farha, F., & Daneshmand, M. (2023). A survey on the metaverse: The state-of-the-art, technologies, applications, and challenges. *IEEE Internet of Things Journal, 10*(16), 14671–14688. https://doi.org/10.1109/JIOT.2023.3278329

Wu, D., Zheng, A., Yu, W., Cao, H., Ling, Q., Liu, J., & Zhou, D. (2025). Digital twin technology in transportation infrastructure: A comprehensive survey of current applications, challenges, and future directions. *Applied Sciences, 15*(4). https://doi.org/10.3390/app15041911

Yaqoob, I., Salah, K., Jayaraman, R., & Omar, M. (2023). Metaverse applications in smart cities: Enabling technologies, opportunities, challenges, and future directions. *Internet of Things, 23,* 100884. https://doi.org/10.1016/j.iot.2023.100884

Zainab, H., & Bawanay, N. Z. (2023, December). Digital Twin, Metaverse and Smart Cities in a Race to the Future. In *2023 24th International Arab Conference on Information Technology (ACIT)* (pp. 1–8). IEEE. https://doi.org/10.1109/ACIT58888.2023.10453803

9

Metaverse for Sustaining City Historic Places

Husniza Husni, Mohd Zhafri Mohd Zukhi,
and Mhd. Zulfansyuri Siambaton

9.1 The Role of Metaverse in Heritage Conservation

Historic places, where history and culture are 'preserved' in old buildings or ancient monuments, hold invaluable values and even mysteries of the past. These places will be lost, forgotten, and damaged over time if not preserved. This is especially true in cities where rapid urbanisation threatens their existence in modern society. Preserving these valuable treasures to thrive and stand tall in the modern world requires meticulous effort and would be costly. With modern technology, the effort to preserve such historic places rests in the hands of digital platforms such as the metaverse. Metaverse can be defined as an immersive virtual ecosystem that seamlessly integrates the physical and digital worlds (Lee et al., 2021). This fusion is enabled by the convergence of the Internet, the web, and extended reality (XR) technologies, including mixed reality (MR), augmented reality (AR), and virtual reality (VR). The metaverse concept has gained unprecedented prominence, particularly following Facebook's rebranding as Meta. As highlighted by CEO Mark Zuckerberg, the metaverse is envisioned as the next evolution of the Internet, surpassing existing social platforms in its scope and impact (Laeeq, 2022).

This transformation has placed the metaverse at the forefront of technological discourse, with major corporations like Microsoft, led by CEO Satya Nadella, emphasising its potential to revolutionise how we perceive reality and actively engage with it. Additionally, companies such as NVIDIA have responded to the rapid advancements in metaverse research and development by creating their virtual ecosystem, Omniverse. The increasing global focus on the metaverse is evident in the significant investments and research efforts undertaken across industries and academic institutions, further accelerating innovation in this domain (Zhang et al., 2022).

More often than not, historic places, be they monuments and buildings or historic sites, reside far off the cities. The historic locations are often based on the ancient population and culture that surround those places. As the world's population grows, the urbanisation process is unavoidable and almost comes 'naturally' as the socio-economic progressively changes to the point where it reaches the historic ground. Some old buildings and monuments stand still in time, surrounded by urban cities such as the famous Champs-Élysées in Paris and the Colosseum in Rome, as depicted in Figure 9.1. These historic monuments or old buildings are examples of complete historic buildings where the structures are still very much intact, most often representing the grandeur of the ancient worlds and the achievements made by our ancestors. These two stand at the heart of the urbanisation in big cities such as Paris and Rome.

There are also historic places within development areas, where the place is not yet a big city but still serves as a prominent city for the locals to do their business. These places can potentially become big, important cities due to the economic growth they currently serve. For such places, the old buildings or historic sites are usually located nearby, where the process of urbanisation is still ongoing and could be affected if actions are not taken to protect and secure their long, rich histories.

9.1.1 The Significance of Historic Places

In preserving history, historic places are crucial as they represent the rich history and the secrets of the ancient worlds. Historic places hold cultural, architectural, archaeological, or social significance, often serving as physical representations of a city's past. Historic places include monuments, buildings, archaeological ruins, religious sites, and districts that reflect a place or population's historical identity, culture, religion, and evolution. Their significance is derived from their age and contribution to historical narratives, social memory, and urban identity. Historical narratives and culture are somewhat intertwined within the historic places. Old buildings, architecture, and ancient monuments are tangible artefacts that stand the test of time. Culturally, historic places act as tangible links to heritage, providing insights into past societies, traditions, and architectural advancements. They serve as living museums, preserving past civilisations' aesthetic and structural ingenuity. Architecturally, they showcase different eras' design philosophies, materials, and construction techniques, illuminating historical periods' technological capabilities and artistic expressions.

Unfortunately, not all survive. Most ancient buildings or monuments are ruined due to many contributing factors, such as weather, natural disasters, artificial mistakes, ignorance, and negligence. Thus, historical preservation activities must be taken seriously to sustain historic places and their weight and value to modern civilisation. One of the potential and most promising approaches is via digitalisation. Safeguarding and preserving the historic places in digital forms bridges the two worlds together – the past and the present – and perhaps carries on the legacy to the future. Nonetheless, there are always hurdles and challenges in such great effort.

FIGURE 9.1
Examples of historic monuments. (a) Champs-Élysées, Paris. (b) The Colosseum, Rome. (Photos From https://www.pexels.com – free licence.)

9.1.2 Challenges in Preservation and Engagement

Despite their significance, historic places in cities or elsewhere face numerous challenges in preservation efforts and public engagement. Urbanisation, environmental factors, and socio-economic changes threaten the integrity and sustainability of these history-rich places. Addressing these challenges would be arduous and thus requires a multifaceted approach that we hope can balance conservation, modernisation, and community involvement.

One of the primary challenges is rapid urbanisation, which has been seen prioritising economic growth and infrastructure expansion over heritage conservation. The demand for land in growing cities leads to the encroachment, alteration, or even demolition of historic sites, just like what had happened to one of the oldest Bujang Valley temples, Kedah, Malaysia, dated back to 500 BCE (Aaltonen, 2017), to make way for new developments. The event that took place in 2013 received major backlash from all over the world, especially from historic conservation communities (The Star, 2013). Without proper urban planning policies, historical structures risk being overshadowed or integrated into modern cityscapes in ways that compromise their authenticity or, worse, are completely demolished in the name of urbanisation and economic growth. Environmental factors such as pollution, climate change, and natural disasters also threaten historic sites significantly. Rising temperatures, heavy rainfall, and humidity contribute to material decay, while air pollution accelerates corrosion and structural weakening, causing damage to the structure and ruins of the sites, just like the temples in Bujang Valley and the Maimun Palace in Medan, Indonesia, the two cases discussed in this chapter. Another challenge is coastal heritage, where the sites face additional risks from rising sea levels and erosion, necessitating urgent conservation measures and sustainable adaptation strategies.

Heritage conservation requires substantial financial investment. Many cities or countries struggle with limited funding and competing budgetary priorities over other essential matters. Restoration projects, maintenance work, and adaptive reuse initiatives often depend on government support, grants, or private donations that are now very challenging and competitive. The challenge lies in creating sustainable funding models that balance preservation efforts with economic viability in this situation. Public awareness and community engagement are essential for the preservation of historic places. However, in many cases, local communities and city residents may not fully recognise the value of their heritage, leading to neglect or inadequate conservation efforts. Educational initiatives, storytelling, and interactive programmes are needed to foster a sense of ownership and appreciation among citizens.

Addressing these challenges requires strong collaboration among policymakers, conservationists, urban planners, local authorities, and communities. In the digital era, leveraging technology for heritage conservation presents opportunities and challenges. While digital documentation and virtual reconstructions can aid in preserving and promoting historic places, the lack of technical expertise, funding, and infrastructure hinders widespread adoption. Many historic sites remain undocumented in digital formats, making them vulnerable to loss in unforeseen disasters or neglect. However, by integrating innovative technologies, sustainable funding models, and inclusive engagement strategies, cities can ensure their historic places' longevity and continued relevance in the modern world.

As the metaverse continues to evolve and expand, it presents a groundbreaking opportunity to reimagine and digitally revive ancient structures that have long been lost. Historical landmarks such as the Pyramids of Egypt, Angkor Wat, and the Bujang Valley Temple are enduring testaments to past civilisations' architectural brilliance and cultural heritage. However, natural decay, environmental factors, and human activities have led to the deterioration of many of these sites, leaving behind only fragments of their former grandeur. Through advanced technologies such as VR, AR, and 3D reconstruction, the metaverse enables the meticulous recreation of these historic wonders in a digital realm. This preserves their architectural essence and allows people from around the world to explore and experience them as they once stood, unrestricted by physical or geographical barriers. Visitors can immerse themselves in interactive environments, walking through reconstructed temples, admiring intricate carvings, and gaining insights into the daily lives of the civilisations that built them.

Beyond mere preservation, integrating historic sites into the metaverse fosters deeper engagement and education. Digital reconstructions give historians, archaeologists, and educators powerful tools to analyse and interpret these structures more effectively. Interactive storytelling, virtual guided tours, and immersive educational experiences make history more accessible and captivating for future generations, ensuring that the legacy of these ancient marvels endures in the digital age. By leveraging the metaverse, we are safeguarding history and redefining how we connect with our past. This innovative approach bridges the gap between ancient and modern, allowing us to appreciate the ingenuity of our ancestors in unprecedented ways while paving the way for new advancements in heritage conservation and cultural appreciation.

9.1.3 Digital Twins and Digital Reconstructions

Integrating digital reconstruction and preservation with archaeological restoration transforms how cultural heritage is studied, preserved, and communicated. Digital image processing and 3D scanning technologies enable researchers to document, analyse, and reconstruct fragile or damaged artefacts without physically altering them (Nencini & Maino, 2011). Addressing a growing niche within architectural preservation by applying metaverse frameworks, VR/AR models, and digital twin technologies in heritage conservation is vital. While traditional methods of documentation and restoration remain invaluable, they are often limited by their static nature and inability to engage diverse audiences effectively. Digital twins, dynamic virtual replicas of physical entities, offer unprecedented opportunities for real-time monitoring, preventive maintenance, and interactive exploration of historical sites (Cruz Franco et al., 2022). For example, projects like VERBuM demonstrate how digital twins integrated with VR can facilitate continuous information exchange in heritage management workflows (Bruno et al., 2022). Similarly, VR and AR technologies enhance visualisation and decision-making processes, enabling users to immerse themselves in reconstructed environments and gain deeper insights into historical narratives (Bevilacqua et al., 2022).

These digital techniques improve the readability of ancient objects and offer a sustainable method for loss compensation through virtual restoration and additive manufacturing (Acke et al., 2024). Furthermore, the digitisation of archaeological sites and artefacts has created high-resolution digital archives, which serve as valuable research tools while providing interactive experiences through virtual reconstructions (Calisi & Botta, 2022). By leveraging digital preservation technologies, archaeologists can ensure that historical artefacts and structures remain accessible to scholars and the public, even in cases where physical preservation is challenging.

9.2 Integration of Digital Reconstruction and Preservation, Interactive Media, and Interactive Storytelling

Integrating digital reconstruction and preservation, interactive media, and interactive storytelling has significantly transformed how cultural heritage is safeguarded and presented in digital environments. Digital reconstruction enables the recreation of historical artefacts and sites, ensuring their preservation for future generations. When combined with interactive media, these reconstructions become more engaging, allowing users to explore virtual cultural heritage sites in an immersive manner (Okanovic et al., 2022). Interactive digital storytelling (IDS) enhances this experience by incorporating narrative elements into reconstructed environments, providing historical context, emotional engagement, and educational value (Rizvic et al., 2020). Through IDS, digital heritage is preserved and revitalised by making historical narratives interactive and participatory rather than static.

One of the key challenges in interactive storytelling for digital preservation lies in adapting traditional storytelling methods to VR/AR environments. Classical storytelling follows a linear structure, whereas digital heritage reconstructions require nonlinear, dynamic narratives that respond to user interactions (Rizvic et al., 2017). Effective IDS requires a multidisciplinary approach that integrates computer science, literature, psychology, and visual arts to create compelling, educational, and emotionally engaging experiences (Abdulhusain et al., 2022).

Another challenge is maintaining historical accuracy while incorporating modern storytelling techniques that appeal to contemporary audiences. By addressing these challenges, IDS bridges the gap between historical preservation and modern digital engagement, making cultural heritage more accessible and meaningful. The potential of interactive storytelling in cultural heritage conservation extends beyond engagement to long-term preservation strategies. By embedding multi-layered narratives within digital reconstructions, IDS allows for representing diverse cultural perspectives and interpretations (Yu, 2024). Additionally, IDS fosters community participation, enabling different stakeholders – such as historians, artists, and the general public – to contribute to digital heritage narratives, ensuring a more inclusive and representative preservation process (Okanovic et al., 2022). Moreover, using artificial intelligence (AI) and machine learning in IDS can enhance personalised storytelling, adapting narratives in real-time based on user preferences and interactions (Yu, 2024). As technology advances, IDS continues to evolve, offering innovative ways to preserve, educate, and immerse audiences in the rich histories of cultural heritage sites.

9.3 Technologies Enabling the Metaverse of Historic Places

Advanced technologies empower historic sites' reconstruction and immersive experience within the metaverse. One such technology is VR. VR has emerged as a powerful tool that enables individuals to engage in diverse digital experiences. However, its role within the broader framework of the metaverse requires further exploration. VR represents just one dimension of the metaverse, a vast ecosystem of technologies designed to replicate, augment, or reimagine real-world experiences. Among these, VR is the most immersive, offering unparalleled opportunities to digitally reconstruct and preserve historical sites lost or damaged over time.

VR is a key component of the metaverse and its application in heritage conservation, demonstrating how users can interact with digital recreations of historically significant yet now-destroyed buildings. While historical preservation and virtual environments may seem unrelated at first glance, their convergence has profound implications for urban planning and cultural heritage management. Traditional historical structures are inherently static, bound by time and physical decay. In contrast, VR offers a dynamic and flexible medium capable of accurately recreating architectural spaces in their prime, allowing for immersive exploration and interaction.

By leveraging VR, researchers, historians, and architects can accurately reconstruct past architectural marvels, providing realistic and interactive experiences that deepen our understanding of their historical significance. Users can navigate through these virtual spaces, comparing past and present historical site states, thereby gaining valuable insights into cultural and structural evolution. As discussions surrounding VR continue to gain momentum and technological advancements push its boundaries further, it has firmly established itself as a cornerstone in historic preservation and architectural visualisation (Chehab & Nakhal, 2023).

9.4 Case Studies of Historic Places

9.4.1 Bujang Valley, Kedah, Malaysia

In this chapter, the Bujang Valley is used as the case to explore how metaverse could be leveraged to 'reimagine' the Bujang Valley temples or, popularly known as 'candi' by the locals. Situated in a sprawling area of 224 square meters in Bujang Valley, near the city of Merbok, Kedah, Malaysia, the historical complex consists of fifty 'candi' or temple sites, with most of the temples now ruined or incomplete (Lembah Bujang, 2024). Bujang Valley is Southeast Asia's oldest civilisation (Mahmud, 2023) under Kedah Tua, which roamed the Malay Peninsula in ancient times. The temple complex was endorsed by UNESCO in 1987, and Malaysia is still nominating Bujang Valley to be listed on the UNESCO World Heritage List in 2013. Figure 9.2 depicts some of the 'candi' sites, with some sites still intact.

This part of ancient civilisation dates back to 500 BCE, 300 years before the Great Wall of China began (Aaltonen, 2017). Hence, many structures were ruined, and only the sites were visibly intact and formed. Hence, it is interesting to explore how the metaverse can be used to reimagine how the temples look like. Based on the remains on the sites, the structure could be similar to Angkor Wat in Thailand (built in 1150, 1650 years after Bujang Valley) and Borobudur in Indonesia (built 800 CE, 1300 years after Bujang Valley). It is worth mentioning that both were Buddhist temples, whereas the candi's etymology suggests influence from both Buddhist and Hindu, where Hinduism was known as the main religion of that region in the era. Hence, the architecture of the candi could be similar to ancient Hindu temples such as the Shore Temple in India, which dated back around the year of the Bujang Valley temples.

For Bujang Valley, the initial effort includes exploring the potential of the metaverse as a platform for the reimagination of ancient structures, in this case, the incomplete candi. By leveraging cutting-edge technologies such as VR, AR, AI, and 3D modelling, this work aims to reconstruct these monuments digitally with unprecedented accuracy and detail. When working

FIGURE 9.2
One of the Candi with some good basic structure at Bujang Valley.

with historical, ancient monuments with little references on many aspects of their entire existence, the two measures, accuracy and detail, become the real deal. The effort of digital preservation of historic temples demands accuracy, but for now, the challenge lies in the fundamental aspects of the reconstruction. What are the fundamentals of cultural heritage for its construction in the metaverse? What are the methodologies to integrate linguistic data and sociohistorical narratives into digital reconstructions of cultural heritage sites? How can we ensure the reconstruction of the temples is valid since cultural and architectural references are from much 'younger' temples, separated by probably a thousand years?

Of course, one could reconstruct it based on other existing temples that are still intact with complete structure, but would that truly show and preserve the ancient world that we are trying to uncover its thousands of years of history? By combining historical research with immersive virtual experiences, this work seeks to bridge the gap between past and present, offering a glimpse into the lives of our ancestors while showcasing the limitless potential of the metaverse as a tool for education, exploration, and cultural preservation. Through collaboration with archaeologists and technologists, we hope to unlock new insights and inspire future generations to explore the wonders of our shared human heritage. We have estimated that there shall be a religious, cultural, and socio-economic influence on reimagining the complete structure of the 'candi'.

Such work is indispensable, as the fundamentals of designing and developing ancient structures in the metaverse hold significant implications for museums, practitioners, and visitors alike. For museums, the goal is preservation and education, especially for the younger generations to appreciate history and how it shaped the modern world we are living in. As the custodians of cultural heritage, having a framework for designing and developing ancient structures in the metaverse allows museums to preserve and present historical artefacts and structures in innovative, interactive ways, alluring more young hearts to dive into history and culture and learn more. This effort enhances their educational mission by providing immersive experiences that engage and educate visitors. By leveraging the metaverse, museums can extend their reach beyond physical boundaries. They can engage with a global audience, reaching individuals who may not have the opportunity to visit the physical museum. It has the potential to broaden its impact and promote cultural exchange on a global scale with innovative, engaging, and interactive or perhaps collaborative digital platforms. The framework enables museums to create innovative exhibitions that blend historical accuracy with interactive elements. Such effort fosters visitor engagement and encourages exploration and learning in a dynamic virtual environment.

As for practitioners, for example, architects, designers, and developers, the work allows them to embark on a creative exploration where the framework provides the fundamentals they need, such as guidelines and methodologies, for creatively exploring ancient architecture in the metaverse with full ethics and responsibility. It encourages ethical experimentation and innovation in virtual design and development, pushing the boundaries of what is possible in digital representation. Designing and developing ancient structures in the metaverse often requires interdisciplinary collaboration between historians, archaeologists, architects, and digital artists. The framework facilitates this collaboration by offering a structured approach integrating expertise from various fields. Professional development is another opportunity for practitioners involved in such digital preservation projects to continue to grow and develop within emerging technologies and digital cultural heritage. They can acquire new skills and expertise that are increasingly valuable in the digital age.

Museum visitors are one of the main targets for the preservation and education of historic buildings. Visitors could benefit from immersive learning experiences that transport them to ancient civilisations, allowing them to explore historical structures in detail and thus appreciate history more. The framework facilitates the creation of interactive simulations and virtual tours that enhance understanding and appreciation of cultural heritage. With the metaverse, access and inclusivity are ensured. The metaverse provides accessible platforms for individuals with disabilities and those unable to visit physical museum spaces. The framework ensures that virtual experiences are designed inclusively, enabling a wider range of people to engage with cultural heritage. Virtual representations of ancient structures in the meta-verse can foster community engagement and collaboration. Users can participate in discussions, contribute knowledge, and share their experiences, creating a vibrant online community centred around cultural heritage.

9.4.2 Maimun Palace, Medan, Indonesia

Being the last-standing, surviving Malay palace in Indonesia, the Maimun Palace sits in the heart of the busy city of Medan. Surrounded by the hustles and bustles of the fourth busiest city in Indonesia, Maimun Palace is indeed a prominent landmark in Medan, the capital city of North Sumatra. Figure 9.3 depicts the surviving Maimun Palace. As if standing strong to narrate the history of hundreds of years of the Deli Sultanate, the palace is now a museum welcoming many visitors, especially tourists, to enjoy its splendour. Its unique interior design originates from a combination of elements of the Deli Malay with Islamic, Spanish, Indian, Dutch, and Italian styles (Sutanto, 2015). Built on August 26, 1888, the palace is 2,772 square metres with 30 rooms. The two-storey palace has three parts – the main building, the left-wing building, and the right-wing building. This palace is currently located opposite the Al-Mashun Mosque, popularly known as the Medan Grand Mosque.

FIGURE 9.3
The Maimun palace, Medan, Indonesia.

With the unique architecture that boasts many cultural influences, the old Maimun Palace faces many challenges of its own. Over the decades, the palace has suffered from structural deterioration due to various environmental factors, such as the tropical climate of Medan with high humidity and substantial rainfall that accelerates the decay of the palace's building material (Sutanto, 2015). With the deteriorating structure, the need to preserve and maintain the palace becomes more and more critical. The responsibility mainly falls on the heirs of the Deli Sultanate, who often struggle with limited funding, where the revenue is mainly generated from tourism and cultural events. This financial shortfall limits the preservation efforts to the decaying grandeur of the palace and arguably causes some irreversible damage to its historical structure soon (Khadry, 2023).

As the capital of North Sumatra, Medan's rapid urbanisation also challenges the Maimun Palace. The modern infrastructure and developments being done in the city threaten the palace's historical landscape (Triratmoko, 2016). Finding the balance between the city's growth and preserving its cultural heritage requires meticulous urban planning that safeguards its historical sites while undergoing rapid development and modernisation. Nonetheless, some of the heritage, such as historical landmarks, are being overshadowed or compromised by modern construction due to the lack of strict policies on heritage conservation (Sutanto, 2015).

Efforts of digitisation at the palace are ongoing, for example, using AR to capture and narrate, more interactively with visitors, the story and history behind some of the prominent artefacts at the palace (Radio Televisyen Malaysia, 2024). In this case, AR technology is preferable, as it is 'visitor-ready', meaning everybody can easily engage with their mobile phones and access the information without relying on other cutting-edge devices. Visitors' engagement and experience with the static artefacts at the palace can be increased and deepen their understanding and appreciation of each artefact's story (Aziz et al., 2024). More advanced technology can be integrated into the palace to attract visitors and create tourism hype, such as using VR or MR. However, such digitisation works require a significant amount of funding that the palace's management has to consider – either to invest in digitisation efforts to attract more visitors or to invest in preserving the palace's deteriorating structure, which has become increasingly apparent over the years.

What can be done to address these challenges involves a multifaceted approach. Collaborative efforts between government bodies, heritage conservation organisations, and the local community are essential. Campaigns to increase public awareness can highlight the palace's historical significance and encourage more community involvement in preservation activities (Khadry, 2023). Private and governmental funding is crucial to maintaining historical sites like Istana Maimun (Triratmoko, 2016). Hence, academicians, alongside industry partners, can be involved in securing funding through grants and partnerships, and tourism can provide the financial support needed for sustainable conservation works. A concerted effort combining structural preservation, financial investment, urban planning, and cultural engagement can ensure this historic palace's endures for future generations. As heritage sites across Indonesia struggle with similar concerns, Istana Maimun's case is a crucial example of the urgent need for sustainable conservation strategies.

9.5 Future Direction and Opportunities

As the preservation of historic sites faces mounting challenges due to urbanisation and resource constraints, the metaverse offers a promising platform for innovation through AI-driven historical reconstruction. By harnessing AI, researchers can unlock new dimensions of accuracy, accessibility, and engagement in preserving cultural heritage, paving the way for transformative opportunities in the field.

9.5.1 The Potential of AI-Driven Historical Reconstructions

Integrating AI into the preservation and reconstruction of historic city places within the metaverse represents a transformative opportunity to sustain cultural heritage in an era of rapid urbanisation. By leveraging AI-driven tools, researchers and practitioners can address challenges related to preservation, accessibility, and public engagement, ensuring that these invaluable sites remain relevant and accessible for future generations.

AI technologies are revolutionising the preservation of cultural heritage by enabling precise and efficient restorations without risking damage to original artefacts. For instance, 3D reconstruction algorithms and deep learning models have demonstrated remarkable potential in restoring damaged or partially destroyed historical structures, as evidenced in the case of Petra's restoration using AI-based techniques (Goussous, 2020). Similarly, AI-driven tools can automate the digitisation and predictive management of historical records, ensuring their long-term preservation and accessibility in the digital age (Ailakhu, 2024). These advancements enhance the accuracy of reconstructions and reduce the costs and resources traditionally associated with manual preservation efforts.

9.5.2 Immersive and Interactive Experiences

The convergence of AI with XR technologies, such as VR/AR and MR, offers exciting new opportunities to create immersive and interactive experiences. These technologies enable users to explore historical sites and artefacts in detail, fostering deeper engagement and understanding. For example, AI-powered platforms can generate personalised content tailored to individual preferences, enhancing the visitor experience in cultural heritage tourism (Lin, 2024). Additionally, AI-driven simulations and virtual tours provide dynamic educational experiences, making history more tangible and inclusive for diverse audiences (Harisanty et al., 2024; Kasprowicz, 2024). Such innovations align with the broader goals of the metaverse to bridge the gap between physical and digital worlds, offering new ways to interact with and appreciate cultural heritage.

9.5.3 Extended Reality and Advanced AI Algorithms

Looking ahead, the future of AI-driven historical reconstructions lies in the seamless integration of XR technologies. These tools can be used for virtual restoration, preservation, and the creation of realistic 3D environments that allow users to explore historical sites in unprecedented detail (Mohan & Kim, 2023). Furthermore, advancements in AI algorithms, such as neural radiance fields (NeRF) and generative AI, will further enhance the accuracy and realism of 3D reconstructions (Zhou et al., 2024). For instance, semi-automatic Scan-to-BIM reconstruction approaches offer innovative ways to interpret and process digital architectural heritage data, making the reconstruction process more efficient and less subjective (Croce et al., 2023). These developments underscore the potential of AI to transform historical preservation into a more scalable and precise discipline.

9.5.4 Ethical and Methodological Considerations

As AI technologies become more prevalent in historical reconstructions, it is imperative to address ethical and methodological considerations. Data privacy, ownership, and the integrity of historical records must be carefully managed to ensure the responsible use of AI (Ailakhu, 2024; Gattiglia, 2025). Researchers and practitioners must take a thoughtful and careful approach to ensure that AI tools do not reinforce biases or introduce inaccuracies when presenting historical narratives (Berson & Berson, 2024; Gattiglia, 2025). Collaborations between technologists, historians, archaeologists, and local communities are essential to balance innovation and authenticity, ensuring that digital renditions respect cultural sensitivities and accurately reflect indigenous knowledge systems.

   AI-driven historical reconstructions present numerous opportunities for enhancing the preservation, accessibility, and engagement with cultural heritage within the metaverse. By leveraging advanced AI technologies and interdisciplinary collaboration, the field can continue to evolve, offering innovative solutions for historical preservation and education challenges. However, addressing ethical and methodological challenges remains crucial to ensure AI's responsible and accurate use in sustaining the city's historic places. As the metaverse redefines how we interact with history, AI-driven tools play a pivotal role in preserving humanity's shared legacy for future generations.

Preserving historic places is crucial to protect, maintain, and sustain the cultural identity, heritage, architecture, and historical narratives for future generations. Rapid urbanisation and modernisation have reshaped a city's landscapes and historic sites as the world progresses and develops, introducing threats and destruction to the ancient heritage we should conserve and preserve. The threats include neglect, destruction, deterioration, and diminishing public interest, as has happened in one of the oldest candi in Bujang Valley, which was demolished for development, and Maimun Palace, which struggles with structural deterioration and financial constraints. These two are among the many cases highlighting the pressing needs and urgency for sustainable strategies, ensuring the historic sites are protected as part of urban development and modernisation.

Metaverse can be one of the options for sustaining historic places and sites, be it in the city or rural areas. Metaverse emerges as a promising digital solution for such preservation by leveraging technologies such as AR, VR, MR, AI, and digital twin, where such technologies provide immersive, interactive, and accessible experiences for visitors. While the technology facilitates the digital reconstruction of the heritage sites' lost, incomplete or deteriorating structure, it could also play an important role in educating and enhancing tourism and public engagement. Despite the potential, the integration of technologies requires substantial funding and stronger government policies that call upon collaboration from various stakeholders. Ethical considerations must also be considered to ensure historical accuracy, cultural sensitivity, and inclusivity of the historical narratives. By embracing digital innovation while upholding the integrity of historical sites, cities can create a harmonious balance between cultural heritage and modern development, ensuring that the rich legacies of the past remain accessible and relevant in the digital age.

Acknowledgement

This work was supported by the International Matching Grant between Universiti Utara Malaysia and Universitas Sumatera Utara, 2024–2025, and the Ministry of Higher Education under the Fundamental Research Grant Scheme (FRGS-EC) FRGS-EC/1/2024/ICT09/UITM/02/3.

References

Aaltonen, G. (2017). *Archaeology: Discovering the world's secret.* Arcturus Publishing Limited.

Abdulhusain, Z., Qaed, F., & Aljawder, H. (2022). Digital storytelling in museums to revive Islamic heritage in the digital museum: A design proposal. *WIT Transactions on the Built Environment, 211*, 51–60.

Acke, L., Corradi, D., & Verlinden, J. (2024). Comprehensive educational framework on the application of 3D technologies for the restoration of cultural heritage objects. *Journal of Cultural Heritage, 66,* 613–627. https://doi.org/10.1016/j.culher.2024.01.013

Ailakhu, U. V. (2024). Digital preservation strategies for historical records in the age of AI and the metaverse. *Library Hi Tech News.* https://doi.org/10.1108/LHTN-10-2024-0175

Aziz, F. A., Husni, H., Nordin, N., Suhairy, M. S., Siambaton, M. Z., & Ahmad, J. (2024). Augmented reality and short videos: Transforming museum experience for visitors. *Asian Journal of Applied Communication, 13*(2), 87–92. https://doi.org/10.47836/ajac.13.02.04

Berson, I. R., & Berson, M. J. (2024). AI in K-12 social studies education: A critical examination of ethical and practical challenges. *Communications in Computer and Information Science, 2150,* 101–112. https://doi.org/10.1007/978-3-031-64315-6_8

Bevilacqua, M. G., Russo, M., Giordano, A., & Spallone, R. (2022). 3D reconstruction, digital twinning, and virtual reality: Architectural heritage applications. *Proceedings – 2022 IEEE Conference on Virtual Reality and 3D User Interfaces Abstracts and Workshops, VRW 2022.* https://doi.org/10.1109/VRW55335.2022.00031

Bruno, S., Scioti, A., Pierucci, A., & Fatiguso, F. (2022). Verbum – virtual enhanced reality for building modelling (virtual technical tour in digital twins for building conservation). *Journal of Information Technology in Construction, 27,* 1–18. https://doi.org/10.36680/j.itcon.2022.001

Calisi, D., & Botta, S. (2022). Virtual reality and captured reality for cultural landscape communication. *International Archives of the Photogrammetry, Remote Sensing and Spatial Information Sciences – ISPRS Archives, XLVI-2/W1,* 113–120. https://doi.org/10.5194/isprs-archives-XLVI-2-W1-2022-113-2022

Chehab, A., & Nakhal, B. (2023). Exploring virtual reality as an approach to resurrect destroyed historical buildings – An approach to revive the destroyed "Egg building" through VR. *Architecture and Planning Journal (APJ), 28*(3). https://doi.org/10.54729/2789-8547.1212

Croce, V., Caroti, G., Piemonte, A., De Luca, L., & Véron, P. (2023). H-BIM and artificial intelligence: Classification of architectural heritage for semi-automatic scan-to-BIM reconstruction. *Sensors, 23*(5), Article 2497. https://doi.org/10.3390/s23052497

Cruz Franco, P., Rueda Márquez de la Plata, A., & Gómez Bernal, A. (2022). Protocols for the graphic and constructive diffusion of digital twins of the architectural heritage that guarantee universal accessibility through AR and VR. *Applied Sciences (Switzerland), 12*(18), 9165. https://doi.org/10.3390/app12178785

Gattiglia, G. (2025). Managing artificial intelligence in archeology: An overview. *Journal of Cultural Heritage, 71,* 225–233. https://doi.org/10.1016/j.culher.2024.11.020

Goussous, J. S. (2020). Artificial intelligence-based restoration: The case of Petra. *Civil Engineering and Architecture, 8*(6), 1350–1358. https://doi.org/10.13189/cea.2020.080618

Harisanty, D., Obille, K. L. B., Anna, N. E. V., Purwanti, E., & Retrialisca, F. (2024). Cultural heritage preservation in the digital age, harnessing artificial intelligence for the future: A bibliometric analysis. *Digital Library Perspectives, 40*(4), 609–630. https://doi.org/10.1108/DLP-01-2024-0018

Kasprowicz, K. (2024). Methodology of history in the era of technological break-throughs of the 21st century [Metodologia historii w dobie przełomów technologicznych XXI wieku]. *Historyka. Studies in Historical Methods, 54*, 329–348. https://doi.org/10.24425/hsm.2024.153710

Khadry, M. (2023). Keberlanjutan dalam pengelolaan Istana Maimun: Menjaga warisan budaya Indonesia. Kompasiana.

Laeeq, K. (2022, February). *Metaverse : Why, how and what.*

Lee, L.-H., Braud, T., Zhou, P., Wang, L., Xu, D., Lin, Z., & Hui, P. (2021). All one needs to know about metaverse: A complete survey on technological singularity, virtual ecosystem, and research agenda. *Journal of Latex Class Files, 14*, 1–66. https://doi.org/10.13140/RG.2.2.11200.05124/8

Lembah Bujang. (2024). Arkib Negara Malaysia. https://pustakailmu.arkib.gov.my/index.php/ms/pustaka-ilmu/mercu-tanda/lembah-bujang

Lin, Y. (2024). Immersive experience design and simulation of Dongguan Nanshe ancient village based on machine learning artificial intelligence technology. In *ACM International Conference Proceeding Series* (pp. 122–127). https://doi.org/10.1145/3671151.3671174

Mahmud, A. H. (2023, July 2). Kedah has Southeast Asia's oldest civilisation and archaeologists barely know its complete history. https://www.channelnewsasia.com/asia/malaysia-kedah-oldest-civilisation-bujang-valley-archeology-history-3589106

Mohan, P., & Kim, J. (2023). From reconstruction to generation: State-of-art approaches for 3D visualisation. *Proceedings – SIGGRAPH Asia 2023 Courses, SA 2023*, Article 8. https://doi.org/10.1145/3610538.3614647

Nencini, E., & Maino, G. (2011). From the physical restoration for preserving to the virtual restoration for enhancing. In *Proceedings of the 16th International Conference on Image Analysis and Processing (ICIAP 2011), Ravenna, Italy, September 14–16, 2011, Part I 16* (pp. 700–709). Springer Berlin Heidelberg. https://doi.org/10.1007/978-3-642-24085-0_71

Okanovic, V., Ivkovic-Kihic, I., Boskovic, D., Mijatovic, B., Prazina, I., Skaljo, E., & Rizvic, S. (2022). Interaction in eXtended reality applications for cultural heritage. *Applied Sciences, 12*(3), 1241. https://doi.org/10.3390/app12031241

Radio Televisyen Malaysia. (2024, August 15). AR development for visitors to explore the attractions of Istana Maimun in Medan. RTM Berita. https://berita.rtm.gov.my/highlights/senarai-berita-highlights/senarai-artikel/ar-development-for-visitors-to-explore-the-attractions-of-istana-maimun-in-medan

Rizvic, S., Djapo, N., Alispahic, F., Hadzihalilovic, B., Cengic, F. F., Imamovic, A., Okanovic, V., & Boskovic, D. (2017). Guidelines for interactive digital storytelling presentations of cultural heritage. In *2017 9th International Conference on Virtual Worlds and Games for Serious Applications* (VS-Games) (pp. 253–259). IEEE. https://10.1109/VS-GAMES.2017.8056610

Rizvic, S., Okanovic, V., & Boskovic, D. (2020). Digital storytelling. In F. Liarokapis, A. Voulodimos, N. Doulamis, A. Doulamis (Eds.), *Visual computing for cultural heritage* (pp. 347–367). Springer. https://doi.org/10.1007/978-3-030-37191-3_18

Sutanto, S. (2015). *Kajian Konservasi Bangunan Bersejarah di Medan (Studi Kasus: Stana Maimun).* [Doctoral Dissertation] Universitas Sumatera Utara.

The Star. (2013, December 10). Candi Lembah Bujang: Destroying history. https://www.thestar.com.my/News/Nation/2013/12/10/Candi-Lembah-Bujang-destroying-history/

Triratmoko, D. (2016). Konservasi Istana Maimun (Kuliah Umum). Institut Teknologi Bandung.

Yu, M. (2024). Interactive digital narrative in cultural heritage conservation: Concepts, system elements, and improving measures. *Documentation, Information and Knowledge, 41*(5), 65–75. https://doi.org/10.13366/j.dik.2024.05.065

Zhang, X., Yang, D., Yow, C. H., Huang, L., Wu, X., Huang, X., Guo, J., Zhou, S., Cai, Y. (2022). Metaverse for cultural heritages. *Electronics (Switzerland), 11*(22), 3730. https://doi.org/10.3390/electronics11223730

Zhou, Z., Liu, X., & Tang, X. (2024). Charting the landscape of multi-view stereo: An in-depth exploration of deep learning techniques. *Communications in Computer and Information Science, 2099,* 152–165. https://doi.org/10.1007/978-981-97-4387-2_12

10

AI Chatbots and Smart Cities: A Case Study of Intelligent Transportation

Mohammed F. Alrifaie, Adib Habbal, Ziyodulla Yusupov, and Dilshod Kodirov

10.1 Introduction

Intelligent Transportation Systems (ITS) have developed with autonomous and networked vehicle technology advancements. The technologies are up-and-coming in shaping travel and pose new challenges alongside opportunities (Lobato et al., 2020). The advent of electric vehicles (EV) technology and advancements in large language models (LLMs) like ChatGPT make digital experiences more interactive and enhance communication and problem-solving. Research into their application in ITS can also enhance connectivity and autonomy (Chen et al., 2023). Adopting new technologies, such as AI-driven traffic management, predictive data analytics for congestion reduction, and V2X communication for connected vehicles, enhances transportation sustainability, efficiency, and safety (Li et al., 2022). The technologies enable smart decisions, effective traffic management, and alleviating congestion and environmental pollution (Abbas et al., 2022). ITS developments also enhance users' experiences and provide customised services and accessibility. Involving EVs in ITS makes it more sustainable but raises challenges in terms of privacy, security, infrastructure, and acceptability (Habbal & Alrifaie, 2024). Overcoming these challenges boosts ITS innovation and improves daily transportation networks (Cao et al., 2022).

Machine learning, a subset of artificial intelligence (AI), allows machines to learn from experience without direct programming. Powered by increased computing power and vast data, deep learning is a prime prediction tool. Compared with classical machine learning, deep learning utilises advanced artificial neural networks that are high in training data requirements but promote generalisation (Qadir, 2023). Transformers, a specialised category of deep learning models, have revolutionised text processing. Transformers outperform older AI models in classification and generation (Berg & Plessis, 2023). Models like Bidirectional Encoder Representations from Transformers (BERT) and Generative Pre-trained Transformers (GPT) are widely adopted for pre-training on vast language corpora. BERT is a master at understanding context, with application in sentiment analysis, whereas GPT is renowned for its contextually appropriate as well as cohesive text output, making it highly appropriate in terms of translation as well as question answering (Shahriar & Hayawi, 2023).

These models represent a paradigm shift in language processing. As part of the LLMs family, they handle vast amounts of information and are fine-tuned for various applications, from automated customer support to advanced research. Before ChatGPT, chatbots relied on language models, but ChatGPT's success stems from reinforcement learning, where human evaluators rank responses to optimise conversational ability. Built upon GPT-3.5 with 175 billion parameters, ChatGPT leverages extensive architectures and training data for improved coherence (Carlini et al., 2021). These models recognise linguistic patterns and associations, enabling effective text generation and interpretation (Brown et al., 2020).

GPT models are trained by predicting the next token in a sequence, learning grammatical structure and semantics. Prompt engineering guides them in specific tasks, ensuring meaningful responses. However, ethical alignment is essential to prevent harmful outputs. Reinforcement Learning from Human Feedback (RLHF) helps refine responses based on human preferences, steering AI towards ethical and useful outputs (Liu & Chilton, 2022; Zhang et al., 2023). ChatGPT can enhance driver assistance systems by analysing driving behaviour and providing tailored safety advice (Wang, 2022). It can also offer real-time feedback on the vehicle's condition and environment using sensors and multimodal technologies. Furthermore, AI models used in autonomous driving, such as deep learning and reinforcement learning systems, can predict the actions of other cars and pedestrians, optimising driving routes (Alrifaie et al., 2021). It supports autonomous driving models by extracting data for training, which helps improve decision-making in complex situations (Wang et al., 2020). Autonomous vehicle companies benefit from ChatGPT's ability to analyse vast driving data to detect trends. Self-driven vehicles are growing clearly in the markets, with over 20 billion devices connected (Chen, 2020), creating significant computational and storage capacity (Karim et al., 2022). Integrating generative AI models like ChatGPT into ITS can revolutionise traffic management, communication, and navigation, leading to smarter, more user-friendly transportation systems (Desai et al., 2021). Figure 10.1 visualises the LLM for ITS.

However, developing an intelligent chatbot for connected and automated vehicles (CAVs) and ITS presents several challenges. These challenges include the need to ensure the accuracy and reliability of the system, the development of a robust natural language processing system, and the integration of various data sources and APIs to provide users with real-time information. The main aim of this study is to explore the application of ChatGPT, an AI-based conversational agent, in ITS, as well as the potential challenges and future research directions in this area.

The team engaged in conversations with ChatGPT to investigate the potential impact of this AI system on CAVs and ITS. We posed a range of general

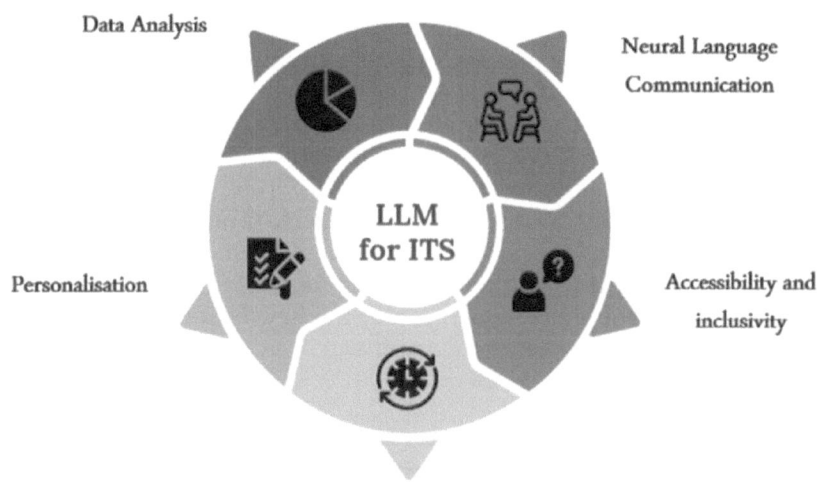

Data Analysis

Neural Language Communication

LLM for ITS

Personalisation

Accessibility and inclusivity

Automation and Optimisation

FIGURE 10.1
Areas that LLM improves on for ITS.

and technical/advanced questions to explore the applications of ChatGPT in this context. We also present several potential applications of the proposed system, including providing personalised recommendations for route planning and traffic management, improving safety and reducing accidents through advanced driver assistance systems, and enhancing accessibility for seniors and people with disabilities. Through the conversation, we have been able to identify several challenges and issues associated with the implementation of ChatGPT in this particular domain.

10.2 Investigating LLM Knowledge on ITS

Given that LLMs such as BERT and GPT have demonstrated impressive processing and generating language capabilities, it is worth exploring their potential in more specialised areas, including ITS. LLMs are trained on vast datasets using statistical methods, machine learning, and deep learning techniques, enabling them to process complex information and provide insights across various fields. Given the rapid advances in ITS and the increasing complexity of CAVs, assessing how well these models can understand and contribute to this evolving discipline is crucial. To this end, we investigate LLMs' understanding, specifically ChatGPT, regarding ITS. In this section, we conducted an interactive session with ChatGPT, where we asked a series of questions to gauge its expertise and capabilities. The goal was to assess whether ChatGPT could generate informed and actionable answers to detailed queries about ITS and CAVs and to identify areas where it could provide valuable insights or guidance. By doing so, we aimed to explore the extent of ChatGPT's knowledge and its potential position in aiding studies and improvement in ITS.

Besides the basic questions, we did ask several advanced/technical questions focused on adopting recent technologies, including digital twin, EV, and metaverse on ITS, using the ChatGPT model to train ITS, the potential for powerful driving models, and how to address current drawbacks and limitations in this area. Overall, these questions highlight the potential impact of ChatGPT on ITS research while identifying key technical challenges that must be addressed to realise its full potential.

10.2.1 Dialogical Questions

The questions in Table 10.1 were used for the conversations. It has six basic questions and three advanced questions.

10.2.2 Chatting Result

The initial testing of ChatGPT revealed that, despite the model's potential for having inaccurate or partial data at the time of the initial query, it could be updated and fixed when new data becomes available. The modified model might need to be distributed and incorporated into the system. Thus, it might take some time before the changes are reflected in ChatGPT's responses. The model could answer most of the questions accurately and relevantly, demonstrating its potential as a helpful tool for researchers studying CAV and

TABLE 10.1

Questions Used for the Conversation

Basic Questions	Advanced Questions
1. Can you define what the intelligent transportation system (ITS) is?	1. How does digital twin enhance ITS?
2. What are the primary uses and advantages of ITS?	2. Is it possible to train a powerful ITS using RLHF as ChatGPT does?
3. In what ways does ITS play a significant role in enhancing traffic flow and decreasing congestion?	3. How can an ITS overcome most of the existing drawbacks?
4. What is connected and automated vehicles (CAVs) and how can the integration of CAV further enhance the current ITS?	
5. What are the potential drawbacks of CAVs?	
6. How might ITS and autonomous vehicles be leveraged to enhance the mobility and accessibility of seniors and people with disabilities?	

Can you define what the Intelligent Transportation System (ITS) is?

Sure! Intelligent Transportation System (ITS) is a collection of advanced technologies, communication systems, and data analytics tools that are used to improve the efficiency, safety, and sustainability of transportation networks. ITS can be applied to all modes of transportation, including roadways, railways, airways, and waterways. The system integrates various technologies such as sensors, cameras, GPS, and communication systems to gather real-time information about traffic flow, weather conditions, and other relevant data. The collected data is then analysed to optimise traffic flow, manage congestion, and provide timely and accurate information to drivers and transportation officials. Additionally, ITS can be used to improve safety by providing advanced warning systems, automated driving systems, and collision avoidance technologies. Overall, ITS plays a crucial role in improving the effectiveness and efficiency of transportation systems while reducing environmental impacts and enhancing safety.

FIGURE 10.2
Answer to Question 1.

ITS fields. Nevertheless, there were times when ChatGPT gave erroneous or insufficient information, especially regarding the most recent advancements and improvements in the industry. Given the dynamic nature of the subject and the regular changes, for example, Figures 10.2 to 10.7 show the answers provided by ChatGPT for Questions 1 to 7.

What are the primary uses and advantages of ITS?

The primary uses and advantages of Intelligent Transportation System (ITS) are:

1. Improved safety: ITS technologies can enhance safety by providing real-time information and advanced warning systems for drivers. This includes collision avoidance systems, emergency response management, and other safety-critical applications.

2. Increased efficiency: ITS technologies can optimise traffic flow and reduce congestion by providing real-time traffic information, intelligent routing systems, and traffic management solutions.

3. Environmental benefits: ITS can reduce the environmental impact of transportation by optimising traffic flow, reducing congestion and emissions, and promoting the use of sustainable transportation modes such as electric vehicles.

4. Enhanced mobility: ITS can provide personalised information and services to users, including real-time transit information, ride-sharing solutions, and other mobility services, making it easier for people to get around.

5. Economic benefits: ITS can reduce transportation costs and improve the efficiency of the transportation system, resulting in economic benefits such as increased productivity, reduced fuel consumption, and decreased maintenance costs.

FIGURE 10.3
Answer to Question 2.

In what ways does ITS play a significant role in enhancing traffic flow and decreasing congestion?

🉐   Intelligent Transportation Systems (ITS) can enhance traffic flow and decrease congestion in several ways:

1. Real-time traffic information: ITS provides real-time traffic information to drivers, allowing them to choose the best routes and avoid congestion.

2. Intelligent routing systems: ITS can provide intelligent routing systems that optimise the use of available road space, reducing congestion and travel time.

3. Traffic management solutions: ITS can enable traffic management solutions that improve the flow of traffic, such as intelligent traffic signals, ramp metering, and lane control systems.

4. Incident management: ITS can help manage incidents such as accidents or road closures by providing real-time information to drivers and rerouting traffic to alternate routes, minimising the impact on traffic flow.

5. Smart parking: ITS can help drivers find available parking spaces quickly, reducing congestion caused by drivers searching for parking.

FIGURE 10.4
Answer to Question 3.

10.3 Discussion of Advanced Questions

In this section, we review a set of technical questions asked on ChatGPT as a case study for LLM to enquire about a specific method or method related to ITS. These questions have been carefully crafted to explore the metaverse's impact on ITS and CAV. When asking ChatGPT: How does digital twin enhance ITS? The answer was that creating a digital twin of a physical system, like a transportation network or a vehicle, enables real-time monitoring and behaviour analysis of that system. There are several advantages to employing digital twin technology in ITS. It can monitor the health of transportation infrastructure, including roads and bridges, and provide early warnings of future failures or repair needs, decreasing downtime and enhancing safety. It also provides better traffic management, which is possible thanks to digital twin's ability to model traffic patterns, forecast congestion, and reduce delays for road users. Digital twin can analyse data in real-time from various sensors and sources, including traffic cameras and weather sensors, giving traffic management employees insights into traffic patterns and facilitating better decision-making. It may test and model various situations, such as

4. What is Connected and Automated vehicles (CAV) and how can the integration of CAV further enhance the current ITS?

Connected and Automated Vehicles (CAVs) are vehicles equipped with advanced communication and automation technologies that allow them to interact with other vehicles, infrastructure, and systems, and to operate with minimal or no human intervention. These vehicles leverage connectivity to exchange real-time information about traffic, road conditions, and hazards, while automation enables them to perform driving tasks autonomously or semi-autonomously. The convergence of connectivity and automation in CAVs opens up possibilities for improved safety, efficiency, and convenience in transportation.

Integrating CAVs into the current Intelligent Transportation Systems (ITS) can significantly enhance system performance in several ways:

1. **Enhanced Traffic Management and Flow:** CAVs can communicate directly with traffic management systems to share data on their location, speed, and intended routes. This data enables ITS to optimise traffic signals, reduce congestion, and manage traffic flow more efficiently, leading to shorter travel times and reduced traffic bottlenecks.

2. **Improved Road Safety:** CAVs can quickly react to real-time data from nearby vehicles and infrastructure, allowing for coordinated responses to potential hazards. The autonomous features also minimise human error, which is a major cause of accidents, thus enhancing overall road safety.

3. **Energy Efficiency and Reduced Emissions:** By optimising driving patterns and reducing idling times through smoother traffic flow, CAVs can contribute to energy savings and lower emissions. Combined with electric vehicles (EVs), CAVs can create a more sustainable transportation network, supporting the goals of eco-friendly ITS.

4. **Personalised and Efficient Mobility Services:** The integration of CAVs into ITS enables personalised services, such as on-demand autonomous shuttles and optimised routing, to provide passengers with tailored, efficient mobility options. This can enhance accessibility for all users, including those with limited mobility.

FIGURE 10.5
Answer to Question 4.

traffic accidents or severe weather, to assess their effects and choose the best course of action without endangering safety or disrupting traffic.

The questions that were asked show the extent of the chatbot's ability to respond to all questions under the supervision of the user. This prompts us to think about creating a chatbot for EV and ITS. Therefore, the question was

What are the potential drawbacks of Connected and Automated vehicles?

There are a few potential drawbacks of Connected and Automated vehicles, including:

1. Cybersecurity risks: As these vehicles rely heavily on digital systems, there is a risk of cyber attacks that could compromise the safety and security of the vehicle and its passengers.

2. Infrastructure challenges: In order to fully realise the potential of Connected and Automated vehicles, significant changes to infrastructure will be required, including improvements to road networks, communication systems, and power grids.

3. Job displacement: As more and more tasks become automated, there is a risk of job displacement for workers in the transportation industry.

4. Privacy concerns: Connected vehicles collect and transmit large amounts of data, raising concerns about the privacy and security of that data.

5. Cost: Connected and Automated vehicles may require significant investments in technology and infrastructure, which could limit their adoption, particularly in developing countries or areas with limited resources.

FIGURE 10.6
Answer to Question 5.

asked: Can a powerful ITS be trained using RLHF as ChatGPT does? The answer indicates that it is possible to train ITS to some extent using RLHF. Using the RLHF approach, an AI system can receive input from human experts and then modify its behaviour.

This feedback could be applied to ITS to enhance system safety, improve traffic flow, and lessen congestion. However, training an ITS with RLHF is more complicated than developing a language model like ChatGPT. ITS consists of many interconnected sensors, actuators, and control systems. Numerous variables, including the environment, traffic patterns, and human behaviour, might influence how these components behave. Identifying particular scenarios and parameters that can be changed depending on human feedback is vital to apply RLHF efficiently in training an ITS. It calls for a thorough comprehension of the system's behaviour and the capacity to model and simulate its performance under various scenarios. When adopting RLHF in an ITS, ethical and legal issues can also be considered.

Although ITS represents a major technological breakthrough in smart vehicles and EVs, it still suffers from many drawbacks, as shown in Figure 10.8.

Therefore, it is evident that we should enquire about a way to avoid these problems and create an improved ITS that addresses the current errors. A thorough strategy that tackles many issues is needed to develop an ITS that can mostly overcome current shortcomings. The following key points can be made to create an effective ITS that handles current drawbacks. Using cutting-edge technologies like AI, big data analytics, machine learning, and

How might ITS and autonomous vehicles be leveraged to enhance the mobility and accessibility of seniors and people with disabilities?

Intelligent Transportation Systems (ITS) and autonomous vehicles have the potential to significantly enhance mobility and accessibility for seniors and people with disabilities. Here are a few ways in which this can be achieved:

1. Increased accessibility: ITS can provide real-time information about accessible transportation options, such as wheelchair accessible buses or taxis, allowing seniors and people with disabilities to more easily plan their trips. Autonomous vehicles can also be designed to be more accessible, with features such as automatic ramps or adjustable seats.

2. Improved safety: Autonomous vehicles have the potential to significantly reduce the risk of accidents, which is particularly important for seniors and people with disabilities who may have limited mobility or visual impairments.

3. Personalised transportation: ITS and autonomous vehicles can provide personalised transportation options based on an individual's needs and preferences. For example, an autonomous vehicle could be programmed to take a senior to their favorite grocery store, or a person with a disability to their place of work.

4. Reduced cost: By improving transportation efficiency and reducing the need for drivers, ITS and autonomous vehicles have the potential to reduce the cost of transportation for seniors and people with disabilities.

FIGURE 10.7
Answer to Question 6.

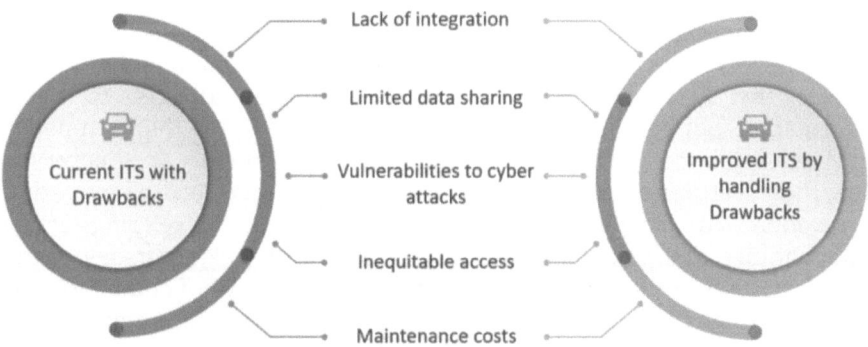

FIGURE 10.8
Current ITS drawbacks.

the IoT can offer real-time data and analysis that can help improve traffic flow and relieve congestion. Working together can help to guarantee that the ITS is created in a coordinated manner that answers the requirements and concerns of all parties involved, including government agencies, commercial businesses, and other stakeholders. An ITS developed with the needs of commuters and other users in mind will be more successful. Convenience, accessibility, and safety are a few variables that should be considered in this strategy. Observing traffic patterns and road conditions in real time might assist in spotting potential problems before they become serious. Additionally, this information can be used to optimise traffic flow and lessen congestion. An ITS ought to consider utilising environmentally friendly modes of transportation such as EVs, public transportation, and bike-sharing schemes. It can increase general efficiency and lessen the harmful effects of transportation on the environment.

10.4 LLM Keys to Enhance User Experience and Accessibility

One of the more intriguing features of AI chatbots in transportation is that they can contribute towards improving the daily life of a commuter. In interviews with urban mobility practitioners, it is observed that these systems deliver a sense of immediacy and a level of personalisation that is not currently available in mass transit. Consider a typical daily routine of a passenger: unexpected interruptions, route deviations, and unexpected setbacks are just par for the course. AI chatbots now provide live advice that is dynamic in its response. Let us imagine a bus is stranded in a jam. The chatbot can at once recommend a different form of travel or a new route, removing uncertainty as much as anxiety. Such interactive engagement has been experienced by many as revolutionary—providing not just ease but a sense of mastery over daily travel.

Furthermore, the universal design of contemporary chatbots is also worth mentioning. In multicultural urban areas, accessibility is paramount. Numerous systems currently have voice recognition and text-to-speech features that allow those with vision impairments equal access to transit information. Support in multiple languages also ensures that non-native speakers can access accurate and intelligible information. It is observed how these features break down barriers in transit usage, leading towards a more equalised transportation system accessible to all. By offering virtual surroundings that meet the needs of elderly and disabled persons, metaverse can help improve the accessibility and inclusivity of transportation networks. It can include tools like audio and visual aids, programmable user interfaces, and assistance- and guidance-giving virtual assistants.

While enhancing user experience is crucial, AI chatbots' overall impact comes from optimising operational efficiency in urban transport networks.

Years of research and field experiments have proved that these technologies can significantly enhance how mass transit operates. Operationally, AI chatbots are live data collectors and processors. They collect data in real-time from various sources—traffic sensors, sensor networks, and commuter feedback. AI chatbots assist in making decisions using this input; for example, they use chatbot-derived insights to modulate traffic lights at rush hour, improving flow and cutting congestion. Such anticipatory management minimises delays, conserves fuel, and minimises environmental impact.

Chatbots also play a key role in areas such as preventive maintenance. Chatbots can predict early signs of breakdown or failure. Transport authorities have reported that early warning allows them to schedule maintenance timely, minimise breakdown frequency, and enhance overall safety. In addition, automating mundane administrative functions such as fare collection and ticketing has allowed human resources to be utilised in more critical areas in mass transit management. The outcome is a more efficient and leaner operation that is more effective both in terms of its impact on mass transit providers and its users.

10.5 Integration with Smart City Ecosystems

The full promise of AI chatbots is achieved once they are envisioned as a component in a much more extensive smart city network. In urban spaces in contemporary cities, discrete solutions are not likely to lead towards lasting outcomes. Instead, adequate progress is achieved by linking multiple digital solutions into a networked approach. AI chatbots are increasingly interfaced with the Internet of Things (IoT), meaning they can draw on data from a network of sensors spread across a city—from parking meters to traffic lights. Such interfacing makes available a complete picture of urban activity, making it feasible to respond quickly to real-time developments. For instance, by consolidating data from various sources, a chatbot can not only recommend the best route for a daily commuter but also aid municipal administrations in dynamically updating plans for traffic management.

A second development regarding AI chatbots' engagement with autonomous vehicles is on the horizon. Autonomous vehicles are experimental in many cities, but chatbots are already beginning to plug gaps between human-led and autonomous networks. In situations where human monitoring is necessary—such as in emergencies or in unexpected failures in a system—the digital assistants step in with ease, ensuring effective communications and overall safety. Urban planning is a key driver in sustainability in cities in the present, and in that context, AI chatbots have solutions with a great deal to promise. In planning travel routings more efficiently and in eliminating wasteful travel, they contribute towards lowered emissions as well as more energy-efficient methods of travel. However, as cities become more data-based, data privacy and cybersecurity concerns are a given. Policy structures and technical measures have a role in staying on par with these developments so that AI does not have a cost in terms of eroded confidence in its application.

10.6 Challenges and Future Directions

Integrating AI in various domains has opened up new opportunities and challenges. This chapter focuses on two specific areas where challenges arise: AI integration and technical considerations. Integrating AI into existing systems requires addressing compatibility issues, data privacy concerns, and ethical considerations (Habbal et al., 2024). Furthermore, technical challenges encompass algorithmic complexity, scalability, and real-time processing requirements. Understanding and addressing these challenges is crucial to harness AI's full potential and ensure its effective implementation in different domains. Next, we will delve into the challenges associated with AI integration and technical aspects, providing insights and potential solutions to overcome them.

One of the key challenges is improving the language understanding capabilities of LLM to accurately interpret and respond to user queries in the context of intelligent driving. It involves training the model to grasp specific driving-related terminology and understand complex queries. It is crucial to protect the security and privacy of user data. Due to the user interactions and potential collection of sensitive information, LLM requires strong data protection measures to guard against misuse or unauthorised access. LLMs require significant computational power, making real-time applications difficult, especially in traditional ITS infrastructure. Frequent retraining adds high costs, posing a challenge to widespread adoption.

ITS relies on immediate responses, but LLMs often struggle with latency, particularly in high-demand environments. Delayed route recommendations can lead to congestion issues and commuter frustration. AI models may be biased due to the data they are trained on, potentially leading to unequal access to transportation services. Ensuring fairness and transparency is essential for ethical AI deployment in ITS.

Integrating AI chatbots into smart urban transport is crucial for making cities more imaginative and more responsive. Engagement with practitioners and research points towards the potential these instruments have in enhancing daily travel experiences and making urban mass transport more efficient. While the promise is enormous, the journey is not free from challenges. Areas that need ongoing attention are data privacy, cybersecurity, and seamless integrations between systems. Future research focuses on crafting effective, multidisciplinary solutions that address these challenges and maximise AI-based solutions' strengths.

Overall, AI chatbots are a dynamic, unfolding dimension of smart transportation. They are poised to revolutionise urban functioning by making urban mobility more cohesive, data-based, and human-centred. The more we transition into smart cities, the vision in this chapter presents us with a glimpse into a time in which urban existence is more entwined with technology, with possibilities far-reaching, more than enhancing the transit system.

References

Abbas, F., Sari, O., Abdulkarem, A., Alrammahi, H., Hameed, A. S., Alrikabi, M. B., Razaq, A. A. A., Nasser, H. K., & Al-rifaie, M. F. (2022). Networks cyber security model by using machine learning techniques. *International Journal of Intelligent Systems and Applications in Engineering, 10*(3s), 257–263.

Alrifaie, M. F., Ismael, O. A., Hameed, A. S., & Mahmood, M. B. (2021, December). Pedestrian and objects detection by using learning complexity-aware cascades. In *2021 2nd Information Technology to Enhance e-learning and Other Application (IT-ELA)* (pp. 12–17). IEEE. https://doi.org/10.1109/IT-ELA52201.2021.9773589

Berg, V. G., & du Plessis, E. (2023). ChatGPT and generative AI: Possibilities for its contribution to lesson planning, critical thinking and openness in teacher education. *Education Sciences, 13*(10), 998. https://doi.org/10.3390/educsci13100998

Brown, T., Mann, B., Ryder, N., Subbiah, M., Kaplan, J. D., Dhariwal, P., Neelakantan, A., Shyam, P., Sastry, G., Askell, A., Agarwal, S., Herbert-Voss, A., Krueger, G., Henighan, T., Child, R., Ramesh, A., Ziegler, D., Wu, J., Winter, C., ... & Amodei, D. (2020). Language models are few-shot learners. *Advances in Neural Information Processing Systems, 33*, 1877–1901.

Cao, D., Wang, X., Li, L., Lv, C., Na, X., Xing, Y., Li, X., Li, Y., Chen, Y., & Wang, F. Y. (2022). Future directions of intelligent vehicles: Potentials, possibilities, and perspectives. *IEEE Transactions on Intelligent Vehicles, 7*(1), 7–10. https://doi.org/10.1109/TIV.2022.3157049

Carlini, N., Tramer, F., Wallace, E., Jagielski, M., Herbert-Voss, A., Lee, K., Roberts, A., Brown, T. B., Song, D., & Erlingsson, U. (2021). Extracting training data from large language models. *USENIX Security Symposium, 6*, 2633–2650.

Chen, Y., Zhang, H., & Wang, F. Y. (2023). Society-centered and DAO-powered sustainability in transportation 5.0: An intelligent vehicles perspective. *IEEE Transactions on Intelligent Vehicles, 8*(4), 7–10. https://doi.org/10.1109/TIV.2023.3264585

Chen, Z. (2020). The combination of battery swapping system and connected vehicles technology in intelligent transportation. *Proceedings – 2020 International Conference on Intelligent Transportation, Big Data and Smart City, ICITBS 2020,* 72–75. https://doi.org/10.1109/ICITBS49701.2020.00023

Desai, J., Saldivar-Carranza, E., Mathew, J. K., Li, H., Platte, T., & Bullock, D. (2021). Methodology for applying connected vehicle data to evaluate impact of interstate construction work zone diversions. *IEEE Conference on Intelligent Transportation Systems, Proceedings, ITSC, 2021-Septe,* 4035–4042. https://doi.org/10.1109/ITSC48978.2021.9564873

Habbal, A., & Alrifaie, M. F. (2024). A user-preference-based charging station recommendation for electric vehicles. *IEEE Transactions on Intelligent Transportation Systems, 25*(9), 11617–11634. https://doi.org/10.1109/TITS.2024.3379469

Habbal, A., Hamouda, H., Alnajim, A. M., Khan, S., & Alrifaie, M. F. (2024). Privacy as a lifestyle: Empowering assistive technologies for people with disabilities, challenges and future directions. *Journal of King Saud University – Computer and Information Sciences, 36*(4), 102039. https://doi.org/10.1016/j.jksuci.2024.102039

Karim, S. M., Habbal, A., Chaudhry, S. A., & Irshad, A. (2022). Architecture, protocols, and security in IoV: Taxonomy, analysis, challenges, and solutions, *Security and Communication Networks, 2022*, 1–19. https://doi.org/10.1155/2022/1131479

Li, W., Wu, L., Wang, C., Xue, J., Hu, W., Li, S., Guo, G., & Cao, D. (2022). Intelligent cockpit for intelligent vehicle in metaverse: A case study of empathetic auditory regulation of human emotion. *IEEE Transactions on Systems, Man, and Cybernetics: Systems, 53*(1), 2173–2187. https://doi.org/10.1109/TSMC.2022.3229021

Liu, V., & Chilton, L. B. (2022). Design guidelines for prompt engineering text-to-image generative models. *Proceedings of the 2022 CHI Conference on Human Factors in Computing Systems.* https://doi.org/10.1145/3491102.3501825

Lobato, W., De Souza, A. M., Peixoto, M. L. M., Rosario, D., & Villas, L. (2020). A cache strategy for intelligent transportation system to connected autonomous vehicles. *IEEE Vehicular Technology Conference, 2020-Novem.* https://doi.org/10.1109/VTC2020-Fall49728.2020.9348553

Qadir, J. (2023). Engineering education in the era of ChatGPT: Promise and pitfalls of generative AI for education. *IEEE Global Engineering Education Conference, EDUCON, 2023-May.* https://doi.org/10.1109/EDUCON54358.2023.10125121

Shahriar, S., & Hayawi, K. (2023). Let's have a chat! A conversation with ChatGPT: Technology, applications, and limitations. *Artificial Intelligence and Applications,* June, 1–16. https://doi.org/10.47852/bonviewaia3202939

Wang, F. Y. (2022). The DAO to MetaControl for MetaSystems in metaverses: The system of parallel control systems for knowledge automation and control intelligence in CPSS. *IEEE/CAA Journal of Automatica Sinica, 9*(11), 1899–1908. https://doi.org/10.1109/JAS.2022.106022

Wang, W., Na, X., Cao, D., Gong, J., Xi, J., Xing, Y., & Wang, F. Y. (2020). Decision-making in driver-automation shared control: A review and perspectives. *IEEE/CAA Journal of Automatica Sinica, 7*(5), 1289–1307. https://doi.org/10.1109/JAS.2020.1003294

Zhang, J., Pu, J., Xue, J., Yang, M., Xu, X., Wang, X., & Wang, F.-Y. (2023). HiVeGPT: Human-machine-augmented intelligent vehicles with generative pre-trained transformer. *IEEE Transactions on Intelligent Vehicles, 14*(8), 1–8. https://doi.org/10.1109/tiv.2023.3256982

11

AI Chatbot and Metaverse

Fady Alkhateeb, Adib Habbal, and Osman Ghazali

11.1 AI Chatbots and Web 3.0

The Internet has experienced significant changes in the last 20 years; Web 1.0 was for reading information, then it became more interactive in Web 2.0 by allowing users to interact with websites through comments and shares. However, with this revolution in Web 2.0, concerns about data privacy and centralisation started to rise (Kshetri, 2022). Then, we start to see another direction for the web to mitigate these issues by becoming decentralised, with a more user-centric Internet and more peer-to-peer interaction, and ensuring data sovereignty (Alabdulwahhab, 2018). This concept is still developing to make Web 3.0. With the rapidly growing Web 3.0, investors and companies have started to put their fingerprints on this area.

As illustrated in Table 11.1, Web 3.0 prioritises wide decentralisation adoption and allows users to own the data (Zarrin et al., 2021). Blockchain technology is widely supported in this new adoption as the decentralised ledger and controller using the smart contract. However, the transition to Web 3.0 has its challenges. We found many concerns that should be handled and under focus, like scalability, privacy, and even more usability (Dunphy & Petitcolas, 2018). Due to these challenges, it was essential to explore more potential solutions that could contribute to Web 3.0.

TABLE 11.1

Comparison between Web 2.0 and Web 3.0

Aspects	Web 2.0	Web 3.0
Architecture	Centralised	Decentralised (Blockchain-based)
Data Ownership	Controlled by corporations	Owned by users
Monetisation	Ads-driven revenue	Crypto-based, decentralised financial (DeFi)-enabled
Security	Vulnerable to breaches	Cryptographic security
Identity Management	Centralised logins (Google, Facebook)	Decentralised identity (SSI)

DOI: 10.1201/9781003619819-14

One of the promising emerging technologies is artificial intelligence (AI). The language model of OpenAI's Chat Generative Pre-Trained Transformer (ChatGPT) is the most promising technology that can assist data scientists and the widespread applications of AI with its powerful ability to converse with humans (Du et al., 2023; OpenAI ChatGPT, n.d.). Its ability to understand and generate human-like text could be leveraged to develop intelligent user interfaces for Web 3.0 applications (Thorp, 2023), potentially improving development, usability, and accessibility (Brown et al., 2020).

OpenAI has released multiple versions of ChatGPT, including GPT-2, GPT-3, GPT-4, GPT-4O, and O1. These versions vary in size, number of parameters, and the number of languages in their pre-training data. GPT-3 was publicly carried out and was trained on a wide range of texts in 95 languages and had 175 billion parameters (Farseev, 2023; Flensted, 2024). ChatGPT is a conversational AI interface that can understand and respond to human queries using natural language processing (NLP). It is powered by deep learning algorithms trained to generate high-quality responses for various queries. ChatGPT uses NLP and machine learning (ML) algorithms to make eloquent and contextually relevant text to achieve this.

The Web 3.0 and metaverse stack have multiple layers working together to enable a decentralised and trustless Internet. At its core, blockchain technology, including platforms like Ethereum, Solana, and Polkadot, serves as the foundation. Smart contracts and self-executing agreements define interactions within decentralised applications, ensuring automated and tamperproof transactions. The InterPlanetary File System (IPFS) facilitates secure and distributed data storage, enhancing data integrity and accessibility. AI and ML contribute by powering advanced chatbots and predictive analytics, improving user experiences and automation. Privacy and scalability are strengthened through Zero-Knowledge Proofs (ZKPs) and other privacy-preserving technologies. Decentralised Identity (DID) and Self-Sovereign Identity (SSI) frameworks also empower users with ownership and control over their digital identities, reinforcing security and autonomy in the Web 3.0 ecosystem.

Web 3.0 is transforming various industries by integrating automation, security, and decentralisation. The finance sector eliminates the need for banks by enabling peer-to-peer transactions, fostering a more direct and efficient financial ecosystem. Further, the healthcare industry benefits from decentralised medical records, ensuring enhanced data security and privacy while giving patients greater control over their information. In education, Web 3.0 facilitates the verification of academic achievements through digital certifications and decentralises learning platforms, making education more accessible and verifiable. Supply chain logistics also experience significant improvements, with increased transparency and better monitoring of supply chains, ensuring authenticity, efficiency, and accountability at every process stage.

11.2 ChatGPT: Enhancing Metaverse Applications

Integrating foundational models like ChatGPT with Web 3.0 offers significant opportunities for enhancing user experience and driving innovation within the Web 3.0 ecosystem. Generative AI, especially exemplified by ChatGPT, holds the potential to revolutionise various aspects of software and content development and consumption, spanning from the fundamental infrastructure to the application layer. Considering the complexity of Web 3.0 technologies, encompassing blockchain, smart contracts, and decentralised applications (dApps), many users might encounter difficulties in their utilisation. Consequently, a new generation of intelligent dApps can be developed with generative models at their core. Leveraging ChatGPT as a conversational interface is motivated to introduce innovative applications such as exchanges, explorers, or wallets embedding conversational capabilities fuelled by advanced language models. For instance, a language-powered explorer would empower ordinary users to enquire about activities like "Have any major institutions transferred funds to Binance?" or seek information regarding similar past occurrences. Furthermore, conversational wallets may empower users to express intentions for transactions, request information, or execute specific tasks using natural language. Additionally, ChatGPT-4's capability to translate raw blockchain data into comprehensible text aids in simplifying the comprehension of complex transactional data, further enhancing user interactions within the Web 3.0 landscape.

In Web 3.0, users wield increased authority over their data, solidifying the path for a more personalised and pertinent content conveyance. ChatGPT, endowed with the capacity to comprehend and generate human-like text, has the potential to be employed for handling personalised and pertinent content based on user inclinations and engagements, thus delivering a distinctive and gratifying user encounter. One of the most overt applications of models like ChatGPT is conceivably the facilitation of a novel breed of non-fungible tokens (NFTs) infused with conversational intelligence. Envision an iteration of your favoured NFT compilation that permits you to enquire about the origin of the creator's inspiration or intricate artistic particulars. This capability extends to asset creation, crafting narratives and stories, and forming 3D avatars in blockchain gaming. Moreover, this technology can conceive immersive 3D environments, pioneer avatar 3D models, generate multiple assets and textures, and innovate avatars within the metaverse.

The revolutionary impact of ChatGPT and other foundational models is poised to profoundly shape the software development process and user experience within the Web 3.0 paradigm. This influence spans various phases: gathering user requirements, designing and developing innovative, intelligent applications, and rigorous testing and security assessment stages. We can find a place for ChatGPT in the layers, as ChatGPT provides an application programming interface (API), creating more opportunities to make it

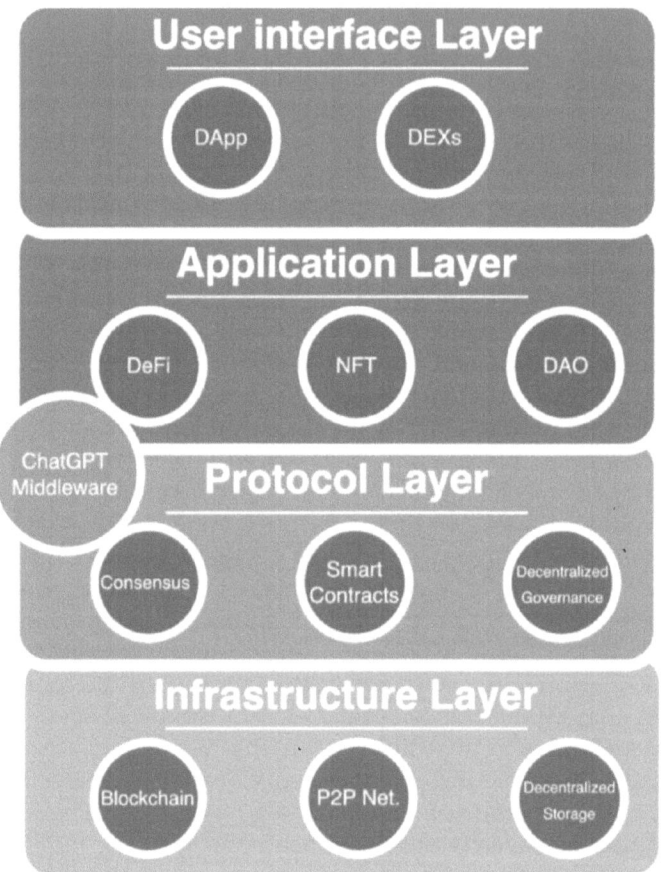

FIGURE 11.1
ChatGPT middleware position in Web 3.0 stack.

a middleware at the Web 3.0 stack, as shown in Figure 11.1. It implies a broad range of automation and request resolution capabilities. It can be integrated into development systems to simplify smart contract creation for developers by translating complex code into understandable conversational language. Besides enhancing the security level of the code, it could also be used to generate smart contract code. Developers can instruct and describe the functionality they want, and it could generate smart contracts to meet the requirements. It can be integrated into development systems to detect vulnerabilities and exploits in smart contract codes and provide suggestions for necessary modifications to improve security. Moreover, it can offer valuable insights and ideas to assist developers in designing Web 3.0 ecosystems that meet particular use case scenarios. So, it can provide several possible applications and enhancements to Web 3.0.

Lastly, but equally important, ChatGPT-4 can serve as a critical resource in enhancing security and privacy within the Web 3.0 realm. It can inform users about potential security risks and guide them in avoiding such hazards. Moreover, it can help users manage their privacy settings, thereby providing a safer and more secure Web 3.0 environment.

11.3 Insights from Conversations with ChatGPT

Five questions to allow us to understand more about Web 3.0 from ChatGPT's perspective, how it can help with use cases, what the challenges are, and how GPT-4 can be exploited in resolving the challenges and enhancing the new ecosystems. After this exploration, query the potential integration of GPT-4 and Web 3.0 technologies, focusing on specific contexts such as metaverse.

11.4 Questions List for ChatGPT-4

Based on Table 11.2, the list of questions for ChatGPT regarding Web 3.0 covers both fundamental and advanced aspects of the technology. The fundamental questions focus on defining Web 3.0, distinguishing it from Web 2.0, and exploring its key features, potential opportunities, applications, and role in infrastructure services and interoperability. These questions help build a foundational understanding of Web 3.0 and its impact. On the other hand, the advanced

TABLE 11.2

List of the Questions for the Conversation

Fundamental Questions	Advanced Questions
1. What is Web 3.0, and how does it differ from Web 2.0?	1. How is Web 3.0 transforming content creation, application development, and user experience?
2. What are the key features of Web 3.0 technology?	2. Web 3.0 is a big umbrella; how can it give opportunities for developing the metaverse?
3. How could Web 3.0 technologies provide new opportunities?	
4. What can we do with Web 3.0 in Infrastructure Services and Interoperability?	3. What are the limitations and challenges in implementing and adopting Web 3.0 technology?
5. What are the current applications and potential use cases for Web 3.0 technology?	4. How to develop an intelligent Web 3.0 system that can overcome most of the Web 2.0 drawbacks?
	5. What are the key areas of ChatGPT that can help in improving Web 3.0?

questions delve deeper into how Web 3.0 is transforming content creation, application development, and user experience. They also examine the role of Web 3.0 in metaverse development, the challenges in its implementation, and strategies to overcome Web 2.0 drawbacks by creating an intelligent Web 3.0 system. Additionally, the table highlights a key question on how ChatGPT can improve Web 3.0, indicating the potential integration of AI in dApps and services.

11.5 ChatGPT-4 Answers for Fundamental Questions

We evaluated the GPT-4 model by asking five fundamental questions about Web 3.0, as we can see in the answers to the first three questions in Figures 11.2–11.4. Although we were on the same chat, it kept repeating some

 What is Web 3.0 and how does it differ from Web 2.0?

 Web3, short for Web 3.0, is often referred to as the next generation of the internet, combining the power of blockchain technology, decentralised networks, and artificial intelligence. While Web1 and Web2 focused on the democratisation of information and user-generated content, respectively, Web3 aims to redefine the internet economy by enabling decentralised and direct peer-to-peer interactions.

Here's a brief comparison of the three stages of the web:

- **Web1** was the "read-only" internet. It was primarily static, with users consuming content rather than creating or interacting with it. Websites were built by people with technical expertise, and content was published for users to read, without much interactivity.
- **Web2** is the "read-write" internet that we're most familiar with today. It introduced interactivity, social media, and user-generated content. It's characterised by platforms like Facebook, Twitter, and YouTube where users can both consume and create content. However, Web2 is also dominated by a handful of large corporations that control the majority of data and information flow.
- **Web3** is often referred to as the "read-write-execute" internet. It's an evolution of the web where services and applications aren't just interactive but also automated and decentralised. The vision of Web3 is a more open and user-centric web, where users own their data and interact directly with each other without the need for intermediaries. It's powered by technologies such as blockchain, smart contracts, decentralised storage and computation, and more.

FIGURE 11.2
Answer to Question 1. (OpenAI ChatGPT., n.d.)

What are the key features of Web3 technology?

 Web 3.0, or the "semantic web," is characterized by several key features:

1. **Decentralisation**: Unlike the centralized servers of Web 2.0, Web 3.0 will rely on decentralised networks. This could lead to a more robust and resilient internet where no single party controls the entire network. Blockchain is the technology most commonly associated with this concept.

2. **Interoperability**: Web 3.0 aims to make data more interoperable, meaning different systems and networks will be able to communicate and exchange data more easily.

3. **User Sovereignty**: A fundamental principle of Web 3.0 is the idea that users should have control over their own data. This contrasts with the model of Web 2.0, where tech giants typically control user data. In Web 3.0, users could control, monetise, and set permissions for their own data.

4. **Privacy and Security**: Web 3.0 is expected to have improved privacy and security. Blockchain and cryptography provide secure ways to verify transactions and identities without needing centralised authorities.

5. **Smart Contracts**: These are self-executing contracts with the terms of the agreement directly written into code. They exist across a decentralised blockchain network, and allow trusted transactions and agreements to be carried out among anonymous parties without the need for a central authority or external enforcement mechanism.

6. **Trustless Systems**: The architecture of Web 3.0 is designed to enable interactions in a trustless environment, meaning you don't need to trust a particular party because the system itself ensures the validity of transactions.

7. **Decentralised Applications (dApps)**: These are applications that run on a P2P network of computers rather than a single computer. They have existed since the advent of P2P networks but have become popular with the rise of blockchain networks.

8. **Artificial Intelligence and Machine Learning**: The use of AI and ML in Web 3.0 will make systems more adaptable and able to understand information like a human would, allowing for more personalised, intelligent functionality.

FIGURE 11.3
Answer to Question 2. (OpenAI ChatGPT., n.d.)

answers and mentioning the limitation for the model to answer because of the trained data bounded with 2021. Regarding our interest in the contribution of Web 3.0 in interoperability and infrastructure services, we found a response about revolutionising these subjects through decentralisation and peer-to-peer interaction. With decentralised storage, users can rent unused storage space or pay to store files across a globally distributed network. Some projects provide more resilient and censorship-resistant storage solutions.

How could Web3 technologies provide new opportunities?

Web3 technologies present a variety of new opportunities, many of which could fundamentally reshape the internet and digital economy as we know them today. Here are a few potential areas of opportunity:

1. **Decentralised Finance (DeFi)**: Web3 technologies are at the heart of the emerging DeFi sector, which aims to recreate traditional financial systems such as lending, borrowing, and trading in a decentralised manner on the blockchain. This could potentially democratise access to financial services and reduce costs by eliminating middlemen.
2. **Digital Ownership & NFTs**: Non-fungible tokens (NFTs) are a type of digital asset that represent ownership or proof of authenticity of a unique item or piece of content, enabled by blockchain technology. This presents new opportunities for artists, creators, and collectors to monetise and trade digital assets in ways that weren't previously possible.
3. **Decentralised Autonomous Organisations (DAOs)**: These are organisations that are governed by smart contracts on the blockchain, with decisions made collectively by its members. DAOs could potentially reshape how organisations are structured and governed, enabling truly democratic decision-making processes.
4. **Data Ownership & Privacy**: Web3 technologies could allow individuals to maintain control and ownership of their personal data, rather than relinquishing it to centralized platforms. This could lead to new business models where users are compensated for the use of their data, or where they can interact with platforms without giving up their personal information.
5. **Decentralised Marketplaces**: Web3 can enable peer-to-peer commerce without the need for a centralised intermediary. This can potentially reduce costs and increase efficiency, as well as open up new models for sharing economy services.
6. **Web3 Infrastructure Services**: As the Web3 ecosystem grows, there will likely be increased demand for infrastructure services, such as decentralised storage, computation, and bandwidth. This could present opportunities for both startups and existing tech companies.
7. **Interoperability and Cross-Chain Services**: With the increasing number of blockchains and other decentralised technologies, services that can bridge these different ecosystems and enable them to interact could be increasingly important.

FIGURE 11.4
Answer to Question 3. (OpenAI ChatGPT., n.d.)

Equivalent concepts apply in the computational power and content delivery networks. Blockchain-based domain name systems (DNS) offer an alternative to traditional centralised DNS.

Cross-chain services can enhance interoperability, enabling smoother interactions between different blockchain networks. Cross-chain bridges are one solution permitting the transfer of tokens and other assets between blockchains. Some protocols are working on an Internet of blockchains for inter-chain security and operation. Also, the rising need for multi-chain decentralised exchanges (DEXs) and cross-chain DeFi protocols can facilitate trades and offer the best features and opportunities across multiple blockchains. These features contribute to the new generation of decentralised, efficient, and flexible web services that Web 3.0 expects.

Based on our analysis, ChatGPT-4 greatly understands the concepts of Web 3.0 and gives accurate responses. It answered all the questions with high accuracy and helpful answers. Upon our enquiry about the potential use cases for Web 3.0 technology, we found answers illustrating applying across various industries, creating new opportunities and potential use cases for Web 3.0 technology. DeFi is a prime application of Web 3.0, leveraging blockchain and smart contracts for lending, borrowing, and exchanges. NFTs, unique digital assets, have revolutionised the concept of digital ownership, applicable from digital art to virtual real estate.

Decentralised Autonomous Organisations (DAOs) employ smart contracts to decentralise decision-making processes. Peer-to-peer marketplaces facilitated by Web 3.0 can operate without a centralised intermediary, reducing costs and enhancing buyer-seller interactions. Web 3.0 also enables SSI solutions, providing individuals control over their identity data, thereby enhancing privacy. Supply chain management can be improved through the transparency and tamper-proof records ensured by blockchain technology. Web 3.0 technologies can also reshape social media platforms, enabling users to control their data and directly monetise their content. It opens new avenues for content publishing and monetisation, where authors can directly earn from their work. Furthermore, decentralised web infrastructure services such as IPFS and Filecoin offer alternatives to traditional web hosting and storage services. Lastly, gaming is another area transformed by Web 3.0, where players can own and trade tokenised in-game assets.

11.6 Advanced Questions Discussion

This section contains a collection of the advanced enquiries we asked ChatGPT-4 regarding Web 3.0 and the potential advantages of ChatGPT-4 to enhance and contribute to Web 3.0 technology. So when we enquired with ChatGPT-4 about the impact of Web 3.0 on content creation, application development, and user experience, the response from ChatGPT-4 confirmed that Web 3.0 has the potential to revolutionise these fields. It highlights the role of decentralisation, smart contracts, and NFTs in this transformation. Web 3.0 primarily empowers content creators by enabling direct monetisation, such as selling art through NFTs and bypassing traditional intermediaries. Creators can also maintain control and ownership over their work. Moreover, it promotes the development of decentralised social media platforms, allowing users to control their data and directly monetise their content.

In application development, Web 3.0 facilitates the creation of dApps on blockchain platforms, thus reducing dependence on centralised services. Developers can exploit smart contracts to automate various application functionalities and interactions. Web 3.0 also promotes interoperability, simplifying data sharing across applications and enabling more complex application development. Furthermore, the open-source nature of blockchain networks fosters permissionless innovation, as developers can build upon existing protocols.

Web 3.0 is set to enhance user experiences by enabling SSI, allowing users to manage their digital identities independently of centralised providers. This technology can provide users with more control over their data, including its accessibility and usage. Web 3.0 also supports more direct peer-to-peer interactions, like trading digital assets on a DEX or purchasing an NFT directly from an artist. It also presents financial services through DeFi, such as earning interest on cryptocurrencies or taking collateralised loans. Finally, Web 3.0 can facilitate novel experiences, such as interaction in a decentralised virtual world or ownership and trading of virtual real estate.

We asked ChatGPT-4 about Web 3.0's potential impact on the development of the metaverse; as Web 3.0 is a big umbrella that includes the metaverse, how can it give opportunities for developing the metaverse? The metaverse refers to a collective virtual shared space. It is often visualised as a digital universe of multiple worlds. Here is how Web 3.0 technologies could impact and create opportunities within the metaverse; first, one significant opportunity lies in user-centric ownership, a fundamental principle of Web 3.0 supported by blockchain technology. It enables users in the metaverse to own their digital assets, such as avatars, virtual real estate, and digital goods. These assets, represented by NFTs, can be created, sold, and traded by users, spurring creativity and economic activity within the metaverse. Web 3.0's key feature, interoperability, facilitates seamless interaction between different systems. This attribute could effortlessly transfer users' digital assets and identities across various platforms or worlds within the metaverse. Enhancing user experience could contribute to realising a fully integrated virtual universe.

The cryptographic principles underpinning Web 3.0 can improve users' security and privacy within the metaverse. The encryption of transactions and interactions guarantees secure exchanges, giving users more control over their data. Moreover, blockchain, a critical element of Web 3.0, offers a transparent and tamper-proof record system. It could foster trust and verification in the metaverse, ranging from verifying the authenticity of digital assets to confirming transactions and user identities. This type of answer inspired us to ask how to develop an intelligent Web 3.0 system that can overcome most Web 2.0 drawbacks. The answer was that developing an intelligent Web 3.0

system involves the integration of various technologies and design principles to address the limitations of Web 2.0. Some strategies can be considered. Firstly, one of the most significant drawbacks of Web 2.0 is the centralisation of data and control in the hands of a few tech giants. Blockchain technology and other decentralised networks can be used to distribute data and control among all participants in the network. It can reduce the risk of censorship and promote data sovereignty.

Secondly, data privacy and security are of utmost importance. Web 3.0 can deploy cryptographic methods to ensure this. Techniques like ZKPs can be used to verify transactions without revealing sensitive information. DID solutions can enable users to control their data and dictate how it is shared. Thirdly, interoperability should be a central focus. In the Web 2.0 era, many services operate in silos and lack interoperability. However, in Web 3.0, standards and protocols can be developed to ensure that different platforms, applications, and blockchains can communicate and interact seamlessly. Next, implementing smart contracts and dApps is essential. These autonomous programmes, running on the blockchain, allow complex operations to be carried out without intermediaries. They can be used to create dApps that provide services similar to Web 2.0 but in a decentralised, trustless manner.

Furthermore, user-centric design is crucial. Web 3.0 should prioritise user experience, with intuitive interfaces and systems designed to educate users about the value and use of decentralisation, privacy, and data sovereignty. Finally, effective decentralised governance mechanisms are paramount for managing upgrades, resolving disputes, and making collective decisions in a Web 3.0 environment. These strategies collectively serve as a blueprint for developing an intelligent Web 3.0 system.

11.7 Applications and Future Directions

We have explored and introduced various potential applications and use cases for integrating generative AI into the Web 3.0 ecosystem, particularly ChatGPT. However, in all these scenarios, Web 3.0 predominantly consumes ChatGPT's capabilities, with the models operating on conventional Web 2.0 cloud infrastructures. This disparity arises because Web 3.0 frameworks have evolved around core elements like decentralised computation, storage, identity, and messaging, with little emphasis on the domain of ML. Within the confines of Web 3.0, infrastructure or technologies have not substantially developed to support ML.

Unsurprisingly, groundbreaking ML advancements, such as transformer architectures and pre-trained models, have not left a mark within Web 3.0 infrastructures. The primary technical hurdle in introducing a native Web 3.0 Generative AI model like ChatGPT lies in the inherent mismatch between the requirements for running foundational models and the specific runtime environment of Web 3.0, particularly blockchain systems. A standard pre-trained foundational model comprises millions of neurons distributed across extensive interconnected layers, typically executing on clusters of graphics processing units (GPUs) or specialised hardware topologies for deep learning. This level of complexity far surpasses any smart contract in the history of Web 3.0. Consequently, it logically follows that a new form of architecture is necessary. Even Web 2.0 infrastructures are undergoing adaptations to accommodate large-scale generative AI models, underscoring the magnitude of changes required within Web 3.0 frameworks.

Scaling Web 3.0 runtime blockchain to meet the demands of these models, which involve billions of parameters and substantial datasets, proves exceedingly costly. This reality has led to the omission of considerations for training or pre-training ChatGPT-4 within blockchain runtimes, given the current inefficiency of blockchains for such compute-intensive tasks and their associated expenses. Furthermore, Web 3.0 infrastructures lack the foundational computing resources, data, and data science frameworks necessary to embrace generative AI fully. Although dApps can certainly integrate generative AI capabilities by interacting with models through Web 2.0 APIs, the prospect of a Web 3.0-native generative AI remains a formidable challenge.

Applying ChatGPT to develop and enhance Web 3.0 and metaverse comes with significant challenges that should be considered. Even though it can generate impressive outcomes, it can occasionally make a mistake and fail to understand conversation specifics and context. Hence, the accuracy of the content generated by ChatGPT or other generative models is another major issue for both the creator and consumer of these contents. Therefore, GPT outputs need more human insight to ensure they generate the correct output, depending on and aligned with the provided input (Dwivedi et al., 2023).

Besides that, ChatGPT currently has a restricted input of exactly 4096 tokens to process (OpenAI ChatGPT, n.d.), which constrains the capability of interacting with use cases that need more data or scenarios to provide the model. This limitation is also tied to the number of requests that we can send to the model via the API; even if it is still improving, it is slow in response, and there is a noticeable time delay that can be considered a significant issue for the use cases in metaverse that need a real-time response. These limitations significantly restrict integrations and the use of GPT as a middleware. Applying ChatGPT to develop and enhance Web 3.0 and metaverse comes with significant challenges that should be considered as shown in Figure 11.5.

Bias is another issue that cannot be overlooked. Like all AI models, GPT is trained on extensive human language datasets. Therefore, it can potentially boost the biases found in these datasets; also, it can be exploitable for targeted content to be trained on it to make the results unreasonable (Yang, 2022). Privacy and security concerns persist with AI models like ChatGPT that generate responses based on user inputs. Employing it in Web 3.0 and metaverse could expose sensitive project details; for example, as ChatGPT

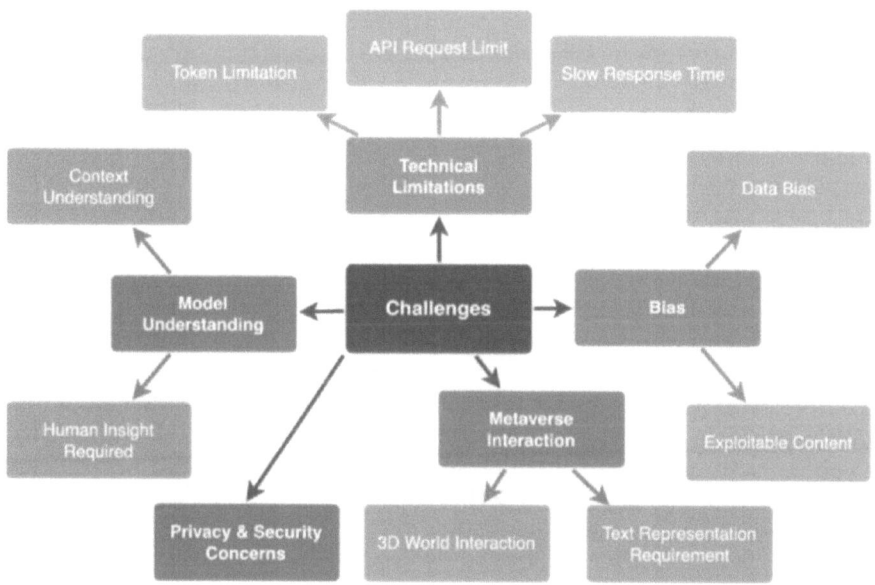

FIGURE 11.5
ChatGPT middleware challenges.

assists developers in writing or reviewing code, it could unintentionally leak sensitive project details. Malicious players could exploit this information. Also, in the metaverse, where digital identities have significant personal and financial implications, ChatGPT's unintentional leak of identity-related information could lead to significant privacy risks.

Finally, as ChatGPT is a text-based model, the 3D world of the metaverse presents a unique integration challenge. So, for the model to understand the contexts and produce relevant results, a way must be found to translate 3D interactions and scenarios into text format. It adds another layer of complexity to the application of ChatGPT within the metaverse.

Addressing these challenges is necessary for successfully applying ChatGPT in the context of Web 3.0 and the metaverse ecosystem. Web 3.0 strives to reshape the Internet, focusing on user-centricity, ushering in decentralisation, heightened security, and increased openness. Foundational models like ChatGPT undeniably hold the potential to introduce a fresh wave of capabilities to dApps. However, this potential is not without its share of limitations and challenges. Concurrently, Web 3.0 can assume a captivating role in the infrastructure underpinning these models.

An illustrative example is the concern of accountability, which looms large as models such as ChatGPT come to the fore. Grappling with the origins of harmful, deceptive, unbiased, or inequitable content has occupied a central position in discussions surrounding the mainstream adoption of ChatGPT and analogous models. The innate decentralisation of Web 3.0. emerges as an apt technological solution, facilitating trustless transparency and the ability to conduct audits for models like ChatGPT. The incorporation of ChatGPT-4 within the Web 3.0 framework signifies a substantial stride towards a more user-centric Internet, poised to revolutionise industries and reshape online interactions. Nonetheless, we must confront diverse constraints and hurdles accompanying utilising ChatGPT's advantages. It is worth noting that while the core of this revolution extends beyond Web 3.0, its ramifications are likely to impact the disparity in innovation, talent, and funding between Web 2.0 and Web 3.0 technologies.

The surge of innovation in open-source foundational models has notably reduced the entry barriers for Web 3.0 platforms to integrate capabilities such as ChatGPT and other generative AI functions. Even more captivating possibilities arise when we contemplate Web 3.0 platforms inherently accommodating generative AI models. Envision open-source foundational models like LLaMA, Dolly, or Alpaca functioning on nodes within a distributed blockchain. The ultimate realisation of this concept entails a blockchain explicitly tailored for the execution of generative AI.

References

Alabdulwahhab, F. A. (2018). Web 3.0: the decentralised web blockchain networks and protocol innovation. In *2018 1st International Conference on Computer Applications & Information Security (ICCAIS)* (pp. 1–4). IEEE.

Brown, T., Mann, B., Ryder, N., Subbiah, M., Kaplan, J. D., Dhariwal, P., & Amodei, D. (2020). Language models are few-shot learners. *Advances in Neural Information Processing Systems, 33*, 1877–1901.

Du, H., Teng, S., Chen, H., Ma, J., Wang, X., Gou, C., & Wang, F. Y. (2023). Chat with ChatGPT on intelligent vehicles: An IEEE TIV perspective. *IEEE Transactions on Intelligent Vehicles, 8*(3), 2020–2026. https://doi.org/10.1109/TIV.2023.3253281

Dunphy, P., & Petitcolas, F. A. (2018). A first look at identity management schemes on the blockchain. *IEEE Security & Privacy, 16*(4), 20–29. https://doi.org/10.1109/MSP.2018.3111247

Dwivedi, Y. K., Kshetri, N., Hughes, L., Slade, E. L., Jeyaraj, A., Kar, A. K., & Wright, R. (2023). Opinion paper: "So what if ChatGPT wrote it?" Multidisciplinary perspectives on opportunities, challenges and implications of generative conversational AI for research, practice and policy, *International Journal of Information Management, 71*, 102642. https://doi.org/10.1016/j.ijinfomgt.2023.102642

Farseev, A. (2023). Is Bigger Better? Why the ChatGPT Vs. GPT-3 Vs. GPT-4 'Battle' Is Just A Family Chat. https://www.forbes.com/sites/forbestechcouncil/2023/02/17/is-bigger-better-why-the-chatgpt-vs-gpt-3-vs-gpt-4-battle-is-just-a-family-chat

Flensted, T. (2024). How Many Languages Does ChatGPT Support. https://seo.ai/blog/how-many-languages-does-chatgpt-support

Kshetri, N. (2022). Web 3.0 and the metaverse shaping organisations' brand and product strategies. *IT Professional, 24*(02), 11–15. https://doi.org/10.1109/MITP.2022.3157206

OpenAI ChatGPT (n.d.). https://chatgpt.com/

Thorp, H. H. (2023). ChatGPT is fun, but not an author. *Science, 379*(6630), 313–313. https://doi.org/10.1126/science.adg7879

Yang, S. (2022). The Abilities and Limitations of ChatGPT. https://www.anaconda. com/blog/the-abilities-and-limitations-of-chatgpt

Zarrin, J., Wen Phang, H., Babu Saheer, L., & Zarrin, B. (2021). Blockchain for decentralisation of Internet: Prospects, trends, and challenges. *Cluster Computing, 24*(4), 2841–2866. https://doi.org/10.1007/s10586-021-03301-8

Section IV

Sustainability and Inclusivity

12

Augmented and Virtual Realities for Special Needs: Fostering Inclusive Education in Urban Sustainability

Husniza Husni, Nurul Izzah Abdul Aziz, and
Emy Hazlinda Mohammad Ridzwan

12.1 Addressing Special Needs through AR/ VR in Urban Environments

Inclusive education is critical for promoting equity and sustainability in today's rapidly evolving urban landscapes. It ensures that all individuals, regardless of their abilities or backgrounds, have access to quality education that meets their diverse needs (UNESCO, 2020). It recognises and values each student's unique contributions, fostering an environment where learners can thrive and develop to their full potential (Ainscow & Sandill, 2010). However, inclusive education faces significant challenges for special needs learners, such as ensuring appropriate accessibility, providing individualised support, and overcoming societal stigma (Slee, 2011). These students often require tailored teaching methods, specialised resources, and consistent collaboration among educators, families, and support services to participate and succeed in mainstream educational settings effectively (Florian, 2014).

Additionally, there is often a lack of adequately trained staff and insufficient funding, which can further impede the delivery of an inclusive and equitable education for special needs learners (Sharma et al., 2013). Despite these challenges, creating an inclusive environment is essential for fostering a sense of belonging and enabling every student to achieve their full potential (Booth & Ainscow, 2011). Technologies like augmented reality (AR) and virtual reality (VR) can play a transformative role in this endeavour by providing innovative, immersive, and flexible learning solutions that cater to the diverse needs of special needs learners (Bossavit & Parsons, 2016).

AR and VR technologies have emerged as transformative tools in educational settings, offering new ways to engage special needs learners and ensuring they can participate fully in the learning process (Cobb & Sharkey, 2007). Through AR and VR, educators can create interactive and personalised educational experiences that are engaging and accessible to students with various disabilities, thereby promoting inclusivity and equity in the learning process (Freina & Ott, 2015). For instance, VR can immerse students with mobility impairments in virtual field trips to historical sites, museums, or natural environments that would otherwise be physically inaccessible to them (Standen & Brown, 2005). It allows these students to explore and learn in ways that are often limited by traditional classroom settings.

Similarly, AR can enhance learning for students with sensory processing challenges or cognitive impairments by overlaying visual cues, auditory prompts, or interactive elements onto real-world objects (Bossavit & Parsons, 2016). For example, an AR app could highlight and label parts of a plant or animal in a science lesson, providing tactile and visual reinforcement that aids in comprehension and retention of information (McMahon et al., 2016). It can be particularly beneficial for students with autism spectrum disorder (ASD), as it allows them to interact with the material in a way that aligns with their learning styles (Bossavit & Parsons, 2016). Moreover, AR and VR can help students with visual impairments by offering enhanced visual and audio descriptions, enabling them to participate more fully in activities such as reading, navigation, or even art (Lahav & Mioduser, 2008). For example, a VR program could recreate a three-dimensional, tactile model of a molecule or a piece of art, allowing visually impaired students to "see" through touch and spatial audio descriptions, making abstract concepts more concrete and accessible (Lahav & Mioduser, 2008). By incorporating these technologies, educators can create a more inclusive learning environment where every student, regardless of their disability, can engage actively, learn effectively, and achieve their full potential (Freina & Ott, 2015). It enriches the educational experience for special needs learners and promotes a culture of acceptance and understanding among all students (Bossavit & Parsons, 2016).

This chapter explores how AR and VR can address the unique challenges faced by special needs learners in urban environments, provides examples of practical applications, discusses the benefits and challenges of integrating these technologies, and proposes directions for future research and community engagement.

12.1.1 Understanding Special Needs Education in Urban Contexts

Urban environments present unique challenges for individuals with special needs, including accessibility barriers, sensory overload, and social isolation (Florian, 2014; Slee, 2011). Traditional educational approaches often fall short in addressing these challenges, making it essential to explore innovative solutions that can adapt to diverse learner needs (Ainscow & Sandill, 2010; UNESCO, 2020). Understanding special needs education within an urban context is a complex endeavour that requires addressing the unique challenges and barriers that students with disabilities face in densely populated environments. Urban schools often grapple with larger class sizes, limited resources, and diverse student populations, which can impact the delivery of special education services (Pak & Parsons, 2020). For instance, consider a scenario where a student with a learning disability in a large urban school struggles to receive individualised attention due to the high student-to-teacher ratio. This student may benefit from assistive technology that can provide personalised learning experiences and support. However, implementing such technology requires adequate funding and training for educators, which can be scarce in urban districts (Sharma et al., 2013).

Recent literature emphasises the importance of inclusive practices and integrating students with disabilities into mainstream classrooms. The Education Endowment Foundation's Guidance Report (2020) suggests that effective inclusion benefits students with special needs by providing access to the general curriculum and fostering a culture of diversity and acceptance among all students. To effectively support students with special needs in urban schools, adopting a collaborative approach involving teachers, parents, and specialists is essential. This collaboration can lead to the development of Individualised Education Programs (IEPs) that are tailored to each student's needs and consider the urban environment's unique challenges (Pak & Parsons, 2020).

In conclusion, special needs education in an urban context requires a commitment to equity and inclusion, adopting assistive technologies, and a collaborative approach to education planning. By addressing these key areas, urban schools can create supportive and effective learning environments for all students.

12.1.2 The Role of AR and VR

AR and VR technologies offer immersive, customisable experiences that can significantly enhance the learning environment for special needs students. By fostering an immersive learning environment, these technologies allow students to learn interactively and improve memorisation compared to only using textbooks (Magomadov, 2020). AR overlays digital information in the real world, providing contextual support and interactive elements that can help students understand complex concepts. Conversely, VR creates entirely virtual environments, allowing learners to engage in scenarios that might be difficult or impossible in real life.

It provides safe, inclusive environments for learning and socialisation for special needs students. For example, VR simulations can assist individuals with autism in improving their social skills by simulating real-life situations in a safe environment. Additionally, students with physical limitations can participate in adventures and activities they might not otherwise be able to. VR can simulate real-world urban settings, enabling students to practice navigating busy streets or using public transportation in a safe, controlled environment. Such simulations can help reduce anxiety and build confidence in real-life situations.

AR can be used in classrooms to provide interactive visual aids and real-time feedback, making abstract concepts more tangible and accessible. Most importantly, AR can trigger or stimulate multisensory learning, which in this case most probably would be visual, audio, and perhaps kinaesthetic when it involves some movements. Therefore, educational institutions should explore integrating AR and VR to enhance the quality and impact of education for learners, whether with special needs or any learners, for more engaging and interactive learning sessions.

12.2 AR/VR Applications for Special Needs Learners in Urban Sustainability

12.2.1 Case Study: AR for Urban Ecology Education

A practical application of AR for special needs learners is its use in urban ecology education. For example, AR apps can overlay information about plant and animal species in urban parks, allowing students to explore and learn about their environment in an engaging, hands-on manner. Such tools can be particularly beneficial for learners with sensory processing disorders, as they provide a controlled way to interact with the environment without sensory overload. By leveraging sensory modalities, AR technology enhances skill acquisition and learning performance for special needs learners in sustainable learning environments (Cavus et al., 2021). It contributes to more accessible and inclusive learning experiences, demonstrating the potential of AR tools to support diverse educational needs.

12.2.2 Case Study: VR for Empathy and Social Skills Training

VR can be a powerful tool for teaching empathy and social skills, which are often areas of difficulty for students with ASD. VR simulations can place learners in scenarios where they must navigate social interactions or understand the perspectives of others, helping to develop critical social skills in a safe, controlled setting. VR can significantly enhance social skills in individuals with ASD, offering practical experiences that mirror daily social interactions (Dechsling et al., 2021). For instance, a study involving students with ASD utilised a VR-based social skills program, resulting in improved social abilities and increased confidence. These findings highlight the potential of VR to provide immersive, controlled settings where young learners can practice and strengthen essential social skills (Ke et al., 2022).

12.2.3 Integrating AR/VR in Urban Sustainability Curriculum

Incorporating AR and VR into the urban sustainability curriculum allows special needs learners to actively participate in projects that require understanding complex systems and interdependencies within urban environments. For instance, students can use VR to simulate the impact of various urban planning decisions on sustainability outcomes, gaining a deeper understanding of how their actions affect the environment. Additionally, AR can overlay digital information onto real-world urban settings, providing interactive educational experiences. For example, students can explore urban ecological systems using AR, which enhances their understanding of sustainability concepts.

This approach makes learning more engaging and supports diverse learning needs by presenting information through various sensory modalities. For instance, the EcoMOBILE project demonstrated that combining AR with environmental problems during field trips enhances students' understanding of ecological concepts (Kamarainen et al., 2013). By providing contextualised and interactive learning experiences, AR helps students better understand complex environmental systems, making abstract concepts more tangible and engaging. Hence, educators can create improved learning experiences that adapt to different learning styles by integrating AR and VR into the urban sustainability curriculum, promoting accessibility and inclusivity in education.

12.3 Benefits and Challenges of AR/VR Integration

12.3.1 The Benefits

Integrating AR/VR into special needs education has its benefits, such as enhancing the students' engagement and motivation to learn and be immersed in the topics they are learning. Such technology enriches the learning experience and provides personalised learning, a much-needed approach to meeting their needs. The technology supports learning by providing safe learning environments for the students, hopefully positively creating meaningful and effective learning sessions.

AR and VR provide interactive, immersive experiences that can make learning more engaging and enjoyable, which is particularly beneficial for students who struggle with traditional instructional methods. According to Alizadehsalehi et al. (2021), students who use AR and VR technology have higher motivation, engagement, and better academic performance. It is due to the immersive nature of AR and VR, which allows students to explore, discover, and engage with their surroundings in more engaging ways.

These technologies allow for the customisation of learning experiences to meet the individual needs of each student, offering tailored support and content that can adapt to their learning pace and style. Familoni and Onyebuchi (2024) state that AR and VR can transform traditional teaching methods and promote innovative learning approaches. These technologies provide immersive, interactive, and personalised learning experiences, fundamentally changing the educational environment. As AR and VR evolve, they are expected to redefine education by creating new opportunities to enhance teaching quality and learning outcomes.

VR, in particular, offers a risk-free environment where students can practice and learn from their mistakes without fearing real-world consequences. Incorporating VR into special education improves learning outcomes and engagement and offers a safe space where students can experiment, explore, and learn from their experiences without worrying about real-world consequences. For instance, VR interventions have positively impacted social skills development in children and adolescents with ASD, providing a controlled environment for practising interactions (Yang et al., 2025).

As a result, by integrating VR and AR technologies, educators can create immersive, engaging, safe, and personalised learning experiences that cater to the unique needs of special needs learners, enhancing their educational outcomes.

12.3.2 The Challenges

Although AR/VR can be beneficial, they do bring some challenges to the table. For instance, the cost of integrating the technologies in classrooms can be a significant challenge, thus limiting the accessibility to such integration. Another challenge could be regarding technological literacy or digital literacy. This challenge is imposed not only on the students with specific needs but also on teachers alike. Not having adequate technological literacy can be a problem in integrating technology into teaching and learning, especially for special needs education. As for the students, their sensory and physical limitations could also pose some challenges to the integration.

The high cost of AR and VR technology can be a significant barrier to widespread adoption, particularly in underfunded schools and communities. This finding is further supported by Mohamudally (2018), who states that VR and AR have not yet succeeded in becoming widely available technologies in many fields, including education. Teachers and students must develop the necessary skills to use AR and VR tools effectively, which requires ongoing training and support. De Paolis and Bourdot (2019) mentioned that many school administrators do not fully understand how the proper use of this technology can improve the classroom. Some experts believe this view is flawed because the technology is ineffective unless the curriculum is adjusted to support its use. Delaying its integration until fully proven may slow progress and cause inaction.

Some students may experience discomfort or adverse reactions to the immersive nature of AR and VR, such as motion sickness or sensory overload. Symptoms such as nausea, dizziness, and disorientation may arise due to sensory incompatibilities in VR environments (Laessoe et al., 2023). Similarly, Souchet et al. (2023) emphasised the risks of VR, including visual fatigue and cybersickness. These findings highlight the necessity of considering sensory and physical limitations when implementing AR and VR tools in education.

AR and VR enhance education by improving engagement, retention, and skills, but overcoming challenges like cost, technological literacy, and sensory and physical limitations is essential for their successful adoption, ensuring more effective and accessible learning experiences. As these technologies continue to evolve, they hold the potential to transform traditional learning methods and create more inclusive and interactive educational environments.

12.4 Community Engagement and Future Directions

12.4.1 Building Inclusive Communities

Community involvement is crucial for successfully integrating AR and VR into education. Collaborating with local organisations, technology developers, and educators can help ensure that the tools and content are accessible and relevant to the needs of special needs learners. Engaging families and community members in designing and implementing AR and VR projects can promote a more inclusive educational environment. For example, community workshops involving parents, educators, and developers can gather feedback and ideas on how AR and VR tools can be tailored to the unique learning needs of special needs students. These workshops can also provide training for educators and parents, empowering them to use AR and VR technologies at school and at home effectively. It ensures the educational tools are relevant and meaningful, increasing engagement and learning outcomes.

12.4.2 Future Research and Development

Future research should focus on developing affordable, user-friendly AR and VR tools that cater specifically to the needs of special education students. Additionally, studies should investigate the long-term effects of these technologies on learning outcomes and social integration. Cai et al. (2021) highlighted the positive impacts of AR games on students with educational needs but also identified design challenges that need to be addressed in future developments. Moreover, Creed et al. (2024) identified accessibility barriers in immersive technologies for individuals with disabilities, emphasising the need for inclusive design in future AR and VR applications.

Cai et al. (2021) discussed the positive impact of AR games on special education students. One challenge is ensuring that AR games are adaptable to different learning styles and skills and identifying design challenges that need to be addressed in future developments. Future research could focus on developing adaptive learning algorithms that adjust the difficulty level in real-time based on the student's performance, providing a personalised learning experience.

Moreover, Creed et al. (2024) identified accessibility difficulties in immersive technologies for people with disabilities, highlighting the importance of inclusive design in future AR and VR applications. For instance, investigating multimodal interaction integration, such as voice commands and gesture controls, could accommodate learners with motor impairments. To improve accessibility for users with visual or auditory impairments, future research could also examine the use of customisable text sizes, colour contrasts, and audio descriptions.

AR and VR offer promising solutions for enhancing the educational experiences of special needs learners in urban environments. By addressing their unique challenges and providing immersive, personalised learning opportunities, these technologies can contribute significantly to inclusive education and urban sustainability. VR and AR offer educational benefits, including increased engagement, motivation, and enhanced learning outcomes. These technologies enable special needs learners to explore virtual environments, interact with digital content, and experience simulations that promote a deeper comprehension of the subject matter. Overcoming these challenges is essential to the impact of VR and AR in education, especially for special needs learners. Investing in the required infrastructure and technology and providing teachers with support and training to use these resources effectively are essential for successful integration. Continued community engagement and research are essential to fully realise the potential of AR and VR in fostering a more inclusive and sustainable future.

References

Ainscow, M., & Sandill, A. (2010). Developing inclusive education systems: The role of organisational cultures and leadership. *International Journal of Inclusive Education, 14*(4), 401–416. https://doi.org/10.1080/13603110802504903

Alizadehsalehi, S., Hadavi, A., & Huang, J. C. (2021). Assessment of AEC students' performance using BIM-into-VR. *Applied Sciences, 11*(7), 3225. https://doi.org/10.3390/app11073225

Booth, T., & Ainscow, M. (2011). *Index for inclusion: Developing learning and participation in schools.* Centre for Studies on Inclusive Education.

Bossavit, B., & Parsons, S. (2016). This is how I want to learn: High functioning autistic teens' grounded theory of how they learn. *Autism, 20*(8), 928–939. https://doi.org/10.1145/2858036.285832

Cai, M., Akcayir, G., & Epp, C. D. (2021). Exploring augmented reality games in accessible learning: A systematic review. arXiv preprint arXiv:2111.08214.

Cavus, N., Al-Dosakee, K., Abdi, A., & Sadiq, S. (2021). The utilisation of augmented reality technology for sustainable skill development for people with special needs: A systematic literature review. *Sustainability, 13*(19), 10532. https://doi.org/10.3390/su131910532

Cobb, S. V., & Sharkey, P. M. (2007). A decade of research and development in disability, virtual reality and associated technologies: Review of ICDVRAT 1996–2006. *The International Journal of Virtual Reality, 6*(2), 51–68.

Creed, C., Al-Kalbani, M., Theil, A., Sarcar, S., & Williams, I. (2024). Inclusive AR/VR: Accessibility barriers for immersive technologies. *Universal Access in the Information Society, 23*(1), 59–73. https://doi.org/10.1007/s10209-023-00969-0

De Paolis, L. T., & Bourdot, P. (Eds.). (2019). Augmented reality, virtual reality, and computer graphics. *6th international conference, AVR 2019, Santa Maria al Bagno, Italy,* June 24–27, 2019, Proceedings, Part II (Vol. 11614). Springer.

Dechsling, A., Orm, S., Kalandadze, T., Sütterlin, S., Øien, R. A., Shic, F., & Nordahl-Hansen, A. (2021). Virtual and augmented reality in social skills interventions for individuals with autism spectrum disorder: A scoping review, *Journal of Autism and Developmental Disorders, 52*, 1–16. https://doi.org/10.1007/s10803-021-05338-5

Familoni, B. T., & Onyebuchi, N. C. (2024). Augmented and virtual reality in us education: A review: Analysing the impact, effectiveness, and future prospects of AR/VR tools in enhancing learning experiences. *International Journal of Applied Research in Social Sciences, 6*(4), 642–663.

Florian, L. (2014). What counts as evidence of inclusive education? *European Journal of Special Needs Education, 29*(3), 286–294. https://doi.org/10.1080/08856257.2014.933551

Freina, L., & Ott, M. (2015). A literature review on immersive virtual reality in education: State of the art and perspectives. In *The International Scientific Conference eLearning and Software for Education* (Vol. 1, p. 133). "Carol I" National Defence University.

Kamaraien, A. M., Metcalf, S., Grotzer, T., Browne, A., Mazzuca, D., Tutwiler, M. S., & Dede, C. (2013). EcoMOBILE: Integrating augmented reality and probeware with environmental education field trips, *Computers & Education, 68*, 545–556. https://doi.org/10.1016/j.compedu.2013.02.018

Ke, F., Moon, J., & Sokolikj, Z. (2022). Virtual reality–based social skills training for children with autism spectrum disorder. *Journal of Special Education Technology, 37*(1), 49–62. https://doi.org/10.1177/0162643420945603

Laessoe, U., Abrahamsen, S., Zepernick, S., Raunsbaek, A., & Stensen, C. (2023). Motion sickness and cybersickness-sensory mismatch, *Physiology & Behavior, 258*, 114015. https://doi.org/10.1016/j.physbeh.2022.114015

Lahav, O., & Mioduser, D. (2008). Haptic-feedback support for cognitive mapping of unknown spaces by people who are visually impaired. *International Journal of Human-Computer Studies, 66*(1), 23–35. https://doi.org/10.1016/j.ijhcs.2007.08.001

Magomadov, V. S. (2020). Examining the potential of VR and AR technologies for education. *Journal of physics: Conference series, 1691*(1), 012160.

McMahon, D. D., Cihak, D. F., Wright, R. E., & Bell, S. M. (2016). Augmented reality for teaching science vocabulary to postsecondary education students with intellectual disabilities and autism. *Journal of Research on Technology in Education, 48*(1), 38–56. https://doi.org/10.1080/15391523.2015.1103149

Mohamudally, N. (Ed.). (2018). *State of the art virtual reality and augmented reality knowhow*. BoD–Books on Demand.

Pak, K., & Parsons, A. (2020). Equity gaps for students with disabilities. *Penn GSE Perspectives on Urban Education, 17*. https://api.semanticscholar.org/Corpus ID:218570252

Sharma, U., Forlin, C., & Loreman, T. (2013). Impact of training on pre-service teachers' attitudes and concerns about inclusive education and sentiments about persons with disabilities. *Disability & Society, 28*(7), 935–949. https://doi.org/10.1080/09687590802469271

Slee, R. (2011). *The irregular school: Exclusion, schooling and inclusive education*. Routledge.

Souchet, A. D., Lourdeaux, D., Pagani, A., & Rebenitsch, L. (2023). A narrative review of immersive virtual reality's ergonomics and risks at the workplace: Cybersickness, visual fatigue, muscular fatigue, acute stress, and mental overload. *Virtual Reality, 27*(1), 19–50. https://doi.org/10.1007/s10055-022-00672-0

Standen, P. J., & Brown, D. J. (2005). Virtual reality in the rehabilitation of people with intellectual disabilities: Review. *Cyberpsychology & Behavior, 8*(3), 272–282. https://doi.org/10.1089/cpb.2005.8.272

UNESCO. (2020). Global education monitoring report 2020: Inclusion and education: All means all. UNESCO.

Yang, X., Wu, J., Ma, Y., Yu, J., Cao, H., Zeng, A., & Ren, Z. (2025). Effectiveness of virtual reality technology interventions in improving the social skills of children and adolescents with autism: Systematic review, *Journal of Medical Internet Research, 27*, e60845. https://doi.org/10.2196/60845

13

Food Sharing for Sustainability and Inclusivity in the Metaverse

Nor Farzana Abd Ghani and Alawiyah Abd Wahab

13.1 Introduction

The digital transformation of food sharing is becoming integral to sustainability efforts in smart cities while extending into innovative virtual environments like the metaverse. As urban areas adopt advanced technologies, food-sharing initiatives help reduce environmental impacts and foster community collaboration (Kearney, 2010). By utilising digital platforms, these initiatives connect individuals and businesses with surplus food to those in need, bridging physical and virtual communities. Prominent applications such as Too Good To Go, OLIO, Karma, FoodCloud, and ShareWaste exemplify how technology effectively addresses food waste and enhances community engagement (Bennett & Smith, 2022; Ritchie & Roser, 2023). These platforms facilitate food redistribution and contribute to a circular economy for sustainable urban development. Food sharing in the metaverse opens new avenues for virtual collaboration, enabling stakeholders to engage in sustainable practices beyond traditional boundaries.

A metaverse is a virtual environment that enables users to interact with one another and digital objects in real-time through customisable avatars. It utilises advanced technologies such as simulation, virtual reality (VR), augmented reality (AR), 3D modelling, artificial intelligence (AI), and blockchain to craft immersive and interactive environments (Wang & Medvegy, 2022; Yaqoob et al., 2023). The immersive experiences in the metaverse enable users to visualise and interact with the food supply chain innovatively. This capability creates new opportunities to address food waste by allowing local food producers, such as restaurants, to share, track, and redistribute surplus food within virtual spaces. Additionally, food sharing in the metaverse can help revitalise urban areas by fostering a more inclusive, resilient, and supportive community, ultimately enhancing the long-term well-being of underserved communities.

This chapter explores the intersection of food sharing and the metaverse, featuring a case study on smart food-sharing initiatives for underserved

DOI: 10.1201/9781003619819-17

communities in Malaysia, strategies for implementing food sharing in the metaverse, and future trends in green technology that can enhance these initiatives.

13.2 A Case Study on Smart Food Sharing for the Underserved Community

Much effort has already been taken to reduce food waste at each stage of the food value chain. However, even if approaches to reduce losses during production and storage stages in developing countries prove successful, these gains may be offset by increases in food waste at the consumption end, especially as the global middle class expands (Hanson & Ahmadi, 2021). Numerous studies have explored ways to reduce or prevent food waste during consumption, mainly through mobile applications (Doğan & Yıldız, 2022). However, most of these studies focus on reducing household food waste (e.g., Barker & McCarthy, 2023; Zhang, 2024). While household food waste management promotes donations, it fails to target the underprivileged.

Food donations should focus on supporting underprivileged groups, commonly referred to as *Asnaf* (Rahman, 2023). According to the Department of Statistics Malaysia (DoSM), *Asnaf* households have a median income of RM3,000 (USD 680) (Usamah, 2024). The concept of sadaqah – donating food to those in need – aligns with Islamic principles, and studies have shown the success of such efforts when food is distributed to the *Asnaf* according to their district (Zaki et al., 2020).

This case study explores the distribution of unspoiled excess food from local food producers by promoting food sharing as an act of sadaqah to the *Asnaf* community through the AsnafFood mobile application. Consultations with *Asnaf* Authority – Lembaga Zakat Negeri Kedah (LZNK) and the Food Safety and Quality Division of the Ministry of Health (MoH) helped develop a comprehensive system concept and food safety guideline. The system workflow and food safety mechanisms were designed and developed based on this collaboration.

13.2.1 AsnafFood Mobile Application

AsnafFood leverages technology to distribute surplus food effectively, enhancing food security in resource-limited areas. To ensure the safety of the food, the researchers take the initiative by providing guidelines on food safety within AsnafFood. Infographics are used in the system to educate the users, as shown in Figure 13.1. All food producers involved in the project were advised to follow MoH guidelines. In addition, the local authority,

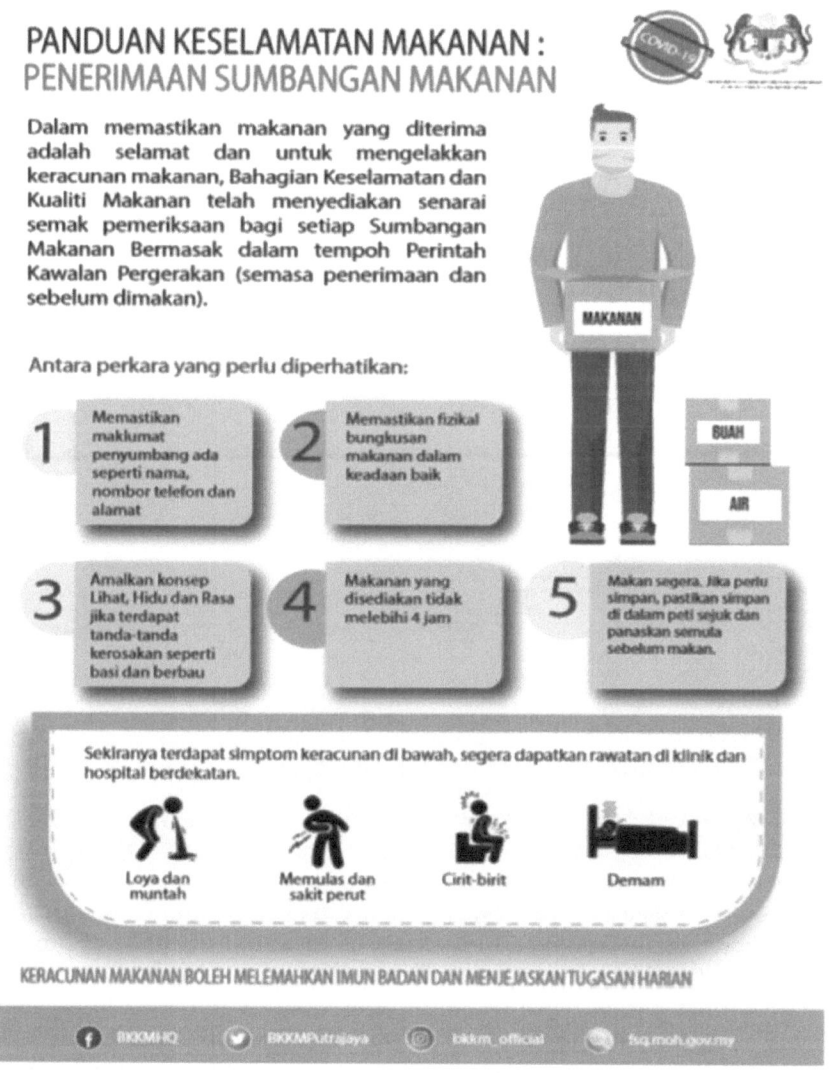

FIGURE 13.1
An example of an article for educating users.

with advice from this department, also monitors the cleanliness of the food premises.

The system workflow was designed after considering *Asnaf*'s e-readiness and deep understanding of the Food Safety Guideline. As presented in Figure 13.2, when food producers confirm their participation (to receive donations and provide free food) by registering their premises and food offers through the AsnafFood app, the system will blast the food offered

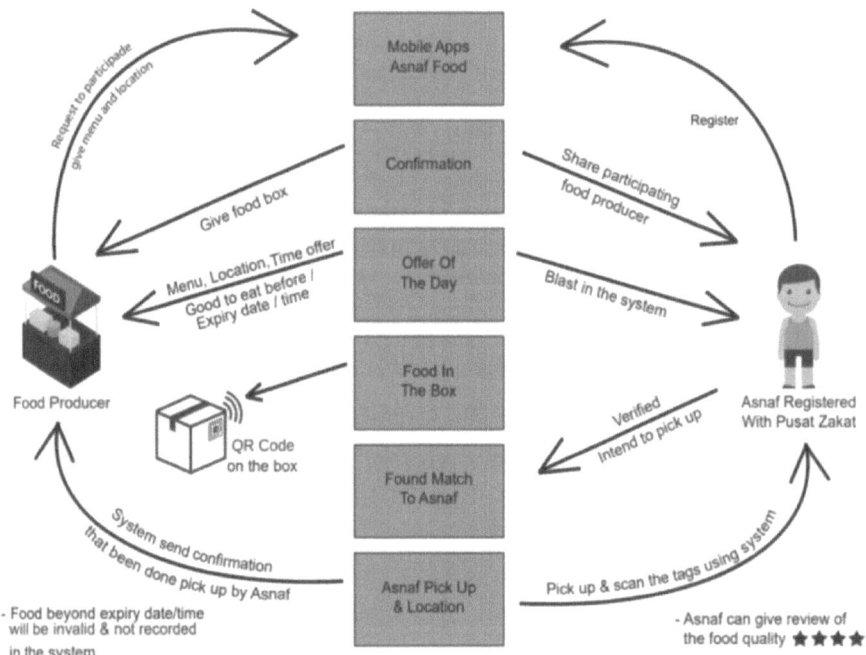

FIGURE 13.2
The system workflow.

to the registered *Asnaf*, as shown in Figure 13.3. Based on the *Asnafs*' preferences, i.e., the nearest location to pick up food, *Asnaf* will go directly to the food premise to self-pick up and scan the QR code to confirm the received food (see Figure 13.4). To ensure freshness and food safety, the food offer time is limited to breakfast (8–11 am), Lunch (12–3 pm), and Dinner (7–10 pm).

Each dining period has a standard offer validity and good-to-eat expiry time. The offer to pick up the food is valid for 3 hours only, and once picked up, the food must be consumed within the food offer time validity hours. For example, if *Asnaf* has picked up the food at the premises at 10 am for breakfast, the system reminder informs *Asnaf* to consume it by 11 am; otherwise, they bear the risk of food poisoning from eating food that is not safe to eat.

The food safety mechanism is designed to prevent foodborne illness. AsnafFood includes a feature that alerts *Asnaf* to pick up the food before it expires. By default, *Asnaf*, who has previously made transactions at any food premises, are automatically subscribed to new food offers. This auto-subscription ensures that if food remains unclaimed before its expiration, the system notifies the nearest *Asnaf* to collect it, reducing food waste. Food past its expiration is no longer valid and is being removed, with a red alert issued. *Asnafs* must tick a consent box in the system to confirm they agree

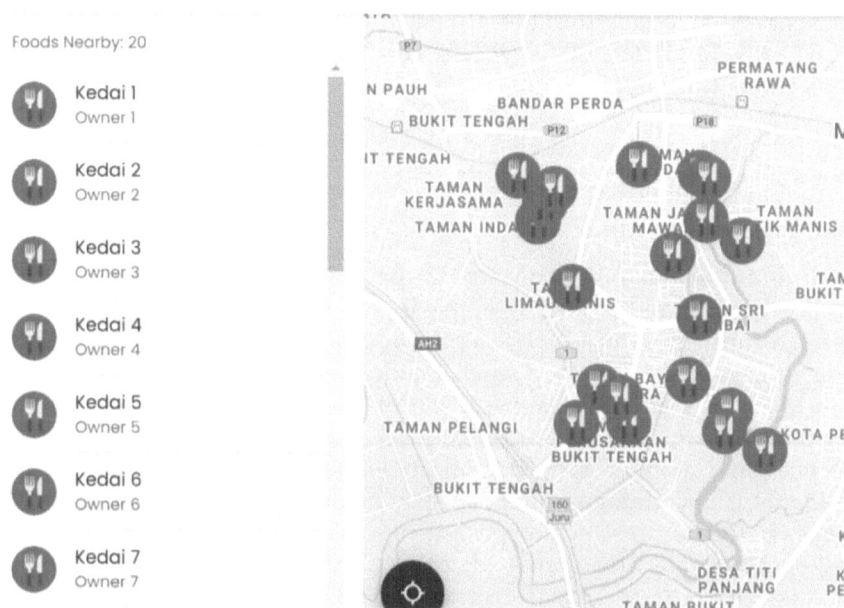

FIGURE 13.3
A map showing nearby food producers.

FIGURE 13.4
Asnaf scans the QR code on the food producer's smartphone during food pick-up.

to consume the food within the stipulated time frame. AsnafFood users are consistently reminded of the food's good-to-eat window through timely alerts and notifications.

13.3 Lesson Learned

Food safety became a key concern during the AsnafFood initiative, particularly regarding redistributing edible excess food. Stakeholders, including research funders, expressed concerns about shared food safety with *Asnaf* groups. To address this, food safety guidelines were implemented to align with MoH standards (Kwok & Lin, 2023). In the future, virtual platforms can provide interactive training for food producers, simulate food safety practices, and monitor adherence to guidelines, ensuring consistent safety standards. Collaborations with other stakeholders enable research and development in food processing and packaging, ensuring donated food maintains freshness and safety (Kumari et al., 2024).

Accessing the right *Asnaf* groups proved challenging due to LZNK's incomplete *Asnaf* profiling. This gap was bridged through collaboration with a local NGO, facilitating connections with *Asnaf* communities. This collaboration extended to the Weekly Outreach Programmes, which uses the AsnafFood app to distribute food and hold weekly community sessions on entrepreneurship, survival skills, and religious talks. This partnership highlights the vital role of community champions in sustaining and expanding outreach efforts.

While LZNK's initiatives, such as the Food Bank, provide critical support, the study identified gaps in awareness among *Asnaf* groups. Integrating platforms like their AsnafCare Website allowed greater accessibility to food donations, connecting donors with food producers. Future efforts could leverage digital innovations, such as virtual engagement tools, to streamline donor-*Asnaf* matching, food distribution, and real-time tracking systems to optimise food donations. Contrary to initial assumptions, food waste was not a significant issue among participating producers, thanks to effective portion control practices. It highlights the importance of engaging experienced food producers in food aid programmes. Leveraging predictive analytics could further enhance food donation patterns and reduce waste.

The AsnafFood app's success was driven by its simplicity, location-based features, and intuitive design. User feedback emphasised the importance of a user-friendly interface and relevant content. Future updates focus on enhancing usability with personalised content recommendations and instant start features to encourage broader adoption. By incorporating robust food safety mechanisms, strengthening collaborations, and adopting innovative solutions, AsnafFood can become a model for sustainable, tech-driven food aid systems (Galanakis, 2024).

13.4 Strategies for Food Sharing in the Metaverse

The e-readiness of underserved populations, particularly *Asnaf* communities, is pivotal in enabling active participation. E-readiness refers to an individual's or group's readiness and willingness to adopt digital technologies, along with the capacity to leverage these technologies to create innovative opportunities and accelerate progress towards achieving goals more efficiently and effectively (Nasution et al., 2018). However, for vulnerable communities, the lack of digital literacy and access to technology presents a significant barrier to participation in the metaverse. Therefore, addressing this digital divide is essential for the success and inclusivity of food-sharing initiatives.

A comprehensive approach is needed to ensure equitable access and bridge this gap. One potential solution is collaboration between the government and private sectors to provide affordable or subsidised VR/AR headsets to underserved communities, enabling them to participate in the metaverse. Such a partnership could also facilitate access to affordable or free Internet services. Furthermore, digital literacy programmes tailored specifically to the metaverse can equip individuals with the necessary skills to navigate virtual platforms effectively. These programmes should focus on metaverse-specific competencies, ensuring that users are familiar with basic technology and understand how to engage with virtual environments for activities such as food sharing.

In addition to access and training, the design of the food-sharing platforms within the metaverse should integrate gamification elements and user-friendly interfaces to enhance engagement and motivation. Research has shown that gamification can improve user participation and foster awareness in food waste reduction initiatives (Yu et al., 2023). By incorporating interactive and appealing elements, these platforms can increase their willingness to engage in sustainable practices within the metaverse.

Another significant challenge impeding the success of food-sharing initiatives is the behavioural barrier posed by social stigma, particularly surrounding the use of free or surplus food. Individuals who receive food donations or rely on free food are often perceived as less fortunate or valuable members of society. This stigma frequently results in feelings of shame, guilt, and a loss of dignity, as DeBate et al. (2024) noted, which may prevent individuals from seeking assistance through food-sharing platforms. However, the metaverse presents a promising solution by offering anonymity through avatars, thereby mitigating this stigma.

The avatar system in the metaverse conceals users' real-world identities, allowing underserved populations, such as *Asnaf*, to access food-sharing platforms without the fear of judgement or discrimination. Research has demonstrated that anonymity in virtual environments can enhance user engagement and reduce the negative effects of stigma (DeBate et al., 2024). Beyond anonymity, the metaverse can be designed to promote cultural sensitivity and inclusivity. Therefore, the metaverse can offer customisable features, allowing users to tailor their experience to their cultural preferences and fostering a more inclusive and respectful environment.

Collaboration among technology companies, government agencies, non-governmental organisations (NGOs), and local community leaders is crucial for developing an inclusive and scalable solution for food-sharing initiatives within the metaverse (Ramli & Mahmud, 2023). Each stakeholder brings valuable resources, expertise, and experience that can significantly contribute to a metaverse that effectively supports food-sharing efforts. For instance, technology companies can leverage their technical expertise to design affordable, user-friendly environments and essential tools that facilitate seamless food-sharing experiences.

The role of government is also vital in shaping the metaverse's growth by establishing policies and regulations that promote responsible innovation, ensure equitable access, safeguard user privacy, and secure food systems. Additionally, the government can foster public-private partnerships that encourage collaboration between NGOs, local communities, and the private sector, thereby enhancing the metaverse's effectiveness (Ramli & Mahmud, 2023). Leading examples of government involvement, such as Korea and China, where government policies and regulatory frameworks have been implemented to coordinate the growth of the metaverse (Ruban, 2023).

Managing the "good-to-eat window" remains a critical challenge in food-sharing initiatives, even within the metaverse environment. The "good-to-eat window" refers to when surplus food remains both nutritious and safe for consumption. This time frame is primarily determined by food safety guidelines, such as those outlined by the USDA (2019), which provide standards for proper food storage, handling, and date labelling. To address this challenge in the metaverse, emerging technologies such as the Internet of Things (IoT), AI, and blockchain offer innovative solutions to enhance food management processes (Galanakis, 2024).

For example, IoT can be employed to provide real-time data on the conditions of surplus food. In the metaverse, food producers could utilise IoT sensors to monitor factors such as temperature, humidity, and freshness, allowing them to make data-driven decisions about whether surplus food is still safe for redistribution. Additionally, AI can be used to predict the remaining shelf life of surplus food, helping food producers plan for the optimal time to distribute or donate items. Blockchain technology further enhances transparency and accountability by enabling the tracking of food from production through to donation, ensuring that all transactions are recorded and verifiable (Lei et al., 2022).

13.5 Future Trends in Green Technology for Food Sharing

Green technology, particularly in the context of food sharing, offers solutions that reduce waste and enhance sustainability and food security. This section discusses future trends in green technology for food sharing, focusing on four critical areas: AI and big data, blockchain, smart packaging, and decentralised platforms. AI and big data are pivotal in optimising food supply chains and enhancing food-sharing initiatives. AI technologies with extensive datasets enable predictive analytics that accurately forecast food availability and consumer demand (Liu et al., 2020). For instance, Kollia et al. (2021) demonstrate that AI and machine learning methodologies can significantly improve the efficiency and safety of food supply chains, ultimately reducing food waste and environmental pollution. By analysing historical consumption patterns and demographic data, AI can optimise distribution networks, ensuring that surplus food reaches those in need promptly.

Furthermore, AI-driven platforms can facilitate real-time inventory management, allowing organisations to dynamically monitor stock levels and expiration dates. Dora et al. (2021) emphasise that AI in food supply chains can address food safety, quality, and wastage challenges by improving transparency and traceability. This data-driven approach maximises resource utilisation and fosters a community-sharing culture, promoting sustainability.

Moreover, big data analytics can enhance personalised recommendations for consumers. By analysing individual preferences and dietary restrictions, AI can suggest available food items for sharing, increasing participation in food-sharing programmes. This personalisation can lead to higher engagement rates and a more robust food-sharing ecosystem, as highlighted by Olan et al. (2024), with the significant role of AI in improving supply chain performance through better information distribution. Blockchain technology is set to revolutionise transparency within food-sharing supply chains, ensuring safety and trust among participants. The decentralised nature of blockchain allows for immutable record-keeping, which is crucial for tracking the provenance of food items. By utilising blockchain, food-sharing organisations can provide verifiable information about food products' source, handling, and storage conditions (Lei et al., 2022). This transparency is essential for building consumer trust, particularly when food safety concerns are paramount.

In addition to traceability, blockchain can streamline logistics by automating transactions and reducing the need for intermediaries. Smart contracts can facilitate agreements between food donors and recipients, ensuring that conditions are met before the transfer of goods occurs. This automation reduces administrative overhead and minimises the potential for fraud and miscommunication. As Modgil et al. (2021) suggested, AI can contribute to enhanced supply chain resilience by ensuring transparency and facilitating last-mile delivery. Moreover, integrating blockchain with IoT devices can further enhance food safety. Sensors can monitor temperature and humidity levels during transportation and storage, with data recorded on the block-chain. This real-time monitoring ensures that food items remain within safe parameters, reducing the risk of spoilage and contamination. Consequently, blockchain technology fosters trust and contributes to the overall safety of food-sharing initiatives.

Smart packaging represents a significant advancement in ensuring food freshness and safe consumption. Sensors and indicators used in the packaging materials allow for real-time monitoring. For example, freshness indicators can change colour based on the condition of the food, providing consumers with immediate visual cues regarding its edibility. This technology enables donors to assess the quality of food items before sharing (Kumari et al., 2024). By ensuring that only fresh and safe food is distributed, smart packaging can enhance the reputation of food-sharing programmes and encourage more individuals to participate. Additionally, smart packaging can facilitate better inventory management by providing data on the shelf life of products, allowing organisations to prioritise the sharing of items nearing expiration (Velázquez-Contreras & López-Cervantes, 2021).

Chen (2024) highlights the critical role of big data in transforming agricultural practices and ensuring food security, which aligns with the advancements in smart packaging. Furthermore, smart packaging integrated with mobile applications can enhance consumer engagement. Users can scan packaging to receive information about the food's origin, nutritional content, and suggested recipes, promoting informed decision-making. This interactive approach educates consumers and fosters a sense of community around food sharing, as individuals can share their experiences and tips through the app.

Decentralised platforms are transforming the food-sharing landscape by increasing peer-to-peer sharing efficiency while reducing overhead costs. These platforms leverage technology to connect individuals directly, eliminating the need for centralised intermediaries. As a result, food-sharing initiatives can operate more flexibly and responsively, adapting to local needs and preferences. It fosters a sense of ownership and accountability within communities, encouraging more people to participate in food-sharing efforts. Community members can take an active role by listing surplus food items, coordinating pick-ups, and sharing resources without relying on traditional food banks or organisations. This model aligns with the findings of Singh (2024), which emphasises the importance of adopting big data analytics using AI and big data.

Decentralised platforms can optimise matching algorithms, ensuring that surplus food is directed to those in need (Liu et al., 2020). Moreover, block-chain technology within these platforms can enhance transparency and trust, as users can verify the authenticity of food items and the credibility of donors (Lei et al., 2022). It can improve operational efficiency and foster a culture of sharing and collaboration within communities. As highlighted by

Doggalli (2024), big data innovations have the potential to address key challenges in the global food system, offering unprecedented opportunities for sustainability.

In conclusion, the future of green technology in food sharing is paving the way for more efficient and sustainable practices. By harnessing AI, blockchain, smart packaging, and decentralised platform technologies, food-sharing initiatives can significantly reduce waste, enhance food safety, and foster a culture of sharing within communities (Galanakis, 2024). As these trends continue to evolve, they play a crucial role in addressing the challenges of food security and sustainability in the years to come.

Acknowledgement

This work was supported by the Universiti Utara Malaysia's ResQ COVID-19 Grant (2020).

References

Barker, A., & McCarthy, M. (2023). Towards sustainable food systems: Exploring household food waste by photographic diary in relation to unprocessed, processed and ultra-processed food. *Sustainability*, 15(3), 2051. https://doi.org/10.3390/su15032051

Bennett, R., & Smith, J. (2022). Digital innovations in food sharing: Impacts on sustainability and community engagement. *Journal of Sustainable Development*, 15(4), 45–62.

Chen, J., Begicheva, S., & Nazarov, D. (2024). The role of big data in advancing precision agriculture and ensuring food security, *BIO Web of Conferences, 121*, 02013. https://doi.org/10.1051/bioconf/202412102013

DeBate, R., Jarvis, J. E., Jones, R., Himmelgreen, D., Conner, K., Dumford, A. D., & Stern, M. (2024). Perceived self- and social stigma among campus-based food pantry users. *Journal of American College Health*, 1–6. https://doi.org/10.1080/07448481.2024.2412067

Doğan, E., & Yıldız, M. (2022). Mobile applications as a next generation solution to prevent food waste. *Ege Akademik Bakış (Ege Academic Review)*, 22(1), 1–12. https://doi.org/10.21121/eab.1181830

Doggalli, G., Kulkarni, S. P., Meti, S. C., Pattar, S. K., Aravind, S. A., Sankati, J., & Singh, D. S. S. (2024). Exploring big data innovations in food and agriculture research: An in-depth analysis. *International Journal of Research in Agronomy*, 7(3S), 330–336. https://doi.org/10.33545/2618060x.2024.v7.i3se.471

Dora, M., Kumar, A., Mangla, S. K., Pant, A., & Kamal, M. M. (2021). Critical success factors influencing artificial intelligence adoption in food supply chains. *International Journal of Production Research*, 60(14), 4621–4640. https://doi.org/10.1080/00207543.2021.1959665

Galanakis, C. (2024). The future of food. *Foods, 13*(4), 506. https://doi.org/10.3390/foods13040506

Hanson, C., & Ahmadi, M. (2021). Mobile applications to reduce food waste within Canada: A review. *Canadian Geographer/Le Géographe Canadien, 65*(3), 400–415. https://doi.org/10.1111/cag.12733

Kearney, J. (2010). The future of food sharing: Innovations and trends in the digital age, *Food Policy, 99*, 101–112.

Kollia, I., Stevenson, J., & Kollias, S. (2021). AI-enabled efficient and safe food supply chain. *Electronics, 10*(11), 1223. https://doi.org/10.3390/electronics10111223

Kumari, S., Debbarma, R., Nasrin, N., Khan, T., Taj, S., & Bhuyan, T. (2024). Recent advances in packaging materials for food products, *Food Bioengineering, 3*, 236–249. https://doi.org/10.1002/fbe2.12096

Kwok, R., & Lin, Y. (2023). Green food packages' effects on consumers' pre- to post-consumption evaluations of restaurant curbside pick-up service. *International Journal of Contemporary Hospitality Management, 36*(6), 2011–2034. https://doi.org/10.1108/ijchm-01-2023-0018

Lei, Y., Zhang, Y., & Wang, Y. (2022). Integration of privacy protection and blockchain-based food safety traceability: Potential and challenges. *Foods, 11*(15), 2262. https://doi.org/10.3390/foods11152262

Liu, Y., Zhang, Y., & Wang, Y. (2020). The role of big data analytics in enabling green supply chain management: A literature review. *Journal of Data Information and Management, 2*(1), 1–15. https://doi.org/10.1007/s42488-019-00020-z

Modgil, S., Singh, R., & Hannibal, C. (2021). Artificial intelligence for supply chain resilience: Learning from COVID-19. *The International Journal of Logistics Management, 33*(4), 1246–1268. https://doi.org/10.1108/ijlm-02-2021-0094

Nasution, R. A., Rusnandi, L. S. L., Qodariah, E., Arnita, D., & Windasari, N. A. (2018). The evaluation of digital readiness concept: Existing models and future directions. *The Asian Journal of Technology Management (AJTM), 11*(2), 94–117. https://doi.org/10.12695/ajtm.2018.11.2.3

Olan, F., Arakpogun, E. O., Jayawickrama, U., Suklan, J., & Liu, S. (2024). Sustainable supply chain finance and supply networks: The role of artificial intelligence, *IEEE Transactions on Engineering Management, 71*, 13296–13311. https://doi.org/10.1109/tem.2021.3133104

Rahman, M. (2023). Analysis of government policies in Padang City in food waste management at the household level. *JIMAT, 2*(1), 1–15. https://doi.org/10.59653/jimat.v2i01.307

Ramli, M., & Mahmud, A. (2023). Metaverse innovation in public service transformation in Makassar metropolitan city. *Journal of Islam and Science PISSN, 10*(2), 105–114. https://tes-ojs.uin-alauddin.ac.id/index.php/jis/article/view/40945

Ritchie, H., & Roser, M. (2023). Food waste: A global overview. Our world in data. Retrieved from https://ourworldindata.org/food-waste

Ruban, A. (2023). *The role of the government in metaverse development in China and South Korea: A comparative analysis.* Università Ca'Foscari Venezia.

Singh, J., Kumar, R., Kumar, V., & Chatterjee, S. (2024). Exploring the dynamics of big data adoption in the Indian food industry with fuzzy analytical hierarchical process. *British Food Journal, 126*(6), 2310–2327. https://doi.org/10.1108/bfj-01-2024-0012

Usamah, W. (2024). *Deepening Malaysia's understanding of poverty.* Khazanah Research Institute.

USDA. (2019, October 2). Food product dating - food safety and inspection service. www.fsis.usda.gov. https://www.fsis.usda.gov/food-safety/safe-food-handling-and-preparation/food-safety-basics/food-product-dating

Velázquez-Contreras, J., & López-Cervantes, J. (2021). Cyclodextrins in polymer-based active food packaging: A fresh look at nontoxic, biodegradable, and sustainable technology trends. *Polymers, 14*(1), 104. https://doi.org/10.3390/polym14010104

Wang, J., & Medvegy, G. (2022). Exploration of the future of the metaverse and smart cities. *ICEB 2022 Proceedings (Bangkok, Thailand)*. https://aisel.aisnet.org/iceb2022/12/

Yaqoob, I., Salah, K., Jayaraman, R., & Omar, M. (2023). Metaverse applications in smart cities: Enabling technologies, opportunities, challenges, and future directions, *Internet of Things, 23*, 100884. https://www.sciencedirect.com/science/article/pii/S254266052300207X

Yu, Y., Yi, S.-X., Xiao, N., Lo, L. Y.-H., Shigyo, K., Xie, L., Wicaksana, J., Cheng, K.-T., & Qu, H. (2023). FoodWise: Food waste reduction and behavior change on campus with data visualisation and gamification. ArXiv (Cornell University). https://doi.org/10.1145/3588001.3609364

Zaki, M. M., Sulong, J., & Ghani, N. (2020). Cabaran amil lembaga zakat negeri Kedah dalam revolusi perindustrian 4.0. *Journal of Contemporary Islamic Law, 5*(1), 1–8. https://doi.org/10.26475/jcil.2020.5.1.01

Zhang, Y. (2024). The impact of dietary preference on household food waste: Evidence from China, *Frontiers in Nutrition, 11*, 1415734. https://doi.org/10.3389/fnut.2024.1415734

Index

Note: Locators in *italics* represent figures and **bold** indicate tables in the text.